REENTRY
ESSENTIALS, INC.

ESSENTIAL REENTRY
SKILLS SERIES

This page intentionally left blank

Content

This page intentionally left blank

Anger Management

This page intentionally left blank

Anger Management

Course Goal: Upon completion of this course, student will acknowledge and control one's anger and appropriately react to others' anger.

I. ORIGIN OF ANGER

OBJECTIVES

II. ANGER CONTROL STRATEGIES

OBJECTIVES

What Is Anger?

Anger is an emotion that tells you something is wrong. It can range from a small feeling of irritation to a blinding rage. Anger is usually a reaction to some kind of threat - emotional or physical.

Anger has three parts:

- **Physical reactions**: These usually start with a rush of adrenaline. Then, you may have increased heart rate, rising blood pressure, and tightening muscles. This is called the "fight or flight" response.

- **Perceptions:** These are the thoughts you have about what is making you angry. For example, you might think something that happened to you is wrong, unfair, or undeserved.

- **Behaviors:** These are the ways you express your anger. There are constructive and destructive ways to express anger. Constructive ways include stating that you are angry, explaining why you are angry, and asking for a break or for something to change. Destructive ways include yelling, slamming doors, and refusing to speak.

Everyone experiences anger, and it can be healthy. It can motivate you to stand up for yourself and seek justice for others. When you manage your anger well, it can help you make positive changes in your life. When you don't manage your anger well, however, it can be unhealthy. When anger is out of control, it can cause you to make poor decisions. These decisions create problems with relationships and at work. People may begin to feel fearful and anxious around you. Unresolved anger can even damage your health, causing high blood pressure, headaches, trouble sleeping, and other problems.

Anger is harmful when:

- You get angrier than the situation calls for.

- You stay angry after the situation is over and can't move on.

- You feel angry all the time or many times a day.

- You're not always sure why you're angry.

- You get angry with those closest to you for very little reason.

- You use physical or verbal aggression.

- You lose jobs, friends, or relationships because of your anger.

- You turn to drugs or alcohol to cope with your anger.

What Is Anger?

Anger is a strong emotion of displeasure or hostility. Everyone experiences anger.

Directions: Answer the following questions.

1. Give an example of a time when your anger was healthy. What effects did it have?

   _____

   _____

   _____

2. Give an example of a time when your anger was unhealthy. What effects did it have?

   _____

   _____

   _____

3. Read the list of signs of harmful anger at the bottom of page 4.

   Are any of those signs true for you? Which ones?

   _____

   _____

   _____

   _____

4. Do you think you have a problem with anger? Explain why or why not.

   _____

   _____

   _____

   _____

Anger Triggers

The situations that cause you to get angry are called anger triggers. These might include being ignored or failing at something new. Sometimes they are situations that remind you of painful situations from your past.

Your anger triggers are unique and based on your life experiences. If you can predict your anger triggers, you can be ready to react appropriately.

Recognizing Feelings Related to Anger

Anger is not always just anger. You may react with anger when what you really feel is embarrassment, fear, or hurt. One reason you might react with anger is because you think being angry makes you look strong and showing those other feelings makes you look weak. Or, feeling angry may seem safer than letting yourself feel those other emotions. Or, it may just be a habit you've had for a long time.

When your anger is triggered, pay attention to the other feelings that come up. If you can name the feelings underneath your anger, you can start to resolve them in a healthy way. Here are some feelings that can be caused by anger triggers.

- Frustration

- Disappointment

- Impatience

- Boredom

- Loneliness

- Sadness

- Shame

- Fear

- Embarrassment

- Hurt

Anger Triggers

Directions: Think of three of your personal anger triggers. Write them in the boxes on the left. Then, think about what feelings might be underneath your anger in each of those situations. Write those feelings in the boxes on the right.

Example:

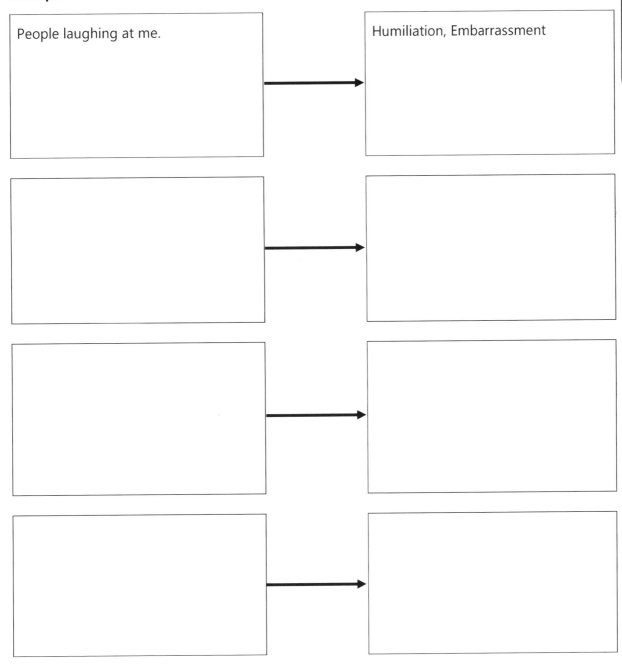

People laughing at me. → Humiliation, Embarrassment

Anger Cues

Another way to recognize anger is by paying attention to your body. Anger cues are physical signs that you are getting angry. It is important to recognize these physical signs before the anger gets out of control. Then, you can pause and try to figure out what other emotions you are feeling underneath the anger.

Once you are honest with yourself about your feelings, you can be honest with others. This is a healthy way to deal with anger.

Anger cues can include the following:

- Racing or Pounding Heart
- Clenched Teeth
- Clenched Fist
- Feeling Hot
- Feeling Cold
- Sweating
- Loud Voice
- Breathing Faster and Harder
- Red Face
- Tensed Muscles
- Trembling or Shaking
- Upset Stomach
- Dry Mouth

Directions: Think about the last time you got angry. How did your body feel? What anger cues were happening? Write them on the lines below.

_____

_____

_____

Group Discussion: Now, discuss what you wrote with a partner. Are your anger cues different from your partner's?

Dealing with Anger

Even though everyone experiences anger, the way people deal with anger can be very different for different people. Lots of things affect when you get angry, how angry you get, and how long you stay angry. The culture you grew up in, your past experiences, and your family life all affect how you deal with anger.

You learned how to respond to anger from your culture and the society you grew up in. Different cultures have different standards for what is appropriate when expressing anger. For example, our society tends to teach us that it is okay for men to show anger but not okay for women to show anger.

You also learned how to express anger from your family. If your parents yelled at you or at each other, you probably yell when you are angry at someone. If your family never talked about how they felt, you probably don't tell people when you are angry at them. In this same way, how you express your anger will shape the way your children express theirs.

There are three main ways people deal with anger. As you read through the list, think about your past experiences and how your family and friends generally deal with anger.

- **Expressing it.** Some people will express their anger verbally or physically. If their anger is uncontrolled, they may yell, throw a tantrum, destroy property, or physically hurt someone when they are angry. If they are in control of their anger, they communicate their anger and take action to solve the problem.
- **Suppressing it.** Some people will hold in their anger or direct it at themselves. While it's okay to suppress anger for a short period, people need to deal with their anger eventually. When people always suppress their anger, they can suffer from depression or health problems, such as high blood pressure. Some people may also try to escape their anger by turning to drugs and alcohol or other self-destructive habits.
- **Managing it.** Some people will take steps to manage their anger and calm themselves down. This requires that they recognize when they are angry and have tools for calming down. Deep breathing, exercise, and positive self-talk are a few ways people manage anger and calm themselves. Once calm, people can express their anger in a controlled way.

In our society, we often see anger expressed with violence. Newspapers, magazines, television shows, and radio broadcasts are full of stories about how anger leads to violence. We see violence in movies, on television, and in video games. We hear about it in the lyrics of popular music. We witness violence in our communities.

Violence can ruin lives. Anger often causes violence, and violence causes more anger. To break the cycle of violence in your life, you must learn to deal with and express your anger in a controlled, assertive way.

Dealing with Anger

The main factors that affect when you get angry and how you respond to the situation include the following:

- How bad the threat or harm is.
- The relationship you have with the person who makes you angry.
- What you think that person's intent is.
- What you think happened during the event that made you angry.
- Your previous life experience and outlook on life.
- The family and culture in which you were raised.
- Your general stress level.
- Genetics (biological traits passed from your parents).
- Your overall mental health (posttraumatic stress disorder, depression, bipolar disorder, anxiety, or personality disorders).

Directions: Think of a time when you were angry. Then, choose three factors from the list above and write them in the boxes on the left. In the boxes on the right, write how each factor might have affected why you got angry and how you reacted in the situation.

Example:

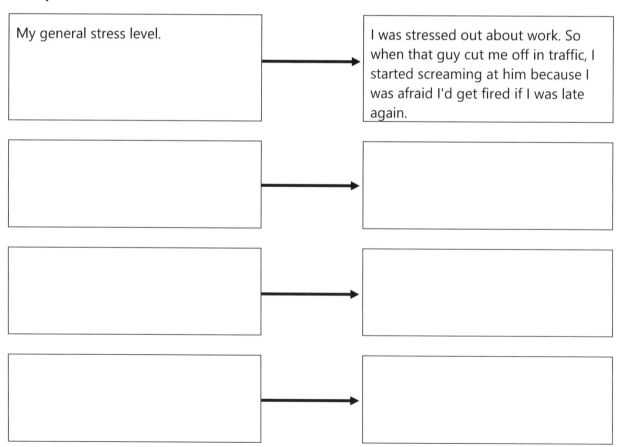

My general stress level.	I was stressed out about work. So when that guy cut me off in traffic, I started screaming at him because I was afraid I'd get fired if I was late again.

Dealing with Your Unresolved Anger

There are several factors that affect when you get angry and how you respond to the situation. Your previous life experiences and the family and culture you were raised in are two of these factors.

Directions: Answer the following questions.

1. What were the people (or person) who raised you like?

   _____

   _____

2. How did they get along with each other and with you?

   _____

   _____

3. How did they show their anger?

   _____

   _____

4. How were you punished when you got into trouble?

   _____

   _____

5. How do you show your anger?

   _____

   _____

6. Was anger involved in the crime that caused your incarceration (the crime you committed)?

   _____

   _____

7. Do you believe that the cause of your incarceration is due to the way you were raised?

   _____

   _____

Reacting Positively

Taking your anger out on another person without thinking about the consequences does not solve the original problem. It can make the problem worse. Running away from anger or pretending that it never existed is also not an effective way to deal with the original problem.

It may be easier to blow up at someone than to have an honest conversation with him or her. It may be easier to blame someone else for your own feelings of shame or disappointment. But learning to look at the real causes of your anger and learning to deal with them in a constructive way are the only ways to have close, healthy relationships.

Life is a lot easier when you know how to deal with anger. Make a plan now that includes the following three steps for handling anger appropriately when it comes up.

1. **Stop and think**. To deal with your anger in a controlled way, you have to be calm enough to think about the situation. Take a deep breath or take a few minutes before responding. When you are calm, identify what is making you angry by completing this sentence: I am angry because.

    Examples: I am angry because Jill lied to me.
                   I am angry because my car won't start.

2. **Identify other emotions.** Anger is often closely related to other strong emotions, such as fear, disappointment, embarrassment, and jealousy. Think about what other emotions may be contributing to your feelings of anger. Be honest.

3. **Take responsibility.** Once you identify what you're angry about and what is causing that anger, you can take responsibility for your feelings. You are the one who is reacting this way, and you can choose to react differently. Think of ways you can deal with or express your anger in a healthy way.

   - Be assertive—use "I" statements to let others know how you feel and what you need.

   - Talk about the situation and feelings with someone you trust.

   - Write about your feelings in a journal or diary.

   - Get active—run, lift weights, jump rope.

   - Find a creative way to express yourself—paint, draw, dance, play an instrument, listen to music.

   - Relax with deep breathing, yoga, or meditation.

These steps can be difficult to follow in a moment of anger. Often, the anger takes over before you can even think about the situation or your feelings. But there are ways you can prevent anger from overtaking you. We will cover several of these strategies later in this book.

Reacting Positively

Directions: Read the three scenarios below. With a partner, answer the following questions for each scenario.

Why do you think this person got angry?

What other feelings might this person be feeling underneath his or her anger?

Is this person taking responsibility for his or her feelings?

Scenario

Pedro buys a trampoline for his daughter's birthday. The night before her big birthday party, he tries to put the trampoline together. When he can't figure out how to get the last piece to fit, he gets angry. His wife tries to help, but he storms out of the room, kicking the trampoline pieces aside.

Scenario

Lydia does not want to meet her boyfriend's friends because she thinks her criminal record will make them dislike her. When her boyfriend calls to ask her over for dinner with them, Lydia gets angry, tells him he's a bully, and breaks up with him. She never stops answering his calls. She never speaks to him again.

Scenario

Charles goes to the corner store to buy some milk. As he is pulling it out of the case at the store, it slips from his hand and smashes on the floor. Milk goes everywhere. Another customer sees it happen and starts to walk toward him. Charles gets angry and yells, "What are you looking at?! Go away!"

Healthy vs. Toxic Self-Talk

As mentioned on page 4, one of the three parts of anger is your perceptions, or your thoughts about the things that are causing you to feel angry. What you tell yourself about a situation is actually more important than the situation itself. When you have negative thoughts, they will only make you feel worse.

Negative thoughts may come from something called toxic self-talk. Toxic self-talk happens when you tell yourself things that make the anger grow. These thoughts may include the following:

- This person should know what I want and what I expect of him or her.

- If I want something, the world owes it to me.

- What is happening to me is not fair.

- If this one thing is true, then this other thing must be true, too.

- This person is out to get me.

- I assume this is true, even if I don't have all the information.

- This person or situation is just like all the others.

It is helpful to practice a more productive way of thinking called healthy self-talk. Healthy self-talk makes you feel more calm instead of more angry. Healthy thoughts include asking yourself to think deeper instead of assuming you know everything. Some of these healthy thoughts may include the following:

- Where are these feelings coming from? Does this situation or person remind me of a situation or person from my past?

- Have I told this person what I want and need? Have I told this person what I expect of him or her?

- What does this person want and need? What are his or her expectations?

- This person is probably doing his or her best in this situation.

- How can I compromise in this situation?

- How can I approach the situation differently?

- I can relax and handle whatever happens.

- This situation is pretty minor in the big picture.

- This misunderstanding is actually kind of funny.

Healthy vs. Toxic Self-Talk

Healthy self-talk makes you feel more calm instead of more angry. Toxic self-talk makes your anger grow.

Directions: Read the statements below. Circle the statements that show healthy self-talk. Draw a line through the statements that show toxic self-talk. Then, rewrite the toxic statements as healthy statements on the lines below.

1. It is unfair that Joe got the job instead of me.

2. I am going to let Sasha know that I want her help cleaning up.

3. Nobody respects me.

4. I don't need that huge TV. I can compromise and be happy with a smaller one.

5. I'm not sure exactly what is happening right now, but I can handle it.

6. If Angela didn't call me, then she obviously doesn't like me.

7. His expectations must be different from mine. I'll ask him what he was expecting.

8. I come here all the time. They should know I hate mustard!

9. I never win, and I'm never going to.

10. This reminds me of the time I got stood up for that date. But this is a different situation with a different person.

_____

_____

_____

_____

_____

_____

_____

_____

_____

_____

_____

_____

Interpret Body Language

Body language is the way we communicate with others through movements and mannerisms. It includes physical signals such as facial expressions, posture, and gestures. Different sets of these physical signals can communicate different things.

Anger often comes from the way you view other people's intent toward you. So, it is important to know what different kinds of body language communicate. Here are some common sets of body language signals.

- **Aggressive Body Language: Showing Physical Threat**

  Aggressive people might frown, sneer, or snarl. People who are about to attack may clench their fists and lower their body for stability. They may also get very close to you, invading your personal space.

- **Bored Body Language: Just Not Being Interested**

  Bored people tend to not look at you. They may doodle or talk with others. They often repeat actions such as tapping toes, swinging feet, or drumming fingers.

- **Closed Body Language: Not Wanting To Open Up**

  People who are closed off may cross their arms across their chest or hold their arms into their body. They may cross their legs or turn their body away from you.

- **Deceptive Body Language: Lying Or Trying To Cover Something Up**

  Deceptive people who are worried about being caught may make sudden movements, have muscle twitches, or change their voice volume and speed.

- **Defensive Body Language: Protecting Self From Attack**

  Defensive people may tend to cover the parts of their body that could get hurt in an attack. They may hold out their arms to fend off an attacker. They may move their eyes from side to side, looking for a way out.

- **Fearful Body Language: Being Afraid**

  When someone's basic needs are threatened, he or she feels fear. Fearful people may break into a cold sweat or tremble. Their face may be pale and their eyes may be damp. They may also look away from you or fidget.

- **Open Body Language: Wanting To Reveal**

  People who are open probably won't cross their arms. They will focus on you and make good eye contact. They may also lean slightly toward you and nod to show they're listening.

- **Relaxed Body Language: Comfortable And Unstressed**

  Relaxed people have steady, slow breathing. Their arms hang in an easy position, and their facial and body muscles are not tensed.

- **Submissive Body Language: Being Prepared To Give In**

  Submissive people may show some of the same signs as fearful people. They will probably try to make themselves look small. They may hold their hands out and palms up to show they mean no harm.

Interpret Body Language

Directions: Work in a group of three to four people. Have each person in the group act out one of the following types of body language without telling the rest of the group what it is, as in a game of charades. When someone names the correct body language, move on to the next actor. Continue like this until the group has guessed all of the body language types below.

Body Language Types:

- Bored

- Relaxed

- Closed

- Deceptive

- Submissive

- Aggressive

- Defensive

- Fearful

- Open

Personal Assessment: Think about your body language right now. How are you sitting? What expression is on your face? What does your body language reveal about how you are feeling right now? Write your answer on the lines below.

_____

_____

_____

_____

_____

_____

_____

_____

Anger Is Normal

Everyone feels anger sometimes. Just like joy or fear, anger is an emotion that can be intense or mild depending on the situation. The emotions you feel tell you about the outside world and motivate you to respond to it.

As you learned earlier, anger is a normal emotion and a useful sign that something is wrong. Anger triggers a "fight or flight" response. When you are angry, you have a rush of adrenaline. Your heart rate increases, your blood pressure increases, and your muscles get ready for action. This physical response can help you defend against an attack or win a competition.

However, anger can be unhealthy if it starts to cause problems in your life or with your relationships. You can learn ways to prevent and control anger so that it does not become unhealthy. You can feel anger and respond in a healthy way - without hurting yourself or the people around you.

Directions: Anger is an emotion that can actually include lots of other feelings. Look at the example of some feelings related to joy below. Then, write some feelings related to anger in the other circle.

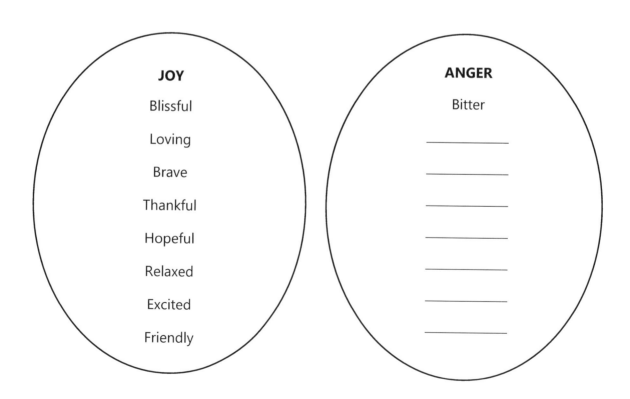

JOY	ANGER
Blissful	Bitter
Loving	_____
Brave	_____
Thankful	_____
Hopeful	_____
Relaxed	_____
Excited	_____
Friendly	_____

Anger Prevention Thought Patterns

Knowing your anger triggers and anger cues can help you avoid many of the situations that cause you to get angry. Of course, knowing your anger triggers and cues can't keep you out of every situation. You must also learn ways to prevent anger from taking over when you are faced with a trigger.

There are some thought patterns you can follow to prevent and control your anger. Patterns 1 and 2 are good to do now, before you get triggered. Pattern 3 is for after you are triggered.

Pattern 1

Think About Who Gets Hurt

- Think about who your anger has hurt in the past.
- Think about the effects your anger has had on your family, friends, and community.
- Use the remorse you feel over hurting others to change your behaviors.

Pattern 2

Plan Ahead

- Try to foresee your anger triggers: Do certain people or places make you more likely to get angry? In what types of situations do you tend to get angry?
- Avoid these people and places, if possible. Seek out healthier places and situations for yourself. If you can't avoid the people and places, think about ways to stay calm and have a plan for handling your anger.

Pattern 3

Stop and Ask

- Before you act, think about the effects your actions will have.
- Ask yourself, "What am I angry about?"
- Think, "I can express myself calmly."

Anger Prevention Thought Patterns

Directions: Read the first thought pattern on the previous page again. Spend a couple of minutes thinking about your answers to each bullet point. Then, write a paragraph on the lines below that describes who your anger has hurt in the past, the effects it has had on the people around you, and how you can use the remorse you feel to change how you deal with it.

_____

_____

_____

_____

_____

_____

_____

_____

_____

_____

_____

_____

_____

_____

Letting Go of Stress

Anger is often caused by stress. Stress is like a mound of firewood and kindling, and your anger triggers are the lit match. One way to prevent anger from flaring up is by reducing your stress level. Reducing stress will not only help prevent anger, but it will also improve your overall physical and mental health. Stress can lead to high blood pressure, heart disease, anxiety, and other problems, so it is important to learn how to manage it. Some ways to reduce stress include the following:

- **Relaxation Exercises:** Learning to relax is key to letting go of stress. It can prevent the harmful effects of stress and anger. Relaxation lowers your heart rate and blood pressure, reduces anxiety, and helps you sleep. There are lots of exercises you can do to relax. Making a daily routine of them is best. On the next page, you'll find one of the most common relaxation exercises.

- **Deep Breathing:** In the middle of a stressful situation, it can be very helpful to take a break. Go somewhere quiet, sit comfortably, and - breathe in deeply. Breathe into your stomach, not just your chest. Hold the air in for a few seconds. Then, let it out slowly. Repeat this five times before you return to the situation.

- **Exercise:** Having a regular exercise routine will help you release stress in a productive way. Try to exercise three to five times per week. Do things that you enjoy so you will keep to your routine. Do you like team sports or working out alone? Do you like being outside or inside better? Do you prefer aerobic exercise, like running, or strength-building exercise, like lifting weights? Base your routine on your answers to these questions. Make sure you talk to a doctor before you start a new exercise routine.

- **Meditation:** Meditation has been proven to help people handle stress better. Each morning or evening, sit in a quiet space. You can sit cross-legged on a pillow with your back straight or sit upright in a chair. Your posture is not as important as your mind. With your eyes open or closed, try to let go of all the thoughts racing through your mind. Just focus on your breath. You don't need to do anything special to your breath - just notice it. It can help to count your breaths to ten and then start over. If your mind wanders, that's okay. Just notice it and let the thoughts go. Then, put your attention back on your breath. Do this for 10 to 15 minutes.

_____

_____

_____

_____

Body Scan Relaxation Exercise

Directions: Follow the directions below to relax your whole body.

1. Get comfortable sitting in your chair. Rest your feet on the ground and your hands on your knees. Close your eyes.

2. Begin with three deep breaths. Breathe deeply into your stomach, and exhale out all of the air slowly. Continue to breathe like this as you go through the next steps.

3. Focus on your forehead. Are your muscles tightened? Is your brow furrowed, or wrinkled? With your next exhale, let any tension go and feel your forehead relax.

4. Focus on the area around your eyes. Notice how your eyes feel. Are they tired? Are they squinting? With the next breath, release any tension from the outer corners of your eyes.

5. Now focus on your mouth and jaw. Notice any anxiety or stress that you are holding in the muscles around your mouth and the bones of your jaw. With your next exhale, let your jaw drop down and your mouth open slightly. Release the tension completely in your mouth and jawbone.

6. Focus on your neck and shoulders. Concentrate on breathing deep into your stomach and, with the exhale, let your shoulders float down toward your feet. Breathe in and feel your neck lengthening, exhale and feel your shoulders drop lower and lower.

7. Focus on your arms, hands, and fingers. Is there any tension there? With your next exhale, release the tension. Feel your arms get heavy as they let go and sink to the floor.

8. Focus on your upper and lower legs. Are you tightening your muscles? Inhale and exhale slowly and completely. With your next inhale, let go of all the worry and stress that you have stored in your lower body. Exhale and let your legs feel heavy against the floor.

9. Finally, notice if there is any tension left anywhere in your body, and release it now.

The Anger Chain

Sometimes, anger can be a chain reaction. When there is a misunderstanding or disagreement, one person's anger can lead the other person to get angry. The anger then builds, with each person getting madder and madder. This is called the **Anger Chain**. Because this chain reaction often leads to violence, it is important to recognize the Anger Chain when it happens.

Luckily, once you recognize the Anger Chain, you can easily cut it off before things turn violent. Here are some ways to stop the Anger Chain.

- **Redirect the Conversation:** If you sense that you or the other person is getting angry, change the subject. Hopefully, you can move on to a more peaceful subject, and the angry party can let his or her anger go. You may be able to return to the original subject later, when both of you are feeling calmer.

- **Ask the Other Person What is Wrong:** If you can tell that the other person is upset but isn't telling you why, just ask. If the other person knows you really care, his or her anger will probably fade quickly. It is important to listen and try to understand the other person's perspective, without getting defensive. Then, you can have a calm discussion about how to resolve the problem or misunderstanding.

- **Ask for a Time-Out:** If you find yourself in a situation where you are both getting mad, or if the other person is being unreasonable, ask for a time-out. This means taking a few minutes away from each other to calm down. During the time-out, think about why you were getting angry. Also try to put yourself in the other person's shoes to figure out why he or she was angry. When you return to the situation; you can talk about your anger calmly.

Directions: Read the scenario below. How would you stop the Anger Chain in this situation? Explain your answer below.

You have plans with Laura to go to a movie, and you go to pick her up at her house. When you get there, she tells you she doesn't want to go anymore. She doesn't explain why. You get frustrated and snap at her, and she calls you a jerk. Suddenly, you realize you and Laura are caught in an anger chain.

_____

_____

_____

_____

_____

Breaking the Anger Chain

Directions: Think of a time you got caught in an Anger Chain. How did you handle it? Were you able to stop it before it got out of hand? How would you handle it now, after learning the strategies on page 23. Explain your answer on the lines below.

_____

_____

_____

_____

_____

_____

_____

_____

_____

_____

_____

_____

_____

_____

_____

_____

_____

_____

Responding to Anger

Let's review the three basic steps for dealing with your anger appropriately.

1. Stop and Think
2. Identify other Emotions
3. Take Responsibility

These are internal responses that will help dissolve your anger. But what about your external response? What can you do to resolve the situation that triggered your anger? There are three basic ways to respond to anger: expressing, suppressing, and managing.

- **Expressing Anger:** You can express anger in either destructive or constructive ways. Expressing anger can be blowing up at, blaming, or physically attacking people (destructive). It can also include explaining your feelings, asking for an apology and change in the relationship, and taking action to solve a problem (constructive).

- **Suppressing Anger:** Suppressing anger can also be either destructive or constructive. It includes bottling up your emotions, withdrawing, and turning your anger toward yourself (destructive). This can lead to health problems or drug abuse. But suppressing anger can also be a positive choice to let something go and forget about it, take a time-out, or move your focus off of the anger trigger (constructive).

- **Managing Anger:** Neither extreme-blowing up or bottling up your emotions is healthy. Managing anger well is about understanding your anger and making healthy choices that benefit yourself and others. When you manage your anger well, you can discuss your wants, needs, and feelings and reach a better mutual understanding with the people around you.

Group Discussion: With a partner, discuss ways you have expressed and suppressed anger in the past. Were they constructive or destructive? How did you feel afterward?

Destructive vs. Constructive Responses

One way to respond to anger is by expressing it. You can express anger in either destructive or constructive ways.

Directions: For each anger response in the left column, write whether it is a constructive or destructive response in the right column.

A Destructive Response is a verbal or physical reaction that damages or destroys something or someone. For example: John was angry at Bob for taking his shoes, so he went into Bob's room and threw all his clothes and shoes on the floor.

A Constructive Response is a verbal or physical reaction that improves, develops, or advances something or someone. For example: John was angry at Bob for taking his shoes, so he decided to take some deep breaths before talking to Bob about it.

Response	Destructive or Constructive
1. kicking the wall	Destructive
2. screaming	
3. asking for an explanation	
4. slamming the door	
5. refusing to talk about it	
6. deciding to let it go	
7. getting drunk or high	
8. hating yourself	
9. asking for a five-minute break	
10. talking to a trusted friend	
11. punching someone	
12. going for a run	
13. taking deep breaths	
14. calling someone names	
15. hanging up on someone	

Anger Cheat Sheet

So far, you have learned what anger is, how to recognize your anger triggers and cues, tips for healthy self-talk, how to read others' body language, and how to prevent and respond to anger. Now, it's time for a short cheat sheet of exactly what to do when you find yourself in a moment of anger.

When you start to feel yourself get angry:

- Take deep breaths.

- Repeat the words "relax" or "it's okay" in your mind.

- Take a time-out.

- Turn a toxic thought into a healthy thought.

- Think about what you are really feeling and what you really want.

When you are calm enough to handle the situation:

- Use "I" statements to take responsibility instead of "You" statements to blame others.

- Admit your anger out loud to others.

- Ask others to help you understand what happened.

- Ask others to explain how they feel about the situation.

- Explain to others how you feel about the situation.

- Express your wants and needs clearly to others.

- Ask others to change their behavior to what you want it to be (but be prepared for them to say no).

- Try to release the tension with a little humor.

Dealing with Anger

Directions: Reread the list of strategies on the previous page that you can use when you start to feel angry. Write your answers to the **following** questions on the lines below.

Which strategy do you think would be the most effective for you?

Which strategy would be the least effective for you?

Can you think of any other strategies that are not listed that would be helpful?

_____

_____

_____

_____

_____

Group Discussion: Now, discuss your answers with the whole group. Does talking to other people about the strategies that work for them make you think differently about your own strategies? Write your answer below.

_____

_____

_____

_____

Anger Management Review

Directions: Circle the letter for each correct answer.

1. Anger is always unhealthy.
   A. True
   B. False

2. Anger is harmful when:
   A. You lose a friend or a loved one because of it.
   B. You stand up for someone in need because of it.
   C. You reflect on your own anger and grow from it.

3. An anger trigger is:
   1. A physical sign of anger.
   2. A situation that sets off your anger.
   3. Your reaction to someone who makes you mad.

4. Sometimes people react with anger when they are really feeling:
   A. Hurt.
   B. Scared.
   C. Both of the above

5. Which of the following is a common anger cue?
   A. Slow breathing
   B. Smiling
   C. Upset stomach

6. Past experiences have no effect on your current anger triggers.
   A. True
   B. False

7. Anger often causes violence, and violence causes:
   A. Justice.
   B. More anger.
   C. Happiness.

8. Which factor affects how you respond to anger?
   A. Your family
   B. Your culture
   C. Both of the above

9. Pretending you were never angry is a _____ response to anger.
   A. Constructive
   B. Destructive
   C. Neither of the above

10. Other people are responsible for your anger.
    A. True
    B. False

11. Which one of the following is an example of healthy self-talk?
    A. That guy should have known better.
    B. I know that she is trying to hurt me.
    C. In the big picture, this doesn't really matter.

12. A pale face and trembling body are body language signs of:
    A. Being afraid.
    B. Being open.
    C. Being bored.

13. Anger is often caused by stress.
    A. True
    B. False

continued on next page

14. Which of the following is a helpful way to let go of stress?
    A. Smoking
    B. Drinking
    C. Exercise

15. Asking for a time-out means:
    A. Taking a few minutes alone to calm down.
    B. Calling in a referee.
    C. Walking out and never coming back.

16. By knowing and predicting your anger triggers, you can:
    A. Be ready to fight when they come up.
    B. Try to avoid the situations that set off your anger.
    C. Feel bad about them.

17. What are the three basic ways to respond to anger?
    A. Expressing, Suppressing, and Raging
    B. Sobbing, Expressing, and Apologizing
    C. Expressing, Suppressing, and Managing

18. The first thing you should ask yourself when you start to feel angry is:
    A. "What about this situation makes me angry?"
    B. "Why is this person doing this to me?"
    C. "How can I get back at this person for wronging me?"

19. Asking others what their intentions were is a healthy way to deal with anger.
    A. True
    B. False

20. When you are angry, you should use "I" statements to:
    A. Blame the other person.
    B. Clearly express what you want and need.
    C. Demand an apology.

REENTRY
ESSENTIALS, INC.

Counseling on Individual Reentry Concerns

This page intentionally left blank

Counseling on Individual Reentry Concerns

Course Goal: Upon completion of this course, student will establish methods conducive to successful reentry into the community by means of understanding the dynamics of the relationships among the individual, family, and members of society.

I. INDIVIDUAL REENTRY CONCERNS

OBJECTIVES

II. FAMILY DYNAMICS

OBJECTIVES

Knowing Your Personal Plan of Action

You are likely anxiously anticipating your prison release. You are thinking about your freedom, your family, and your friends. Every year, thousands of **prisoners** are released from local state and federal prison systems. Within five years, more than 50 percent are back in prison because of parole violations or newly committed crimes. How will you make sure that you are part of the 50 percent of released **prisoners** who get on the right track and stay out of prison?

Directions: Read each "Basic" in the left column. Complete "Your Plan of Action" on the right.

BASICS	YOUR PLAN OF ACTION
Employment/Earning Income:	
Do I have the necessary paperwork to find a job (social security card, driver's license)?	
Have I obtained any certification or job skills in prison that I can use to find a job?	
Will my wages be enough to support myself?	
Housing:	
Where will I live?	
Are my living arrangements short-term or long-term?	
Will my housing be approved by my parole officer/probation agent?	
Support:	
Do I have friends/family available for emotional support?	
Will I be able to figure out health care?	

Group Discussion: Talk with a partner or small group about your specific plan(s). Take turns asking each other questions about the things you think might and might not work.

Preparing for Release

To prepare for your release, you need to think about what you have learned during your incarceration. You also need to figure out your specific plans for after your release.

Directions: Think about some of the programs that you have taken advantage of in prison. These programs will help you be better equipped to reenter your community. Answer the following questions.

1. What educational programs/courses have you taken advantage of in prison?

   _____

   _____

2. Have you participated in any substance abuse programs in prison? If so, describe them.

   _____

   _____

3. Do you have a plan to continue substance abuse treatment when you are released? What is your plan?

   _____

   _____

4. Have you taken any medications while in prison? If yes, what are they?

   _____

   _____

5. How will you get your medications after you are released from prison?

   _____

   _____

6. Have you received any faith-based services or counseling in prison? If so, describe them.

   _____

   _____

7. Will you seek out any faith-based services when you are released? If so, what will they be?

   _____

   _____

Budget for Expenses

Financially, things may be difficult when you are released from prison. You will have to come up with a reasonable budget. It will need to include all of your income as well as all of your monthly expenses.

Keep in mind that you may apply for Social Security benefits, the Supplemental Nutrition Assistance Program (SNAP), or other social services that will help you cover your monthly expenses.

Directions: Complete your expected monthly expenses below.

My Monthly Expenses

Housing	
Groceries	
Utilities	
Transportation Gas, Bus Pass, Car Payment	
Insurance	
Savings	
Childcare (If applicable)	
Other Expenses	
TOTAL MONTHLY EXPENSES	

Now, think about any additional financial goals you may have. Would you like to start saving money to buy a car or a house? Would you like to take a trip to visit a friend? Would you like to obtain additional schooling? Write your goals on the lines below.

_____

_____

_____

Personal Responsibility

Personal responsibility means "owning" your actions. It means taking responsibility for your actions and your mistakes. It means not blaming other people.

In an October 10, 2012, *Talk of the Nation* special titled "Programs that Keep Inmates from Returning to Prison," former inmates were asked to call in and talk about what kept them out of prison. They were asked why they were able to get out and stay out of prison when over 50 percent of prisoners return to prison within five years of their release. Most of the prisoners stated the same thing: "I decided to stay out of prison. I did not want to go back."

To stay out of prison, you are going to make the decision that you want to keep yourself out of prison for good. Only you can make this important decision. After you make your decision, you are going to have to "own" it. You have to make the choice to follow the law and take action to stay out of prison. You are going to have to take personal responsibility for yourself. You can get out of prison and stay out of prison.

Directions: Work with a partner. Read each of the quotes about personal responsibility. Discuss what you think each one means and whether you can relate to it. Then, answer the questions below.

> *"The great end of life is not knowledge but action."*
> - Thomas Henry Huxley -

> *"No pleasure is comparable to the standing upon the vantage-ground of truth."*
> - Francis Bacon -

> *"The work must be done; we cannot escape our responsibility."*
> - Theodore Roosevelt -

> *"We learn wisdom from failure much more than from success. We often discover what will do by finding out what will not do; and probably he who never made a mistake never made a discovery."*
> - Samuel Smiles -

> *"Perseverance is more prevailing than violence; and many things which cannot be overcome when they are together, yield themselves up when taken little by little."*
> - Plutarch -

1. Which quote do you like the best? Why? _____

   _____

   _____

2. Which quote do you like the least? Why? _____

   _____

   _____

Your Personal Concerns

What are your biggest worries about your reentry into your community? Are you worried about returning to your old neighborhood? Seeing your old friends? Finding a job? Keeping a job? These are all natural concerns. Exploring them now will help you better cope with your reentry when you are released.

Directions: Answer the questions below.

1. What are some of your fears about being released from prison? Why do you have these fears?

   _____

   _____

   _____

   _____

2. Are there any services currently available to you in prison that you think might be able to help you work toward solving your personal concerns before you are released?

   _____

   _____

   _____

   _____

3. What personal concerns do you feel the most confident about dealing with after your release? Why?

   _____

   _____

   _____

   _____

Group Discussion: Talk with a partner or in a small group about your answers to these questions. Do you share the same fears? Do you have confidence about the same things?

Positive People

What defines a positive person? How can you develop a positive attitude and the strategies you need to reenter society successfully?

Positive people view the glass as half full rather than half empty. Positive people meet the world with a "Can do!" attitude rather than a "Why me?" attitude. Positive people look hard to see the best in people and situations.

Readjusting to society, finding work, and reconnecting with your family and friends will require hard work. It will require a positive attitude as well as patience with yourself and others. Here are some "Positive People" ideas that will make your transition go more smoothly.

- **Productive regret is good.** Everyone has some regrets. Regrets are a part of life. Productive regret will help you change a behavior into something that works positively for you. Productive regret also means learning from your mistakes and finding better ways to do things. Remember, everyone makes mistakes. As long as you learn from your mistakes, you can have productive regret about the things you did wrong. When you focus on productive regret, you will also be able to have more empathy—or understanding—for other people. Empathy will help you forgive yourself and others for their mistakes. You need to learn to forgive yourself for the mistakes you have made and also forgive the people around you for making mistakes.

- **Be proactive, not reactive.** Positive people are proactive. Proactive people make changes when they need to. They work toward what they want. Reactive people respond to a situation or person based on what the other person is doing. Proactive people figure out what they want out of a situation or a relationship and then work hard to achieve it. You can't change other people, but you can change how you respond to other people. When you choose to respond proactively, you fix what you can control in each situation and then move on.

- **Be grateful.** Look around. Count your blessings. Life is good—even when it is hard. Some studies have shown that people who are grateful actually live longer, healthier lives. Notice the good around you. Talk about the things and people that you are grateful for. Notice a garden of flowers, the sun on your face, and your first bite of breakfast. People like to be around positive people—share your gratitude with them.

Change Your Way of Thinking

Developing positive strategies and attitudes to adapt to society will take practice.

PRODUCTIVE REGRET MEANS LEARNING FROM YOUR MISTAKES.

Directions: On the lines below, write about what you have learned from something you did that you regret.

1. _____
   _____
   _____

POSITIVE PEOPLE ARE PROACTIVE RATHER THAN REACTIVE.

Proactive: Creating or controlling a situation by causing something to happen rather than responding to it after it has happened.

Reactive: Acting in response to a situation rather than creating or controlling it.

Directions: Circle the proactive response.

2. During your first day at work, a co-worker spills his coffee all over your new pair of work pants.

   A. You yell at your co-worker and ask him why he is so careless.

   B. You ask your co-worker to help you find some supplies so you can clean yourself up.

3. You can't find your car keys, and you are late to meet your parole officer.

   A. You call your parole officer and let him or her know you are running late.

   B. You scream at everyone in the house to come help you come find your keys right this minute.

POSITIVE PEOPLE ARE GRATEFUL PEOPLE.

Directions: Make a list of four things you are grateful for.

4. _____
   _____
   _____

Group Discussion: Share the list of things you are grateful for. Listen to the things others are grateful for. Discuss why you think grateful people might be healthier than ungrateful people.

Positive Coping Skills

One thing is for certain—when you are released from prison, your life will not be problem free. Everyone has problems. You had problems before you went to prison, and you will have problems after you are released from prison. You have to learn how to cope, or deal, with your problems.

Good coping skills are important. These skills will help you deal with your problems in a healthy way. They will help you keep a good perspective and live successfully in your community. Having good coping skills will help you R-E-C-O-V-E-R from the setbacks that will happen to you.

R - Relax. Take a deep breath. Pause. Try practicing yoga or meditation.

E - Exercise. Run. Walk. Swim. Bike. Move your body. It can change your perspective and help you cope more effectively with life's ups and downs.

C - Create hobbies. Find things you like to do. Hobbies help you get your mind on other things. Hobbies help your perspective, or your understanding about how things or facts affect each other. They build your confidence. They are fun!

O - Outreach. Outreach programs—like counseling services, spiritual and faith programs, and mental health services—can help you stay on track and find the resources you need.

V - Value yourself. Don't be too hard on yourself. Everyone faces setbacks and makes mistakes. Everyone fails sometimes. Remind yourself that you are valuable. You matter. You don't have to drink or do drugs to cope. You can deal with problems and difficult situations. You can recover and learn from hard times.

E - Enjoy friends. Relationships matter. Make friends with positive, law-abiding people. Be a friend. Spend time with people who care for and support you. Lean on them when you are having hard times. Let them lean on you when they are having hard times.

R - Rest. The whole world looks better when you have had enough sleep. Make sleep a priority. It reduces stress levels. It helps you eat healthier, feel better, and deal with problems more easily.

Directions: Why do you think having good coping skills is important? Write your answer on the lines below.

_____

_____

_____

Good Reactions

In the past, you may have used some self-destructive coping skills like using alcohol, drugs, or violence to cope with situations that seemed difficult. Using the R-E-C-O-V-E-R strategies for coping with obstacles will be hard at first, but it will get easier with practice. Also, when you meet and cope with your problems sober, you can actually work toward solving them rather than trying to forget that they exist.

Some of these coping skills will work better for you than others. Try different coping skills and figure out the one(s) that work best for you.

Directions: Read each activity. Write the coping skill from page 41 that it best represents.

For example: Call a friend: <u>Enjoy friends.</u>

1. Go for a run. _____

2. Remind yourself that you are important. _____

3. Find a support group. _____

4. Go to sleep earlier. _____

5. Schedule a meeting with a positive, law abiding friend. _____

6. Play soccer. _____

7. Take a deep breath. _____

8. Go for a long walk. _____

9. Start a rock collection. _____

10. Learn how to paint. _____

Group Discussion: With a partner, discuss a coping strategy that has helped you in a difficult situation in the past.

Being a Successful Person

Stephen Covey wrote a best-selling book called *The Seven Habits of Highly Effective People*. In his book, Covey concludes that successful people are all of the following:

- **Proactive.** They work to change a situation they don't like. Successful people take charge and make a new plan whenever they face a setback.

- **Goal setters.** They continually set goals. Successful people start with the end in mind and then follow specific, well-planned steps to get to where they need to be.

- **Good at prioritizing.** They are good at setting their priorities and following through with their plan. Successful people put their list in order from highest priority to lowest priority and then work hard to achieve each item on their list.

Directions: Complete the items below.

1. Write about a time you have been proactive in a situation.

   _____

   _____

   _____

   _____

2. Describe two goals you have set for yourself this year.

   _____

   _____

   _____

   _____

3. Make a list of three things you need to do to reach your goals. Prioritize them. Number the items in your list from 1 to 3, with number 1 being the most important.

   _____

   _____

   _____

   _____

Preventing Recidivism

Recidivism in the context of the jail system is defined as inmates returning to prison. The national recidivism rate is more than 50 percent of prisoners. As you prepare to exit prison, one of your primary goals should be to stay out of prison in the future. How will you do this? What choices will you make to make sure that you reach your goal?

You will likely be returning to your same neighborhood. You will likely be around many of the same people you were around before your arrest. Even if you have changed, many of your friends may not have. How should you deal with some of the peer pressure that you may face after your release?

- **Keep your values and goals in mind**. Write them down. Read them every day. Post them somewhere where you can see them. Remember, you cannot achieve your goal(s) if you return to prison.

- **Find things you can be good at.** Learn a new skill or how to do a specific job. Take a class. Find a new hobby. Play a sport. Gaining confidence in yourself will help you keep your goals in mind and to not give in to peer pressure.

- **Surround yourself with people with similar values.** Accept the fact that you may have to find different friends after you are released from prison. Do not put yourself in dangerous situations where you might fall back into old habits and give in to peer pressure. Surround yourself with positive, law-abiding friends who will pressure you to do the right thing—not the wrong thing.

- **Practice doing the right thing.** Think about some difficult situations that you might find yourself in. Practice saying no and not giving in to peer pressure. This role-playing will help you be better prepared when you find yourself in situations where you need to stand your ground.

Directions: Did negative peer pressure play a role in your being incarcerated? If yes, how? Write your answer on the lines below.

_____

_____

_____

_____

_____

_____

Staying Out of Prison

The circumstances into which you are released have a great impact on your likelihood of recidivism. Who are the most important sources of support? Families are. Inmates who have kept family ties during their prison terms and have strong family support and/or involvement are less likely to return to prison. Having a mentor can also increase your chances of staying out of prison.

Situations that will increase your chances of staying out of prison include the following:

- Living with a spouse or partner.

- Finding a job.

- Living in a rural or less populated area upon your release.

- Living in an area with a low poverty rate—assuming you are employed.

Directions: Circle each situation that will increase your chances of staying out of prison. Cross out each situation that will increase your chances of returning to prison.

1. Not being able to find a job.

2. Living on a large farm in a rural area.

3. Living with your spouse or partner.

4. Returning to your old neighborhood.

5. Making new friends who make good choices.

6. Hanging out with old friends who make bad choices.

7. Getting a job at a grocery store.

8. Getting a job as a diesel mechanic.

9. Doing drugs.

10. Having a mentor.

Changing Behaviors

Your transition from prison back into society is going to require you to abandon some of your prior lifestyle choices for new ones. It is going to mean adopting new behaviors and ways of thinking. It is going to require you to change some of your behaviors.

Howard J. Shaffer created the Stages of Change Model (SCM). It focuses on change as a process that each individual has to progress through at his or her own pace. Here are the stages of progress.

- **Precontemplation.** You are not even aware you need to make a change.

- **Contemplation.** You know there is a problem, but you are not sure if you want to change it.

- **Preparation/Determination.** You are getting ready to make a change.

- **Action/Determination.** You actually make the change.

- **Maintenance.** You maintain the new behavior.

After you progress through all the stages, there is the possibility of relapse, or returning to old behaviors and forgetting the new ones.

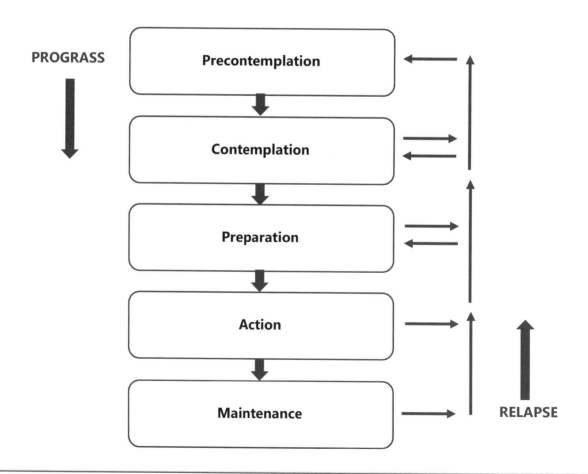

Moving in a New Direction

Directions: Think about a lifestyle choice that you need to change to make sure you stay out of prison. Write the change you want to make on the line.

_____

Now, complete the chart with as much information as you can about the lifestyle change you plan to make when you are released from prison. Include the steps you will take during the last three stages of change.

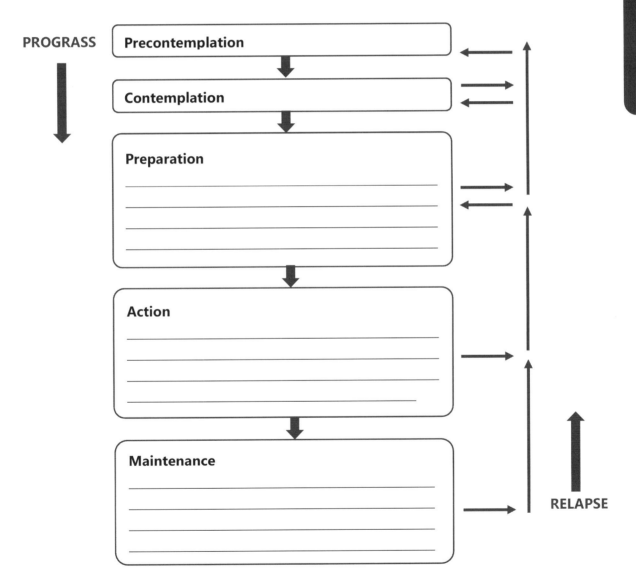

Group Discussion: Discuss the changes you want to make and how you plane to make it.

Moving Back in with Your Family

After your release from prison, you may move back in with your family. Here are a few important things to remember when you move back in.

- Get a job! Find a job and then contribute some of your earnings to the household.

- Talk to your family members about how they are feeling about having you home.

- Help! Cook dinner, make your bed, and do your own laundry. Make contributions around the house that will make your family's lives easier.

- Be patient. Moving is a big adjustment. It takes time to get settled.

- Try to have realistic expectations. Life will not be perfect when you move back home—don't expect it to be!

- Be thoughtful and respect the values of others in the house.

Directions: It will be important to get along with others in your household. Interview someone in your family about his or her values and the things that are most important to him or her. Write what you learn on the lines below.

_____

_____

_____

Personal Assessment: A Venn diagram shows the way things are alike and different. Use the Venn diagram to show which of your values match those of your family member and which do not. Write your shared values, or those that are alike, in the space in the middle where the circles overlap. Then write the values that are different in the spaces that are separate the left circle for your values, and the right circle for your family member's values.

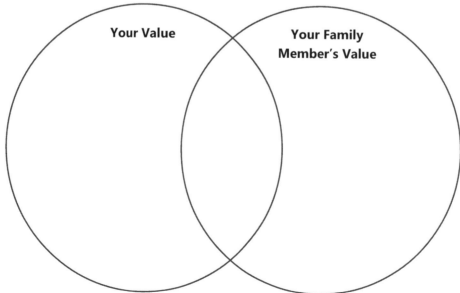

Your Value

Your Family Member's Value

Your Family

Directions: Answer the questions below.

1. Who do you consider your family? List these people in the box.

2. Has your family supported you while you have been in prison? What kind of help do you expect to receive from your family when you are released from prison?

    _____

    _____

3. Your family may also have expectations of you when you are released from prison. They might expect you to:
    *   Get a job
    *   Help pay for rent, utilities, and other household expenses
    *   Help with childcare
    *   Come in at a certain hour—keep a curfew
    *   Stay away from old friends or "troublemakers"
    *   Go to religious services
    *   Do chores
    *   Attend substance abuse classes

How will you make sure that you have a clear understanding with your family members about their expectations of you after your release? You will need to talk with family members at length so that you can come up with a plan that works for everyone.

What expectations do you think your family has of you after your release?

_____

_____

_____

_____

A Clear Plan

Here are some questions to consider if you plan on moving in with family members after your release. How will you adjust to living with your family again? How will the people in your family adjust to living with you again? The transition may be difficult—especially if you have not set clear expectations of one another. Coming up with a clear plan and sticking to it will make transition from inmate to family member easier.

Directions: Write a letter to the family member that you will be moving in with. Ask the family member to write to you with his or her expectations of you. Tell your family member anything else you think he or she should know. Ask questions about any concerns you may have.

Dear _____,

_____

_____

_____

_____

_____

_____

_____

_____

_____

_____

_____

_____

_____

Sincerely,

_____

Compliments

Previously, you learned about how being grateful can improve health and happiness. Giving compliments to others can also improve your well-being. You can compliment others on many different things—their clothing or hairstyle, their actions, or their personality traits. You can compliment others on whatever you like about them, as long as you remain appropriate.

Directions: At the top of each box, write the name of one family member or friend. Then write three to five things you like about that person in the box.

Name
_____

Name
_____

Name
_____

Name
_____

Parenting

More than 2.3 million children in the United States have incarcerated parents. If you have children, hopefully you have been able to have contact with them during your time in prison.

Love. Time. Energy. More love. Being a parent is hard work. But it is worth it. Being a parent is the most valuable job you can have. It is important to listen to and get to know your children. Time is the most valuable gift you can give them. Spending time getting to know your children again is a good way to show them how loved they are.

Directions: Complete the items below.

1. My children's favorite colors are _____.

2. My children's favorite things to do are _____.

3. My children's favorite songs are _____.

4. My children's favorite friends are _____.

5. My children's favorite sports are _____.

6. My children don't like to eat _____.

7. My children don't like to play _____.

8. My children's favorite seasons are _____.

9. I would like to take my children to _____.

List ten ways you would like to spend time with your children after your release.

_____

_____

_____

_____

_____

_____

_____

_____

Putting a Positive Spin on Rules

Your children not only need you to spend time with them, but they also need you to set clear boundaries and expectations. Clear boundaries and expectations will make your children feel more secure and confident. Coming up with three to five house rules is a good idea. Post the rules in a high-traffic area of your house. Make sure to set a positive tone with the rules. For example, use a positive house rule such as "Be kind to one another" instead of "No name-calling."

Directions: Draw a line from each rule on the left to the rule on the right that has a more positive tone.

1. Don't mess with anyone else's stuff.	Use good table manners.
2. Don't run inside the house.	Take care of your things.
3. Don't talk with your mouth full.	Respect other people's property.
4. Don't interrupt.	Tell the truth.
5. Don't lie.	Listen.
6. Don't leave your toys out.	Use walking feet indoors.

You have posted the rules and talked about the rules. At some point, one of them will be broken. There are three types of consequences for breaking a rule.

- **Natural consequences** are a direct result of not following the rules. For example, if your child is running inside, he or she may trip and fall and scrape a knee.

- **Logical consequences** are consequences related to the rule that was broken. For example, if your child doesn't put away a toy, then it will be taken away for the rest of the day.

- **Losing a privilege** means taking away something unrelated to the misbehavior. For example, if your child doesn't tell the truth, he or she might lose TV privileges for the rest of the day.

Keeping Your Cool

Have you ever given your children a time-out for not following the rules? Sometimes, parents need time-outs, too. What should you do when your children make you angry? Try the following ways to calm down.

- Take several deep breaths.
- Take a time-out for yourself.
- Listen to music.
- Go for a walk.
- Talk to a friend about it.
- Take a break outside.
- Think about why exactly you are angry.

Directions: Complete the items below.

1. What other strategies help you "keep your cool" when your children make you angry?

   _____

   _____

   _____

2. Write about a time you "lost your cool" when your children made you angry. What could you have done differently?

   _____

   _____

   _____

3. Write about a time you "kept your cool" even though you were angry with your children.

   _____

   _____

   _____

Spending Time with Your Children

It is important to spend quality time with your children. Be sure to set aside time to do activities together.

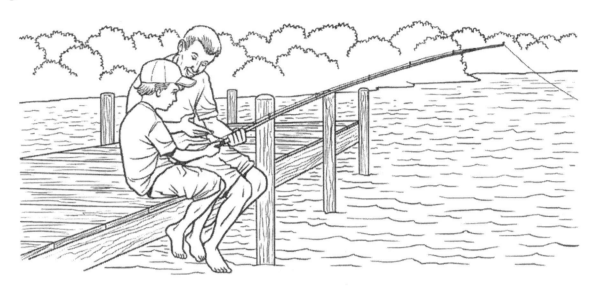

Directions: Circle the activities in the box below that you would like to do with your children. Then write four ideas of your own on the lines.

Go to The Park	Sing Songs	Rake Leaves
Ride Bicycles	Watch A Sporting Event	Play Tennis
Take A Walk	Paint	Draw
Visit A Museum	Make Breakfast	Roller-Skate
Go to The Zoo	Shop for Groceries	Ice-Skate
Play A Board Game	Play Catch	Laugh
Walk the Dog	Play Soccer	Go to The Library
Listen to Music	Go Out for Ice Cream	Go Fishing

_____

_____

_____

_____

Praising Your Children

It is important to remind your children that you love them and tell them why they are special. Not only will this strengthen your relationship with your children, but it will also help build up your children's self-esteem. What can you say to praise or encourage your children?

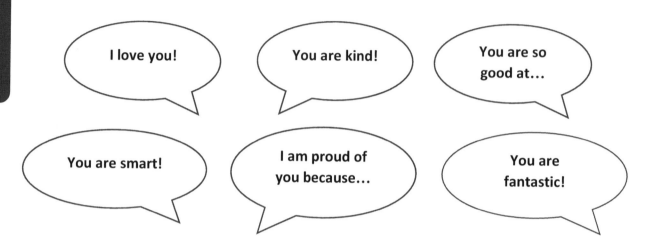

Specific, real praise is the best kind. Instead of, "You are so good at sports," try "I loved it when you dribbled up the court and made the shot right before the half." Spending time with your children, listening to your children, and praising your children are all things that will strengthen your relationship with them.

Directions: Complete the items below and share your answers with a partner.

1. Write about something you think you are good at as a parent.

   _____

   _____

   _____

   _____

2. Write about something you hope to improve upon as a parent.

   _____

   _____

   _____

   _____

Renewing Relationships

Reconnecting with family members after incarceration is not easy. Some of your family members may have trouble trusting you. Some of your family may be angry with you or feel embarrassment or shame about the fact that you spent time in prison.

You cannot change the fact that you are an ex-inmate. Now, you just have to work hard to prove yourself to the people you love again. You need to prove that you are trustworthy and dependable. You need to show your family that you learned from your mistakes and will work hard to stay out of prison in the future.

- **Communicate with your family.** Talk about life in prison and the changes you are going to make so that you don't return to prison.

- **Look for a support group.** There are many groups that offer support to ex-offenders and their families during reentry. These support groups allow you an opportunity to talk openly with one another as well as meet people in similar situations.

- **Don't fall into the same bad patterns and habits.** Stay away from the friends and situations that were part of your life before you went to prison.

- **Give yourself and your loved ones time to build trust.** You hurt your family by breaking the law. Work hard to earn back their trust and be patient that it will happen.

Directions: Describe three things that you can do to prove that you are trustworthy and dependable on the lines below.

1. _____

2. _____

3. _____

Spending Time with Your Family

Spending time with your family will help you reconnect and renew your relationships with them.

Directions: Read the ideas of things to do with your family in the box. Circle the ones you plan to do. Then write four of your own ideas on the lines below.

Turn off the television and talk to your family.

Eat dinner together. Go around the table and have everyone say one thing he or she is grateful for.

Look at pictures together.

Go to religious services together.

Shop for and cook a family dinner together.

Hike a trail together. Stop and admire the view.

Plan a date night with your spouse or partner.

Ride bicycles together.

Have everyone draw a picture of one person in the family—then put them all together as a "family portrait."

Rent a movie together and pop popcorn.

Have family game night and play board games or cards.

Cook a family dessert together.

Counseling on Individual Reentry Concerns Review

Directions: Circle the letter for each correct answer.

1. You should figure out where you are going to live before you are released from prison.
   A. True
   B. False

2. Personal responsibility means:
   A. Blaming other people.
   B. "Owning" your actions.
   C. Returning to prison.

3. Productive regret will help you:
   A. Feel really guilty.
   B. Change bad behaviors.
   C. Stay the same.

4. Proactive people:
   A. React to what other people are doing.
   B. Make changes when they need to.
   C. Both of the Above

5. Which of the following is not a coping skill?
   A. Exercising.
   B. Deep breathing.
   C. Yelling.

6. Positive people see the glass as half empty.
   A. True
   B. False

7. According to Stephen Covey, successful people:
   A. Hope for the best.
   B. Ignore laws.
   C. Set goals

8. What percentage of prisoners return to prison within three to five years of their release?
   A. Less than 25 percent.
   B. More than 50 percent.
   C. More than 75 percent.

9. The _____ into which you are released have a great deal of impact on your likelihood of recidivism.
   A. Seasons.
   B. Circumstances.
   C. Neither of the above.

10. The Stages of Change Model (SCM) focuses on change as a process.
    A. True
    B. False

11. Make sure to set a _____ tone with your rules for your children.
    A. Positive.
    B. Negative.
    C. Neutral.

12. Natural consequences are a direct result of:
    A. Losing a privilege.
    B. Not following the rules.
    C. Following the rules.

13. Recidivism means returning to prison.
    A. True
    B. False

14. What are the three basic things you need to have figured out before your release?
    A. Employment, housing, support system.
    B. Employment, housing, a new car.
    C. Childcare, car payment, exercise plan.

15. "Keeping your cool" means:
    A. Blaming others.
    B. Getting angry.
    C. Staying calm.

16. Children need a lot of freedom and little discipline.
    A. True
    B. False

17. _____ is one of the most important things you can give your children.
    A. Art.
    B. Time.
    C. Money.

18. One way to show your family you have learned from your mistakes is to:
    A. Avoid friends and situations that tempt you to get in trouble.
    B. Join a support group.
    C. Both of the Above.

19. Your family will likely have no expectations of you when you are released from prison.
    A. True
    B. False

20. How many children in the United States have incarcerated parents?
    A. 1 billion.
    B. 10,000.
    C. 2.3 million.

Employment Skills

This page intentionally left blank

Employment Skills

Course Goal: Upon completion of this course, student will understand soft skills needed to enter the workforce and how these skills are implemented on the job.

Getting Along

Being able to communicate with your boss is an important aspect of your job. Having a positive relationship with your boss will help you keep your job and be happy in it. Work hard to build a relationship with your boss based on the following guidelines.

Establish Trust.

- Trust is key to building a successful relationship with your boss.
- Do what you say you are going to do, when you say you are going to do it.
- Never steal or falsify records.
- If you make a mistake, admit it, apologize, and learn from it. Reassure your boss that you have learned from the experience and won't make the same mistake again.

Make no Excuses.

- Arrive at work on time.
- Be ready to work hard and do your part.
- Leave personal problems at home.

Ask Questions.

- If you are not sure what to do, ask.
- If you are not sure that you are doing something correctly, ask how to do it!
- Don't make assumptions.
- Asking questions is a good way to learn how to do your job correctly. Doing your job correctly is the best way to keep your job.

Follow Directions.

- Do what you are asked to do.
- Doing your job correctly and efficiently will make your boss look good.
- Making your boss look good is an excellent way to build a positive relationship with him or her.
- When your boss looks good, you look good.

Help or Hurt?

Directions: Read the list of actions below. Circle the actions that would help you build a positive relationship with your boss. Draw a line through the actions that would not help you build a positive relationship with your boss.

1. At the end of her shift, Maria is expected to make sure the cash in her drawer and the receipts match. Today, however, Maria wants to meet her friends after work. Her cash has always matched the receipts in the past, so she doesn't check the receipts and quickly clocks out.

2. Thomas doesn't hear his alarm and arrives to work late.

3. Mary asks her boss exactly how he wants the return address to read even though she thinks she knows.

4. Raul spends time on the phone at work paying his electricity bill and setting up a time to get his cable hooked up.

5. Marcus signs off on a mileage report he is unsure about because he needs to get home soon and thinks it is close enough.

6. Leila knows she is going to have to attend a funeral next week. She tells her boss right away.

7. Sam had another fight with his wife this morning. When he gets to work, though, he decides to focus on his job instead of stewing about the argument.

8. Marty takes computer paper, staplers, and colored pencils from the office supply room so that he can complete a personal art activity he is working on at home.

9. Samantha sets up a time to meet with her boss because she has questions about the project she is working on.

10. Lou is really hungry. He decides to stop at the coffee shop for a quick breakfast even though it will make him several minutes late to work.

Communicating Effectively

It is important to communicate effectively and have a positive relationship with your boss. Establishing trust, making no excuses, asking questions, and following directions are four important parts of building this successful relationship.

Directions: Read each sentence on the left. Decide if the action is an example of establishing trust, making no excuses, asking questions, or following directions. Write your answer in the column on the right. Some actions may have more than one answer.

Example; Tom calls his boss as soon as he realizes his car won't start.	Establishing Trust or Making No Excuses
1. Lou calls his boss to clarify which file should be sent.	
2. Ingrid double-checks the receipts with her cash drawer.	
3. José admits his mistake.	
4. Mary tallies up Evan's hours before signing off on his time sheet.	
5. Sam asks what to do next after he completes his first job.	
6. Chris rereads the checklist on how his company wants him to make a chocolate sundae to make sure he does it correctly.	
7. Peyton divides the tip jar evenly among himself and the other employees.	
8. Paul finds a babysitter for his daughter so that he can get to work on time.	

Working Together

Getting along with co-workers is also important. Thinking about yourself and your co-workers as a T-E-A-M can help you work more effectively with your co-workers.

> **T- Thoughtful.** Get to work on time, don't miss work, speak to your co-workers, smile, don't gossip, and be considerate. It's also important to appreciate differences among people and cultures. Don't make jokes or comments that single out or stereotype any one group of people.
>
> **E- Effective**. Do your work, do a good job, and pull your weight.
>
> **A- Avoid Alcohol and Drugs.** Never use alcohol or drugs at work. Show up to work sober.
>
> **M - Motivated.** Be energetic, figure out what needs to be done at work, and do your part.

Being a T-E-A-M player helps everyone. Employees' attitudes and behaviors are contagious and affect productivity. Being positive is important!

Directions: Answer the questions below.

1. Why do you think employees' attitudes and behaviors are contagious?

   _____

2. What does the "A" in T-E-A-M mean?

   _____

3. What does "pull your weight" mean?

   _____

4. Why do you think being present at work every day and getting to work on time are part of being a thoughtful co-worker?

   _____

5. Why do you think it is important not to gossip at work?

   _____

6. Give an example of being able to appreciate differences among people and cultures.

   _____

T-E-A-M

A large part of being a good co-worker is working together to do a good job for your boss and company. Being a good T-E-A-M member means working effectively. It means staying motivated and on task.

Good co-workers help each other work hard.

Working hard, being positive, and effectively communicating with co-workers are important parts of your job.

Directions: The employees in the situations below are not being T-E-A-M players. Read each situation. Then, write which part of T-E-A-M would help the co-worker(s) make the right choice. Explain why you chose that answer.

1. Chuck and Rita are at an all-day training session for their company. Between the afternoon and evening training session, Chuck invites Rita to go to the bar next door for a few pitchers of beer.

   _____

   _____

   _____

2. Phillip works as a data entry clerk in a large accounting firm. His work can get pretty boring. He downloads his favorite game off the Internet and takes a break to play the game for an hour or two.

   _____

   _____

   _____

3. Manny still has a lot of personal shopping to do before the holidays. Since he has just finished one project, he plans to spend all day Friday completing his holiday shopping online from his computer at work.

   _____

   _____

   _____

Staying Calm

Have you heard the saying, "The customer is always right"? Some customers can be hard to work with. The best way to deal with difficult customers is by keeping your cool. Often angry customers just want to feel heard. They want to feel like they are right. They want to feel like you understand.

Since customers are a key ingredient to a successful business—just like your boss and co-workers— they are very important people to get along with. When communicating with customers in person:

- Stay calm and be polite.
- Listen and give customers your full attention.
- Try to figure out a solution or a place to direct them so a solution can be found.
- Document what was said and make sure to give your notes to your boss.
- Smile.

Some jobs involve speaking on the telephone to customers. Being polite and responsive to customers on the phone is very important. When communicating with customers over the phone—

- Stay calm and be polite.
- Listen and focus on what the customers are saying.
- Try to figure out a solution or connect them with a supervisor who can help them solve their problem.
- Always ask customers if you can put them on hold or transfer them before you do it.
- Smile—even while speaking with customers on the phone.

Directions: Each item below gives two possible responses for speaking with customers. Circle the best telephone response.

1. Hold the line.   Will you hold a moment, please?

2. Do you mind if I transfer your call to Ms. Jones? I think she will be better able to help you.   I'm transferring you to Ms. Jones.

3. Mr. Guerra will be back in an hour. May I have him call you back?   Mr. Guerra is out playing golf.

   May I please ask who is calling?

4. Who is this?

Figure It Out

Listening, staying calm, and trying to help customers figure out workable solutions are all important aspects of being able to effectively communicate with your customers. Keeping a positive attitude and a smile on your face are also helpful. Frequently, all a customer needs is to feel like you are on his or her side.

Directions: With a partner or small group, read each situation. Then read each of the possible responses. Talk about which responses might work best and why.

Situation 1: You work at a clothing store. Your store has a giant sale every February. A customer comes to your register angry that the pants he bought in December have recently gone on sale for half price. He demands a refund on the pants even though he has been wearing them regularly for two months.

Possible Responses:

 A. *Tell your customer that he has been wearing the pants for two months and he is just going to have to deal with the fact that sometimes things go on sale.*
 B. *Reassure your customer that his situation sounds frustrating and offer to call the manager.*

Situation 2: A customer says she wants to return a television because it is the wrong size for her apartment. She does not have the receipt or the credit card it was purchased with.

Possible Responses:

 A. *Tell your customer that it sounds like she is in a difficult situation and that you will have to call the manager to help her figure out how to solve it.*
 B. *Tell the customer that she should have measured the space for the television before she bought it and that without a receipt there are absolutely no returns—ever.*

Situation 3: Your store is very busy at lunchtime. Several customers have to wait in line for more than 10 minutes before checking out. They are angry and ask you why the service at your store is so terrible.

Possible Responses:

 A. *Agree with the customers that the lunchtime wait was an inconvenience and reassure them that your store is working to improve the situation.*
 B. *Tell your customers that you are tired of the situation at your store, too. Explain to them that you don't feel like dealing with people with bad attitudes either and that they should show a little more appreciation for the cashiers.*

Situation 4: Have you ever dealt with an unsatisfied customer at a job? Discuss what happened and how you worked to solve it.

What Is Sexual Harassment?

Sexual harassment is inappropriate behavior that makes you feel uncomfortable. It is unwelcome and affects the workplace in a negative way. If you are being sexually harassed in your workplace, it is important that you clearly communicate—verbally, in writing, or by your actions—that you want the harassment to stop immediately. If the sexual harassment does not stop, it is important that you document the facts and report them to your boss right away.

What does sexual harassment look like?

Sexual harassment can sometimes be hard to define. At first something might seem funny or harmless. Then it starts to make you more and more uncomfortable. It makes it hard for you to concentrate at work and do your job effectively.

Sexual harassment might be **verbal, visual, physical**, or **written**. Here are some examples.

- **Verbal:** telling inappropriate sexual or sex-based jokes, repeatedly asking someone out, joking about wanting sexual favors, making comments about someone's physical appearance, or spreading rumors about a person's sex life

- **Visual:** looking up and down someone's body, making sexual gestures at another person, or secretly watching a person

- **Physical:** inappropriate touching, stroking, patting, or hugging; blocking someone into a space, assault

- **Written:** posters, emails, social media postings, drawings, pictures of a sexual nature

Why do people sexually harass others?

Most people who sexually harass others are trying to prove their power. The harasser's goal is usually to intimidate or control—not to have a relationship with the person being sexually harassed. People who sexually harass others in front of their co-workers may be trying to get attention or approval.

What can you do to try to prevent sexual harassment in the workplace?

Do not tolerate it. If you hear others making sexual or sex-based jokes and comments at the office, remind them that jokes or comments like that are not appropriate at work. Do not laugh or take part in the conversation. Dress in an appropriate manner for the office. Inform your boss quickly and clearly if co-workers behave in an inappropriate way at the workplace.

Defining Sexual Harassment

Directions: For each sentence below, decide whether it is an example of verbal, visual, physical, or written sexual harassment. Write your answer on the line.

1. Your co-worker tells rude, sex-based jokes during lunch. _____

2. Your co-worker pats your bottom as you walk to the copier. _____

3. Your co-worker secretly blows you kisses after an important meeting. _____

4. Your boss posts how "hot" you looked at work on his Facebook page. _____

5. Your boss repeatedly asks you to come over to her apartment after work for a drink.

    _____

6. Your boss strokes your leg under a table at a meeting. _____

7. Your co-worker shows you pictures of himself in his underwear. _____

8. Your boss follows you to the bus stop and watches you wait for the bus. _____

9. Your co-worker rubs up against you every time she passes you in the hall. _____

10. Your boss emails you to tell you he is thinking about how sexy you are. _____

Group Discussion: Have you ever felt sexually harassed in your workplace? How? Talk about this experience.

Dressing for Work

Making a good impression at your workplace is important. Clothes, accessories, and even shoes can influence how you are perceived at work.

The good news is that something as simple as wearing the right clothes to work can lead people to trust and respect you.

What should you wear to work? The answer depends on what job you have. If you are working as a nurse in a hospital, it may be perfectly acceptable to wear tennis shoes since you are on your feet all day. If you are meeting with clients in an office, tennis shoes probably are not the best choice. Here are some things to consider:

- Does your workplace have a dress code? Find out fast. If there is a dress code, make sure to ask for a copy and read it. If you aren't sure about wearing a certain item, ask your boss. Ask about tattoos and piercings, too. Some employers will want tattoos and piercings to be covered up at the workplace. If there is not a dress code, pay attention to what others are wearing at work to determine what is acceptable.

- Do you need to purchase a uniform for your job? Some workplaces may have strict requirements about what color shoes to wear. Other workplaces may require shirts to be starched and dry cleaned. Make sure to find out all of the details so that you can be dressed appropriately.

- Are there any safety requirements about what you can and can't wear to work? For example, many jobs require that workers wear closed-toe shoes. Get the details before your first day. When you show up to work, you want to be able to work safely.

- Look around at what your boss and co-workers are wearing. Try to dress to the same level as them. Wear a tie if your boss and co-workers are wearing ties.

- Plan what you are going to wear your first few days on the job so you don't have to scramble in the mornings. If you don't have appropriate clothing, see if you can borrow some from a friend or buy a few essential items to get you through the first week. Then, set aside money to buy more as your budget permits.

Clothes influence how people see you, so they are an important part of being successful at work.

Closet Connections

Directions: Read Clarissa's and Jeremiah's job descriptions. Then, go through their closets and circle the things that you think would be appropriate workplace attire.

Clarissa's Closet

Clarissa is an accountant for a large accounting firm. She works in a high-rise office building in downtown Boston. She works in the front office and is often the first-person clients meet when they enter the accounting office.

Blouse	High Heels
Business Suit	Dress Shoes
Slacks	Pantyhose
Blue Jean Skirt	Mini-Skirt
Flip-Flops	Dress Pants
Dress	Running Shoes
Sleeveless Shirt	Sweater
Jean Jacket	Athletic Pants
Shorts	Jacket
Jewelry	Dressy Skirt

Jeremiah's Closet

Jeremiah is a production worker in an automotive parts factory. He works long days with his co-workers and frequently has to work underneath cars. His job requires him to wear closed-toe shoes.

Cowboy Boots	Tuxedo
Business Suit	Sweater
T-Shirt	Jeans
White Button-Down Shirt	Dress Pants
	Jewelry
Running Shoes	Open-Toe
Tie	Sandals Dress
Flip-Flops	Shoes
	Shorts

Personal Assessment: Now, name a place you would like to work. _____

List appropriate workplace attire for your job.

_____

_____

_____

_____

The Basic Ten

Do you greet your grandmother the same way you greet your boss? Do you talk to your co-workers the same way you talk with your friends when you are out on a Saturday night? Behavior and manners change depending on where you are, what you are doing, and who you are with.

Being professional in the workplace is important. Following the Basic Ten will help you be successful interacting with your co-workers and boss.

1. Actively listen to your boss and co-workers: look at them while they are talking, think about what they are saying, and take notes if you need to.

2. Keep your personal life out of your workplace.

3. Do not criticize other people's work or offer advice unless it is asked for.

4. Respect diversity. Don't criticize other people's beliefs or expect others to share your own beliefs. Don't judge other people based on their ethnicity, religion, or appearance. Respect different work styles.

5. Do not talk about people. Office gossip only creates problems. Avoid situations where other people are gossiping. Never repeat office gossip that you hear. It has no place in a successful workplace.

6. Stay out of office politics. Don't get involved.

7. Say "please" and "thank you" often.

8. Say "hello" and "good-bye" to your co-workers and people you see in the elevators, in the halls, and on the stairs.

9. Don't complain. Be positive.

10. Work hard.

Working Well

Directions: Circle the acceptable work behaviors. Cross out the unacceptable work behaviors.

1. You say "hello" to your co-workers when you arrive at work.

2. You ask your co-worker to repeat what she just said so you can make sure you understand.

3. You have a beer with a co-worker over lunch.

4. You tell your co-worker all about how hard your job is.

5. You look at your boss while he is talking to you and concentrate on what he is saying.

6. You complain about having to do more work than anyone else in the office for the same pay.

7. You thank your co-worker for making extra copies for you.

8. You repeat a very surprising office rumor to your co-worker at lunch.

9. You explain to your co-worker the many ways his presentation could be improved.

10. You make a joke about your co-worker's religion.

11. You work hard and stay focused at work even though things at home are difficult.

12. You curse loudly at your boss several times when you get a poor performance review.

13. You ignore what the co-worker you don't like says during a work meeting.

14. You make a joke about the outfit your boss is wearing to a large group of co-workers at lunch.

15. You stay a few minutes late to help your co-worker find the file he is looking for on the computer

Business or Personal

Your work relationships are much different than your personal relationships. You may want to share every detail of your Saturday night date with your best friend, but this same information is not appropriate to discuss with your co-worker during business hours.

Three topics to avoid at work are:

- Religion
- Politics
- Personal Problems (relationships, health issues, money problems)

Directions: Read each situation. Then, write your answers on the lines.

1. Pretend you are going to lunch with your best friend. List three things you might talk about.

   _____

   _____

   _____

2. Pretend you are going to lunch with your boss, List three things you might talk about.

   _____

   _____

   _____

3. Do you think you would talk about the same things? Why or why not?

   _____

   _____

   _____

Personal Hygiene

Personal hygiene means keeping your body clean and healthy so you can look and feel your best. Having good personal hygiene is part of being a good employee. It is important that you look and smell good every day.

Simple things like taking a shower, brushing your hair and teeth, and not putting on too much cologne or perfume are all things that are going to make people perceive you positively. They are also things your co-workers and boss will appreciate.

Another reason personal hygiene is important in a workplace is because it keeps workers healthy. The healthier workers stay, the less often they have to miss work. The less often they miss work, the more they are able to accomplish. The single best way to stay healthy is to wash your hands—but other grooming habits are important, too. Good personal hygiene will keep you healthy and your co-workers and boss happy.

Directions: Rate yourself on a scale of 1 to 10 for each statement below, with 10 meaning that the statement is always true, and 1 meaning that it is never true.

_____**1**. Sometimes I wear my clothes several days before washing them.

_____ **2**. I brush my hair every morning.

_____ **3**. I keep my fingernails short.

_____ **4**. I bite my fingernails.

_____ **5**. I always wash my hands after using the restroom.

_____ **6**. I wear deodorant every day.

_____ **7**. I chew on my shirt sleeves.

_____ **8**. When I sneeze or cough, I always cover my mouth.

_____ **9**. I never floss my teeth.

_____ **10**. I brush my teeth twice a day.

Group Discussion: With a partner or small group, talk more about personal hygiene. What aspects of personal hygiene are most important to you? Why? What aspects of personal hygiene are less important to you? Why? Why do you think personal hygiene is important at work?

Good Grooming

Taking care of yourself and having good personal hygiene are also related to your self-image. Taking care of yourself and having good personal hygiene can improve your self-esteem and increase your confidence. Good personal hygiene also shows others that you respect yourself, you want to make a good impression, and that you expect to be taken seriously.

Directions: Check each item that describes something you need to do to have good personal hygiene.

☐ **1.** Take a shower weekly.

☐ **2.** Wash your face nightly.

☐ **3.** Shampoo your hair daily if needed.

☐ **4.** Brush your teeth once a day.

☐ **5.** Shave monthly.

☐ **6.** Cut your fingernails yearly.

☐ **7.** Get a haircut once a year.

☐ **8.** Brush or comb your hair weekly.

☐ **9.** Never use deodorant.

☐ **10.** Practice good posture monthly.

Partner Activity: Now, with a partner go back and reread each sentence. Change each unchecked sentence to a correct sentence. For example, the statement "Floss your teeth weekly" could be changed to "Floss your teeth daily."

Being an A-W-E-S-O-M-E Team Player

Most jobs require you to work with a variety of people. You will like some of your co-workers more than others. Part of your job is learning how to work effectively with all of your co-workers. Learning how to be a team player with a positive attitude will help you become more successful at work.

Being positive at work is important. A good attitude is contagious. If you are working hard to be a positive team player, it is likely your co-workers will want to be positive players, too.

What does a positive team player look like? A positive team player looks A-W-E-S-O-M-E!

A - Always Wear a Smile. Keep a smile on your face even when you are having a hard day. Smile even when you are having personal problems. "Fake it until you make it" in the workplace.

W - Work Hard. Be willing to do your part. Don't be afraid to do more than your share. Take the initiative to figure out what needs to be done every day.

E - Even-Tempered. Keep your cool at work. Don't lose your temper, get too emotional, make snap judgments, or criticize others. If something upsets you while you are at work, try to find a private place to deal with your emotions. Once you have calmed down, you have a better chance of resolving the issue in a professional manner.

S - Stay Focused. Think about your job and how to effectively get it done. Don't spend your work time on personal tasks.

O - Only You. Don't blame or criticize others for your mistakes or problems. Focus on yourself and how you can get better at your job.

M - Mistakes. Admit your mistakes when you make them and move on. Use your mistakes as learning experiences and think about how you can avoid making those mistakes again.

E - Encourage. Encourage the people around you. Notice other people's good work. Celebrate your co-workers' and boss's successes.

A-W-E-S-O-M-E

Directions: Answer each question on the lines provided.

1. What do you think "fake it until you make it" means? Why is this a good strategy to use in the workplace?

   _____

   _____

2. What does the "M" in A-W-E-S-O-M-E stand for? Why do you think this is important?

   _____

   _____

3. How do you think encouraging others makes you a positive team player?

   _____

   _____

4. How could getting too emotional at work hurt your productivity?

   _____

   _____

5. What does the "W" in A-W-E-S-O-M-E stand for? Why do you think this is important?

   _____

   _____

6. Do you think a good attitude is contagious? Why or why not?

   _____

   _____

The Right Job for You

Most people will spend about one-third of their life working, so it is very important to think about the type of work you might enjoy. Do you like math or history? Do you prefer to work in a group or by yourself? Take time to think about the things you like to do. Spend time researching the different jobs you think you would like to do.

Directions: Check the statements below that apply to you.

☐ **1.** I prefer to be inside.

☐ **2.** I prefer to be outside.

☐ **3.** I like change.

☐ **4.** I like sitting still.

☐ **5.** I like working with computers.

☐ **6.** I like working with people.

☐ **7.** I like sports.

☐ **8.** I like animals.

☐ **9.** I am comfortable being in a hospital.

☐ **10.** I like moving around a lot.

☐ **11.** I prefer to work during the day.

☐ **12.** I prefer to work at night.

☐ **13.** I like learning new skills.

☐ **14.** I like to do the same thing over and over.

Group Discussion: Based on your preferences, can you think of a job you might like? Why? What job do you think you might not like? Why?

Applying for a Job

Applying for a job can be a humbling experience. It takes a lot of time and effort to apply for jobs.

Applications are long. You might apply for many jobs online and/or in person that you don't get. Sometimes, you'll hear back from employers, and sometimes you won't. Sometimes it can feel like your application is going in a deep, dark hole.

Stay optimistic! You will find a job. Often the application process takes time. Filling out a **job application** is the first step. A job application is a form that tells the employer who you are. It asks you questions such as the following:

- What is your current address?

- How long have you resided at your current address?

- What schools have you attended? List the names and addresses of each of the schools you have attended.

- What jobs have you had? Where have you worked? List your past employers and the names of your former bosses. Include their addresses and phone numbers.

Since each job application requires filling in a lot of information, making a written copy of this information is a good idea. Saving this information on your computer is also a good idea. That way, each time you are ready to apply for a job, you will be able to access this important information easily.

You will also need to prove who you are when you are applying for jobs. You will often need the following items when you are filling out a job application:

- Social Security Card

- Birth Certificate

- Passport, Driver's License or Identification Card

Getting the Right References

References are important. References are people who know you well and who will recommend you to an employer. An employer will call and talk to your references before they formally offer you a job. If your references do not know you well or do not give you a good recommendation, it is unlikely you will be hired for the job.

Who makes a good reference?

A good reference will speak highly of you and your work ethic. Consider listing the following people as references:

- A former employer who thought highly of you.

- A former co-worker who enjoyed working with you.

- A former teacher who enjoyed having you as a student.

- A family friend who has positive things to say about you.

- Someone you have done work for in the past.

- Someone you have done volunteer work with.

Who does **NOT** make a good reference?

A bad reference may result in an employer rejecting your application. Do **NOT** list the following people as references:

- A family member or intimate friend.

- A casual acquaintance.

- Someone you have done work for in the past who would not be willing to rehire you .

Contact Your References

Before you begin filling out a job application, make a list of the people you want to use as references. Gather their current job title, telephone number, and address. Contact them and make sure they are comfortable being a reference for you. Giving them a little warning that someone might call and ask about your work performance will give them time to think about your good qualities and the things they enjoyed about working with you. If any of the people you contact are not comfortable recommending you, take them off the list and do not use them as a reference.

You want to make sure your references are all people who will speak highly of you and your ability to be an effective employee.

The Right References

Directions: Circle the people in the box that might make a good reference on your job application.

1. Your sister-in-law.

2. A former teacher who thought you were gifted in math.

3. A former boss who fired you for being late too much.

4. A former boss who gave you a promotion.

5. Your dad.

6. A former art teacher who inspired you to learn to sculpt.

7. A former boss who was impressed by your work ethic.

8. A former boss who won't call you back.

Personal Assessment: Think of someone in your life who would be a good reference. On the lines below, write 1 - 2 sentences proving why this person would be a good reference.

Good reference: _____

_____

_____

Now, think of someone who would NOT be a good reference. On the lines below, write 1 - 2 sentences proving why this person would NOT be a good reference.

NOT a good reference: _____

_____

_____

Avoiding Common Mistakes

Filling out an application form is not hard, but it can be stressful and frustrating. These hints and tips can help you avoid the common mistakes many job applicants make.

- If you can, pick up the application and take it home to fill out so you aren't rushed. If you must fill out the application in person, remember to bring all support documents—identification, list of prior jobs with dates, list of references, etc.—you need to fill out the application completely.

- Make sure you fill out the entire application. If a question on your application does not apply to you, write "N/A," which means "not applicable." This will let your employer know that your application is complete.

- Always tell the truth on your application. If the application asks if you have ever been convicted of a felony, an acceptable answer would be, "Will discuss at an interview." All of the information on your application must be true.

- Most applications will ask about your education. If you didn't graduate from high school, but you have successfully passed the tests of General Educational Development (GED®), make sure to list this under the "Education" section of your job application. Completion of your GED® shows potential employers that you have the same credentials as a high school graduate. It also shows employers that you are able to successfully work toward achieving a goal. Also, make sure to list any certifications or special training you have under "Education." For example, if you have certification as a welder or electrician, make sure to include this information on your job application—even if it is not directly related to the specific job for which you are applying.

- Reread your application. Check for careless mistakes and spelling mistakes. Check your spelling using a dictionary or a spell checker on your computer. An employer wants to see that you can do quality work. Your application should be error free.

- Make sure your application is neat and easy to read. If you take the application home to fill out, keep it as clean as possible. Make sure you do not spill grease or food on your application.

- Do not give any specific salary amounts if your job application asks you how much you want to get paid. Write "negotiable" on this line.

- Sign and date your application. By doing so, you are agreeing that all of the information on your application is true.

Job applications frequently will specify what color pen you should use. Black ink is often required. Buy erasable pens so that you can correct errors on your application easily while still keeping it neat. It is also good to have correction tape or fluid on hand.

Sample Job Application

Directions: Complete this sample job application.

Job Application

Company
Employment Application
An Equal Opportunity Employer

Company is an equal opportunity employer. This application will not be used for limiting or excluding any applicant from consideration for employment on a basis prohibited by local, state, or federal law. Applicant requiring reasonable accommodation in the application and/or interview process should notify a representative of the organization.

Please print and complete all sections.

Applicant Information

Applicant name _____

Home phone _____ Alternative phone _____

Email address _____

Current Address:

Number and street _____

City _____ State & ZIP _____

How were you referred to this company? _____

Employment Positions

Position(s) applying for: _____

Are you applying for?

- Temporary work, such as summer or holiday work? ☐ Y or ☐ N

- Regular part-time work? ☐ Y or ☐ N

- Regular full-time work? ☐ Y or ☐ N

What days and hours are you available for work? _____

If applying for temporary work, when will you be available? _____

If hired, on what date can you start working? _____/_____/_____

Can you work on the weekends? ☐ Y or ☐ N   Can you work evenings? ☐ Y or ☐ N

Are you available to work overtime? ☐ Y or ☐ N   Salary desired: $ _____

Personal Information

Have you ever applied to/worked for this company before? ☐ Y or ☐ N

If yes, please explain (include dates): _____

Do you have any friends, relatives, or acquaintances working for this company: ☐ Y or ☐ N

If yes, state name & relationship: _____

If hired, would you have transportation to/from work? ☐ Y or ☐ N

Are you over the age of 18? ☐ Y or ☐ N

(If under 18, hire is subject to verification of minimum legal age).

If hired, will you be able to present evidence of your U.S. citizenship or proof of your legal right to work in the United States? ☐ Y or ☐ N

If hired, are you willing to submit to and pass a controlled substance test? ☐ Y or ☐ N

Are you able to perform the essential functions of the job for which you are applying, either with/without reasonable accommodation? ☐ Y or ☐ N

If no, describe the functions that cannot be performed: _____

_____

_____

(Note: This company complies with the ADA and considers reasonable accommodation measures that may be necessary for eligible applicants/employees to perform essential functions. It is possible that a hire may be tested on skill/agility and may be subject to a medical examination conducted by a medical professional.)

Have you ever been convicted of a criminal offense (felony or misdemeanor)? ☐ Y or ☐ N
If yes, please describe the crime—state nature of the crime(s), when and where convicted, and disposition of the case.

_____

_____

_____

(Note: No applicant will be denied employment solely on the grounds of conviction of a criminal offense. The date of the offense, the nature of the offense, including any significant details that affect the description of the event, and the surrounding circumstances and the relevance of the offense to the position(s) applied for may, however, be considered.)

Education, Training, and Experience

High School:

School name: _____

School address: _____

Number of years completed: _____

Did you graduate? ☐ Y or ☐ N

Degree/diploma earned: _____

College / University:

School name: _____

School address: _____

Number of years completed: _____

Did you graduate? ☐ Y or ☐ N

Degree/diploma earned: _____

Vocational School:

School name: _____

School address: _____

Number of years completed: _____

Did you graduate? ☐ Y or ☐ N

Degree/diploma earned: _____

Military:

Branch: _____

Rank in military: _____

Total years of service: _____

Skills/duties: _____

Understanding the Interviewing Process

Interviewing for a new job is stressful. Being prepared and knowing exactly what to expect at your interview can make things easier.

Since different types of businesses have different types of interviews, make sure that you ask about exactly who is going to interview you before you arrive for your first interview. In some situations, you may speak directly with the person who will be supervising you. In other situations, there may be rounds of interviews, and you may speak with different groups of people. For example, one group might include potential managers, while another group might include potential co-workers.

Some businesses have a Human Resources Department, which will often be your first point of contact. Human Resources representatives may want to have a phone interview with you before they recommend an in-person interview to your potential manager. Even though you won't be working directly with the Human Resources representative if you get the job, it is important to be professional and courteous with him or her.

Ask questions before you arrive at your interview to make sure that you understand that company's interview process. Before you arrive at your interview, ask the following questions:

- Whom will I be interviewing with?

- How many rounds of interviews will there be?

- How long will my interview last?

- What is your company's dress code?

- Do I need to bring anything (Social Security card, driver's license, list of references) ?

- Are there any additional forms I need to fill out?

Preparing for Your Interview

Congratulations! You have been invited to interview for a job. Preparing for an interview is important because you only get one chance to make a good first impression.

Before the Day of Your Interview:

- Pick out what you are going to wear. Make sure it is comfortable, clean, and fits you well.

- Practice shaking hands, smiling, and greeting your interviewer. A roommate or friend might be willing to play the part of your interviewer so that you can gain confidence.

- Research the company you are interviewing with. What does the company do? Look online and read the newspaper. Do you know anyone who works there? If so, ask this person about the company's culture. Research the job you are interviewing for. Make sure you know what skills you need to be successful at the job you are interviewing for.

- Practice selling yourself. The person interviewing will likely ask you questions about yourself. He or she might say, "Tell me about yourself. Why would you be a good fit for this job? What are your strengths? What are your weaknesses?" Practice answering these types of questions.

- Print out a map detailing exactly where you are going for your job interview.

- Get a good night's sleep.

On the Day of Your Interview:

- Get up early. Eat a healthy breakfast.

- Take a shower. Get ready.

- Read over your notes about the company you are interviewing with and the position you are interviewing for. Review your resume.

- Leave home early to make sure you have plenty of time to get to your interview on time.

- Relax. You are going to do great!

The Day After Your Interview:

- Follow up with a note thanking the person who interviewed you, and remind him or her why you are the best candidate for the job.

Remember that selling yourself is an important part of a successful job interview.

Possible Interview Questions

The best way to prepare for an interview is to practice. If possible, have a friend or roommate play the role of the person interviewing you. This will help you learn to think on your feet, and it will make you more relaxed when you arrive at your interview.

- Practice introducing yourself at the start of the interview.

- Make sure you look directly at the person who is interviewing you and state your name clearly.

- Shake hands firmly with the person interviewing you before you take your seat.

- Smile—being upbeat and enthusiastic is important.

- Practice talking clearly during your interview—you want to make sure the person interviewing you understands exactly what you are saying.

- Remember to actively listen—you can learn important things about the company and its expectations during your interview.

Directions: Imagine that you have an interview scheduled for a new job. Identify the job on the line below. Then, work with a partner and practice answering each of these questions. Write your responses on a separate sheet of paper.

Job:

_____

1. Tell me about some of your strengths.

2. Tell me about some of your weaknesses.

3. If your former co-workers had to describe you, what do you think they would say?

4. What did you like most about your previous job? Least?

5. Describe your work style.

6. Do you work well with other people?

7. What interests you about this job?

8. Do you prefer to work on your own or with a team?

9. How well do you handle pressure?

10. Do you like to work under pressure?

11. Describe a typical work week for you.

12. Why should we hire you for this job opening?

An Honest Interview

When you are invited for an interview, it is important that you discuss your past with the person interviewing you. This includes discussing your felony conviction.

Take Responsibility for Your Actions. Admit your mistake. Talk about what serious consequences your bad choice had on you and your family. Explain to your interviewer how you have changed. Reassure your interviewer that you have changed.

Talk About What You Learned from Your Experience. Have you rebuilt your life with your family? Have you earned your GED® or college degree? Have you learned how to play an instrument? Have you become an artist? Talk about how a bad choice helped you learn how to make better ones. Talk about what you accomplished while you were incarcerated and since your release.

Talk About How You Have Changed Since Your Experience. How have you changed since you were released? Do you value your freedom more? Do you look at working at a job as a gift? Are you more responsible? Talk about specific changes you have made that will direct you toward success. Talk about how determined you are to make the right choices from now on.

Talk About the Skills You Have That Will Make You Successful at Work. Explain how these skills make you especially qualified for the task(s) at hand. Talk about specific things that you will do to improve the workplace and be successful at your job.

Mention That A Federal Tax Break Is Available to Companies Who Hire Former Felons. Both the Federal Bonding Program and the Work Opportunity Tax Credit (WOTC) will offer benefits to your employer for hiring you. The federal government wants you to find a job! The Federal Bonding Program provides free insurance to employers to protect them from employee theft. You can print the bonding program brochure and take it with you to your interview. This brochure will help answer questions your employer may have about the program. Also, print a WOTC brochure. This brochure provides details about how your employer can apply for and receive a tax credit after hiring you as a new employee.

Take Time for a Thank You

Make sure you send a thank-you note within 24 hours after your interview. A handwritten note on simple stationary is a good way to go. What should you say? You should say that you enjoyed interviewing for the position. If you shared a joke or something else meaningful, you could mention that. Remind your interviewer again about what a good fit you are for the job opening.

It is important to follow up with a thank-you letter after a job interview whether you were hired for the position or not. Below is a sample thank-you letter. This letter can be reworded if necessary to express appreciation for just being given the opportunity to interview.

6000 Main Street
Portland, Maine 02140

Mr. Joe Peterson
General Repairs
P.O. Box 94064
Portland, Maine 02140

Dear Mr. Peterson:

Thank you for taking the time to interview me yesterday for your heating technician opening. I enjoyed meeting you.

I think my recent training and experience working with both gas and electric heaters makes me an excellent fit for your company, General Repairs. Regardless of your final decision, I enjoyed meeting you and learning about your company.

I look forward to hearing from you.

Respectfully,
Joe Johnson

If it is not possible to send a handwritten letter, at least follow up the interview with an email or a phone call. Even if you don't get the job, sending a thank-you note is the right thing to do. Also, you never know—the same company might have another opening that you ARE the perfect fit for.

Your Personal Thanks

Directions: Read the scenario below. Then, write a thank-you note to Mr. Cambridge.

Yesterday, you interviewed for a job you really want. You felt you had a good connection with the man who interviewed you. When you walked into his office, you noticed he had a Pittsburgh Steelers mug. The Steelers happen to be your favorite team, too. You knew all the team's stats, and the two of you spent a few minutes talking about the team before starting the interview.

You believe you are very qualified for his company's job opening. He needs someone to work full-time in his shop, TV Tronics. Your recent classes taught you all the latest television repair technology. In fact, you really don't think that there is a television that you can't fix. You want to thank Mr. Cambridge for interviewing you yesterday.

276 Maple Avenue, Apartment #3C
Wheeling, West Virginia 89877

Mr. Mike Cambridge
TV Tronics
76 Main Street
Wheeling, West Virginia 89877

Dear Mr. Cambridge:

_____

_____

_____

_____

_____

_____

_____

_____

_____

_____

Respectfully,

_____

Employment Skills Review

Directions: Circle the letter for each correct answer.

1. What is the key to building a positive relationship with your boss?
   A. Being aggressive.
   B. Establishing trust.
   C. Making assumptions.

2. What does the "A" in T-E-A-M stand for?
   A. Ask your teammates to help you often.
   B. Always smile.
   C. Avoid alcohol and drugs.

3. What should you try to do first when dealing with an angry customer?
   A. Stay calm.
   B. Walk away.
   C. Call security.

4. Telling inappropriate or sex-based jokes at work is what type of sexual harassment?
   A. Visual
   B. Physical
   C. Verbal

5. Your boss is inappropriately stroking your hand during a team meeting. Which type of sexual harassment is this an example of?
   A. Visual
   B. Physical
   C. Verbal

6. Clothes, accessories, and even shoes can influence:
   A. How much you want to work.
   B. How you are seen at work.
   C. Where you eat lunch during work.

7. Which of the following is NOT one of the Basic Ten?
   A. Keeping your personal life out of your workplace.
   B. Honoring diversity.
   C. Complaining quietly.

8. A positive team player looks:
   A. W-O-N-D-E-R-F-U-L.
   B. A-W-E-S-O-M-E.
   C. F-R-I-E-N-D-L-Y.

9. Part of being a good team player is:
   A. Being very competitive.
   B. Trying to help co-workers solve all of their problems.
   C. Admitting your mistakes when you make them.

10. Which of the following people would make a good reference?
    A. A longtime family friend.
    B. Your dad.
    C. A former boss who fired you because you got in a fight at work.

11. Which of the following is NOT something to do the night before a job interview?
    A. Practice answering questions you might be asked during the interview.
    B. Print directions to the location and put them by the front door .
    C. Stay out late having drinks with your friends.

12. Which of the following is a part of personal hygiene?
    A. Eating enough fruits and vegetables.
    B. Flossing your teeth.
    C. Making sure you arrive at work on time.

13. Being on time to work shows:
    A. That you value your co-workers.
    B. That you went to bed on time.
    C. That you have had many different jobs.

14. What is something you should do before you start filling out your job application?
    A. Read all the directions carefully.
    B. Find a pencil.
    C. Both of the above

15. What should you do if you don't understand what your boss asks you to do?
    A. Make an assumption.
    B. Ask him a question.
    C. Try to reassign your task to your co-worker.

16. If you have a felony conviction, you should try to keep it a secret.
    A. True
    B. False

17. The Work Opportunity Tax Credit (WOTC) may give your employer a tax credit for hiring a felon.
    A. True
    B. False

18. You should wear a business suit for all jobs you have.
    A. True
    B. False

19. You should write "negotiable" if your job application asks:
    A. If you have been convicted of a felony.
    B. Where you live.
    C. What you want to be paid.

20. What is one of the things you should think about before you decide what job(s) to apply for?
    A. What you like do.
    B. What your friends and family like to do .
    C. Both of the above

21. About how much of a lifetime do most people spend working?
    A. $\frac{1}{3}$ C. $\frac{1}{4}$
    B. $\frac{1}{2}$

22. Having a positive attitude at work is important because:
    A. A good attitude is contagious.
    B. It helps you get along with co-workers.
    C. Both of the above

23. Which of the following is an example of staying out of office gossip?
    A. Telling someone exactly what someone else just said about them.
    B. Staying away from people who enjoy talking about others.
    C. Asking your co-worker to tell you whom everyone likes and dislikes at work.

24. Which of the following does NOT involve being a thoughtful co-worker?
    A. Smiling at your co-workers.
    B. Appreciating differences among your co-workers.
    C. Gossiping with your co-workers.

25. After you interview for a job, you should always:
    A. Send a thank-you note.
    B. Post good things about the company you interviewed with online.
    C. Deliver a batch of homemade cookies to the office where you interviewed.

REENTRY
ESSENTIALS, INC.

Job Placement Assistance

This page intentionally left blank

Job Placement Assistance

Course Goal: Upon completion of this course, student will use available resources to successfully research, identify, and attain employment.

I. CAREER INTEREST INVENTORY

OBJECTIVES

II. BUILDING A RESUMÉ

OBJECTIVES

III. JOB-SEEKING SKILLS

OBJECTIVES

Jobs vs. Careers

The average United States worker will have about fifteen jobs in his or her working lifetime. It is not a bad thing to change jobs. However, it doesn't help you to move between jobs randomly. If you develop goals and a plan, you can change jobs strategically to build a career.

Your job is what you are doing today. Your career is how your jobs build upon each other to create a progression. Having a career means setting a professional goal and figuring out what you have to do to get there. Having a career requires planning for the future.

A job has the following characteristics:

- It is the position in which you are currently employed.
- It is work performed for a regular paycheck.
- It is a temporary situation.
- It is a place to build useful skills.

A career has the following characteristics:

- It is a chosen profession or occupation.
- It is the general course of your working life or your professional achievements over time.
- It includes jobs you have had that are similar to each other or in the same industry.
- It involves making connections with people who can help you achieve your goals.
- It is a way to put your skills to use.

When you start planning your career, you have to think long-term. To start thinking long-term, consider the following:

- Everything you do counts.
- What you do today affects you tomorrow.
- Mistakes can haunt you for a long time.
- It is important to make good decisions.
- Before you act, ask yourself, "What's my next step, and why?"

Not all jobs will fit into your career goals. You may take some jobs just to make money. That's OK— while you are gaining skills in that job, you can figure out your career goals and plan for the next job.

In any job, you should always do your best. If you go the extra mile beyond your minimum job description, you will be respected and appreciated by your employer. This may lead to a promotion. It will certainly lead to a good reference when you decide to change jobs.

Jobs vs. Careers

Directions: Read each situation in the left column and decide whether the person is pursuing a career or working at a job. Then write "job" or "career" in the right column.

Activity	Career or Job?
1. Jeannie operates the vacuum at a car wash to make ends meet.	
2. Scott gets a culinary degree and becomes a cook at a local restaurant.	
3. Rafi works his way up from mail clerk to office manager at a law firm.	
4. Rhonda works at a department store in the mall on the weekends.	
5. Gary loads trucks in a distribution warehouse while he goes to a vocational school.	
6. Lydia has worked as a medical transcriptionist for several different companies. She gets a promotion to manager of the transcription department at her current company.	
7. Minto receives an award from his company for his outstanding achievements over the ten years he has worked there.	
8. Laura takes a job as a door-to-door salesperson to make some quick cash.	
9. Ed wants to be a concierge in a hotel. He takes the first hotel job he can find and begins to make connections with the concierges.	
10. Chanté gains valuable customer service skills as a dispatcher in a phone bank.	

Identifying Your Career Type

Each of us is different, and we enjoy doing different things. You probably think some of your friends' jobs sound awful, while others sound great. It is important to get to know your own personality and interests before you choose a career path. Research shows that the more your personality traits match up with your chosen career, the more likely you are to be happy in your jobs. You will probably also stay in each job longer.

When you are deciding on a career, there are steps you can take to make sure you make the right choice.

1. **Think about what you like doing.** What do you do for fun? What makes you happy? What were you doing the last time you completely lost track of time? Make a list of these interests.

2. **Think about what you are good at.** What skills do you have? What jobs have you done well at in the past? What do people turn to you for because you are good at it? Make a list of these skills. It may help to ask friends or family to help, because you may not recognize all of your talents. Once you have a list of your skills, you can use a skills profiler to find careers that match up with your skills.

3. **Explore your options.** The U.S. Bureau of Labor Statistics has an online service called the Occupational Outlook Handbook that allows you to explore hundreds of potential careers. You can learn what people in each occupation do, what conditions they work in, how much they get paid, and what kind of training they needed to enter the occupation. The Occupational Outlook Handbook can be found at http://www.bls.gov/ooh/.

4. **Take a career personality test.** You can find numerous career personality tests online. A popular test is the Myers Briggs Type Indicator, based on Carl Jung's typology theory. It asks you a series of questions about your feelings and behaviors to determine your main personality type. Knowing your personality type can help you rule out certain careers that won't be a good fit for you.

5. **Take a career interest inventory test.** You can find these online as well. Through a series of questions that determine your likes and dislikes, a career interest inventory test can predict some careers that you would enjoy doing.

Identifying Your Interests

The first step to figuring out what career path is right for you is identifying your interests. The best jobs will allow you to do things you enjoy doing.

Directions: Think of three activities you have enjoyed doing. The activities can be things you have done alone or with others, at work, with family, or with friends. They can be mental or physical. Write each activity you enjoyed in a bubble on the left.

In the first bubble next to each activity, write a specific reason why you liked it.

In the second bubble next to each activity, write a skill you learned or used during the activity.

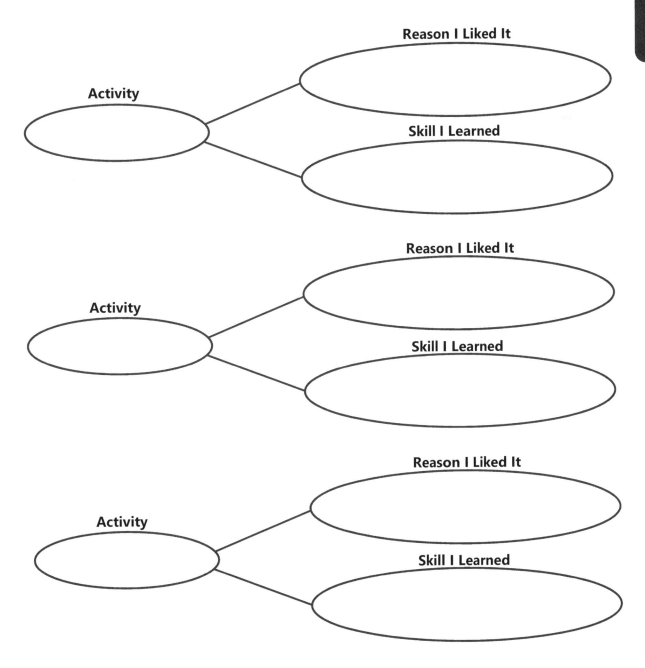

Career Interest Inventories

Let's look more closely at the career interest inventory tests that are available to you. In addition to simple online inventories, there are several paper tests you can order. These paper tests go deeper into your history and interests to get an accurate prediction of specific careers that would suit you. If you are struggling to plan for your future career, these tests are a great way to get on track. They are all based on research and have proven to be effective for many people.

Some of the paper inventory tests you can take include the following:

- **The Career Exploration Inventory.** This test helps you explore and plan three major areas of your life—work, leisure, and learning. With the Career Exploration Inventory (CED, you reflect on 128 activities and consider your past, present, and future interest in them. Scores connect to sixteen career interest areas. Interest areas include relevant jobs, education and training options, and leisure activities. The test is also available in Spanish.

- **O*NET® Interest Profiler**. The O*NET® Interest Profiler (IP) is a career exploration tool that can help people discover the type of work they would enjoy and find exciting. Test-takers identify and learn about broad interest areas most relevant to themselves. They can use their interest results to explore the different careers.

- **O*NET® Values Interest Inventory.** This inventory helps you explore over 900 O*NET® job titles based on your work values and motivators. Once you have identified your most important work values, the inventory guides you to match your results to potential careers. Then you can explore those careers using the inventory's suggestions for further research. You can also print out a Job Information/Action Plan worksheet to help you plan to reach your goals.

- **The Job Search Attitude Inventory.** This test measures how motivated and successful you will be in looking for a job. It calculates where you are on four factors related to successful job searching: luck vs. planning; uninvolved vs. involved; help from others vs. self-help; and passive vs. active. If you receive a low score on this test, then you probably need to seek outside help in finding a job.

Career Interest Inventories

Career interest inventories will ask you questions about a wide range of things, such as what you enjoy doing with your time, who you enjoy spending time with, and what environments you prefer. The CareerShip® website uses six broad interest areas to describe preferred working styles: realistic, investigative, artistic, social, enterprising, and conventional. When you choose the style that fits you best, the website gives you a list of careers that match that working style. Then you can see the required duties, skills, education, and even typical salary of each career.

Directions: Read the descriptions of the CareerShip® working styles below. Then put a star next to the one that appeals to you most.

Realistic — Realistic occupations frequently involve work activities that include practical, hands-on problems and solutions. They often deal with plants, animals, and real-world materials like wood, tools, and machinery. Many of the occupations require working outside and do not involve a lot of paperwork or working closely with others.

Investigative — Investigative occupations frequently involve working with ideas and require an extensive amount of thinking. These occupations can involve searching for facts and figuring out problems mentally.

Artistic — Artistic occupations frequently involve working with forms, designs, and patterns. They often require self-expression, and the work can be done without following a clear set of rules.

Social — Social occupations frequently involve working with, communicating with, and teaching people. These occupations often involve helping or providing service to others.

Enterprising — Enterprising occupations frequently involve starting up and carrying out projects. These occupations can involve leading people and making many decisions. Sometimes they require risk taking and often deal with business.

Conventional — Conventional occupations frequently involve following set procedures and routines. These occupations can include working with data and details more than with ideas. Usually there is a clear line of authority to follow.

Group Discussion: As a group, try to match the careers listed below with the working styles described above. Many careers will match more than one style. Circle the careers that match the working style you starred.

Animal Trainer	Lawyer	Welder	Accountant	Film Director
Real Estate Agent	Stone Mason	Cashier	Fashion Designer	Computer
Librarian	Coach	Writer	Counselor	Programmer
Teacher	Dancer	Engineer	Manager	

Thinking About Careers

There are lots of career options for people who have some high school, have passed the GED® tests, or have a high school diploma. These careers may be the easiest for you in which to find a job. As of February 2019, the fastest-growing careers include the following:

Cement, Brick, and Stone Masons	Automotive and Watercraft Service Attendants
Home Health and Personal Care Aides	Painters
Cargo and Freight Agents	Paperhangers
Medical Assistants	Plasterers
Occupational Therapy Aides	Trash Collectors
Physical Therapist Aides	Food Services
Dental Assistants	Retail Salespersons
Paramedics	Roofers
Construction Workers	Pest Control Workers
Drywall and Ceiling Tile Installers	Plumbers
Glaziers (Install Glass)	Pipe Layers
Medical Secretaries	Fitness Trainers
Insulation Installers	Electricians
Non-Farm Animal Caretakers	Insurance Salespersons

Directions: Circle the careers above that might interest you. Then, with a partner, discuss the skills, experience, and training you think you would need for each career.

Developing a Career Plan

You have a clear picture of your interests and skills. You also have some ideas for careers that would be a good fit for you. Now, it is time to develop a career plan. A career plan will help you focus on what you want to do and how to get there. It is a plan for your future.

Here are the steps to developing a career plan:

1. **Decide your career goal**, which can help you focus more clearly on possibilities available to you. A career goal can be a specific job, such as x-ray technician or welder, or a particular field you want to work in, such as medicine or construction. There are several job possibilities within any career field. For instance, if you choose a medical career, you may want to get a job as a nurse's aid, an x-ray technician, or a doctor.

2. **Determine what you need to do to prepare for your chosen career.** Will you need special training? If so, find out what schools offer the training you need. Will you need experience in the field to be successful in your career? If so, find some ways to get that experience. Internships are a great way to get work experience in a career field. Volunteering is another way to gain work experience.

3. **Write your career plan.**

Writing Your Career Plan

Writing a career plan involves four simple steps:

1. **State your career goal.** This may be a job or a general career field. Be as specific as you can. Make sure your goal is realistic—you may make an excellent rocket scientist, but you may not have the time or money to get the education you would need to achieve that goal.

2. **List the required training and skills you will need to achieve your career goal.** These may include education, on-the-job training, and specific skills that are necessary to succeed.

3. **List the skills and training you already have that may be relevant to the career you have chosen.** These may include training courses or classes you have taken, work or volunteer experience, and skills you have learned.

4. **Write your plan for the next steps.** What school or training program will you attend? Will you find an internship, find a volunteer opportunity, or get experience another way? How long will each of these steps take? Be sure to include landing your dream job as the final step!

Writing Your Career Plan

Directions: Answer the questions below.

1. What is your career goal? If you are not certain, choose something that you think you would like to try. Why do you think you will enjoy this career?

   _____

   _____

2. What special skills or training do you think you will need for this career? How might you go about getting those skills and training?

   _____

   _____

   _____

3. What skills or training do you already have that would relate to your chosen career?

   _____

   _____

4. Based on your answers above, write your career plan. Write each step, starting with where you are right now and ending with entering the career you have chosen.

   _____

   _____

   _____

   _____

   _____

   _____

   _____

   _____

Describing Your Skills on a Resumé

Once you have written a career plan, you are ready to begin building your resumé. A resumé is a document that you use to present your skills, experience, and career goals to potential employers.

One of the major sections of a resumé is the Skills section. In it, you will include all of the skills you have gained through past jobs, volunteering, or education that might be relevant to the job you want to apply for. For example, office skills like using a computer and a copy machine are relevant to jobs you would do in an office, but they are not at all relevant to field construction jobs. An ability to fix a car is relevant to auto mechanic jobs, but it is not relevant to sales jobs.

Look at the career plan you wrote on the previous page and think about the following questions:

- What career did you choose?
- What job will you apply for within that career path?
- What required skills did you list for that job in your career plan?
- What other skills do you think would be beneficial to have in that job?
- Finally, which of those skills do you have?

Your answer to the final question should be the skills you include on your resumé. Keep in mind that not all of the skills you list need to be tangible things like typing or welding. Employers want to know about other skills, such as being good with details ("detail-oriented"), being able handle several tasks at the same time ("multitasking"), or being good with people ("team player" or "people skills"). These are non-tangible skills.

Here is a list of some other non-tangible skills you may possess:

- Organizational Skills
- Sales Skills
- Communication Skills
- Customer Service Skills
- Supervisory/Management Skills
- Always Meet Deadlines
- Always on Time
- Dependable
- Very Motivated

The important thing to remember is to be honest. Never lie about the skills you have. But think hard about the ones you do have—you probably have more than you think!

Explore Your Skills

Directions: Complete the items below.

1. List six of your tangible skills (for example, sewing, using a copy machine, fixing a car, etc.) on the lines below.

   _____

   _____

   _____

2. List six of your non-tangible skills (for example, hardworking, organized, dependable, etc.) on the lines below. If you can't think of six, ask others in the room to help you think of non-tangible skills you have that you didn't list.

   _____

   _____

   _____

3. Circle the tangible and non-tangible skills above that apply to the career in which you want to work.

4. On the lines below, write how you think you would use those skills in your chosen career.

   _____

   _____

   _____

   _____

   _____

   _____

   _____

   _____

   _____

   _____

   _____

Formatting Your Resumé

Employers often look at dozens, if not hundreds, of resumés to fill each job. This means your resumé has to impress them. The information it contains is what will get you the job in the end, but the format of your resumé will determine whether the employer even considers you.

A resumé should be short and to the point. Try to keep it to one page. It should also be organized in a way that makes it easy for employers to find the information they're looking for. Use a basic, legible computer font like Times New Roman, at least 11 point size. Put sufficient space between sections so that it is readable. Do not include fancy graphics or colors on your resumé (unless you are applying for an art design job).

There are different theories about how best to format a resumé, but the following basic facts should be included.

1. Put your **contact information** at the top. Include your:
   a. Name
   b. Phone number
   c. Physical address
   d. Email address
   e. LinkedIn profile URL or professional website address, if you have them. *Don't* include MySpace, Facebook, or Twitter profile address

2. State an **objective** (optional). This is a statement about who you are, what job you want, and what value you will bring to the company. It should mention your total number of years of experience, professional specialties, and major accomplishments.

3. List your **relevant skills and qualifications**. Include only skills that are applicable to the job you are applying for. Use the job posting to learn the specific duties and required skills of each job.

4. List your **work experience**. This can include past full-time and part-time jobs and volunteer experience.
   a. Make the list chronological, with your most recent experience first. However, if your most impressive experience is not your most recent, you can put that first.
   b. For each experience, include your job title, the employer's name and location, and the dates you worked there.
   c. For each experience, also include a bulleted list of your job duties and accomplishments. List the duties that are most relevant and impressive, even if you did not perform them every day. Try to include tangible accomplishments—use dollar amounts, percentages, and numbers whenever you can.

5. List your **education.** Indicate if you have a high school diploma, have passed the GED® tests, have taken any college courses or vocational training, or have earned any degrees or certifications.

Sample Resumé

John Doe is a manager in the food services industry. He has decided to leave his current job at a school district and apply for jobs at catering companies. He wants to find a job with a more flexible schedule and higher pay than his current job.

John Doe
1234 Pleasant Lane, Town, LA 99999
(555) 555-5555
johndoe@internet.com

OBJECTIVE

A talented and accomplished food service professional with more than 10 years of experience. Specialize in high-volume restaurant and cafeteria settings. Seeking management position in the catering industry to put menu planning and management skills to use.

SKILLS AND QUALIFICATIONS

Extensive nutritional and recipe planning skills

Detail-oriented food preparation skills

Outstanding customer service and communication skills

English/Spanish bilingual

Effective multitasker under stress

Computer skills: Word processing programs, databases

WORK EXPERIENCE

Town Independent School District, Town, LA (2007—2013)

Food Services Manager

- Performed all menu planning for school district with over seventy schools.
- Balanced nutritional requirements with student preferences.
- Acted as liaison between school administration and parent groups about all food service issues
- Worked with student committees on student concerns, such as menu variability.

Regional Food Bank, Town, LA (2005—2007)

Food Services Technician

- Assisted in daily management of three food bank locations serving the public.
- Prepared meals for approximately 100 homeless and needy families per day.
- Conducted all food and supply purchasing on weekly basis.
- Managed and organized all food inventory.

Starshine Restaurant, Town, LA (2002—2005)

Line Cook

- Prepared meals in a high-volume kitchen with exceptional quality.
- Developed new food and beverage recipes.
- Restaurant was awarded Best New Restaurant in Louisiana, 1996.

EDUCATION AND TRAINING

Associate's Degree in Culinary Arts, Culinary Institute of America

Training courses in inventory management

Appropriate Resumé Format

John Doe's resumé shows his progression from line cook at a restaurant to food services manager in a school district. You can clearly see the jobs he held and his duties and accomplishments within them. Though his jobs differed, he has consistently followed his career goal of working in the food service industry. With each job, he gained more skills, responsibilities, and respect.

Directions: Answer the questions below.

1. Why do you think the format of your resumé matters?

   _____

   _____

2. What do you think the benefit of listing your jobs in chronological order is?

   _____

   _____

3. What is an objective statement on a resumé? Do you think it is important to include?

   _____

   _____

4. What kinds of skills should you include on your resumé?

   _____

   _____

5. What kinds of duties should you include in the Work Experience section of your resumé?

   _____

   _____

Group Discussion: Discuss your answers with a partner. Which of your answers are different from your partner's?

Beginning to Craft Your Resumé

Before you jump into typing your resumé, it's best to get all the basic information down first. This gives you a chance to spend time reflecting on your skills and past experiences. It may take some time to remember that really impressive thing you did at a job you had ten years ago or that skill you learned as a high school volunteer.

Give yourself the time and space to think about what you want to include on your resumé. This will be based on what jobs you are applying for. Getting a job is a numbers game: the more jobs you apply for, the more likely you are to get one. Since not all of those jobs will be exactly the same, you may need to create more than one version of your resumé. For example, a resumé targeted to a hotel front desk attendant job should be different from a resumé targeted to a hotel concierge job. Both jobs are in the hospitality industry, but they have different duties. List only your skills that relate to the duties of each job on its resumé. Save each version of your resumé as a separate word processing document. Clearly label each one for the job it targets.

Make sure you are highlighting your most relevant skills. Computer skills and bilingual skills are especially useful in many jobs. They will be impressive to most employers. Show the best version of yourself.

Once you have the basic information set, you can fine-tune your resumé and get the wording just right. As you are fine-tuning your resumé, take care to use active voice. Active voice means stating what you did directly. For example, it is better to say, "I answered twenty service calls a day" rather than "Twenty service calls were answered per day." Active voice sounds more powerful and impressive. Using strong verbs is another way to impress employers. Instead of weak verbs like "tried" or "took," try to use strong verbs like "managed," "achieved," or "initiated."

Finally, make sure your resumé is clean. Even though your qualifications may be impressive, the employer will not be impressed with a sloppy resumé. It is very important that you proofread your resumé for typing errors, spelling errors, and grammar mistakes. After you proofread it, have at least one other person proofread it.

Addressing the Gaps in Your Employment

Do not address the gaps in your employment due to your incarceration in your resumé. That can be discussed when you interview in person. At that point, you may want to explain the reasons for your incarceration and ways that you have changed. Discuss any training or skills you got while you were incarcerated. You can also reassure the person interviewing you that you are honest, trustworthy, and hardworking.

Creating Your Resumé

Directions: Fill in the information you will include on your resumé under each heading below.

Objective

_____

_____

Skills and Qualifications

_____

_____

_____

_____

_____

_____

_____

_____

Work Experience

_____

_____

_____

_____

_____

_____

_____

Education

_____

_____

Crafting a Cover Letter

It is important to include a cover letter with every resumé you send to employers. A cover letter is how you introduce yourself to a company when you respond to a job posting. A cover letter is a chance to show who you are and why you think you are the best fit for that job. It is also a great way to show your knowledge about the company to which you are applying.

You will send a different cover letter for each job. Each cover letter should refer directly to the job for which you are applying. It should also refer to the resumé you have attached for that job.

Here are some steps to creating a good cover letter:

- **Think about why you would be good at this job.** Why should this company hire you for this job? What have you done well in the past that proves you would be good at this job?
- **Think about why you want this job.** Is there something special about the position or company? Do you enjoy the tasks you would be doing in the job? Would it Challenge you in new and interesting ways? Note: Don't discuss pay in your cover letter—that will be determined later in the hiring process.
- **Do some research about each company you want to work for.** It will help you to be sure you want the job. It will also make you stand out from other applicants who have not done the research. Usually, a simple Internet search on the company name will give you the information you need. Look at the company's mission, contact information, and job openings on its website.

Include the following elements on each cover letter:

- Your **name and contact information**
- The **company's name and address** (address the letter to the specific person doing the hiring, if possible)
- The **date**
- An **introduction paragraph**: State the job you are applying for and how you are qualified to do it.
- One or two **brief paragraphs explaining why you want the job and why you are the best candidate for it.** You may want to include a bulleted list in one of these paragraphs.
  - Explain your past work experience and relevant skills in a narrative, or story-like, way. Don't go into too much detail—employers will read your resumé for the details. Connect your skills and experience with the job duties to show that you can fulfill the job requirements.
  - Show that you have done your research and are knowledgeable about the company and the position. Include any positive personal experience with the company.

- A polite **conclusion paragraph**: Show enthusiasm for the job, remind the employer why he or she should hire you, and request an in-person interview.
- Your **signature**

Sample Cover Letter

Here is the cover letter that John Doe sends in with his resumé to apply for a Food Services Manager job at a catering company.

John Doe
1234 Pleasant Lane
Town, LA 99999

February 10, 2013

Ms. Anna Smith
Food Services Director
New Taste Catering Town, LA 99999

Dear Ms. Smith:

I am writing in response to your job posting for the position of Food Services Manager at New Taste Catering. My ten years of food service experience and excellent customer service skills make me an ideal fit for the position.

Along with my past experiences as a food services technician and line cook, my work as the Food Services Manager at Town Independent School District (TISD) particularly qualifies me to succeed in New Taste Catering's Food Services Manager position. At TISD, I was responsible for the planning and preparation of food requests within the school district. My Spanish-language skills helped me communicate effectively with various groups of people. I worked with teachers, parents, and students to create meals that met nutritional and taste requirements. In this and other positions, I gained valuable communication, planning, and management skills.

I have always admired New Taste Catering's commitment to providing high-quality, custom catering for a reasonable price. Several friends of mine attended a party catered by New Taste last month, and they raved about both the food and the service. I would be honored to contribute my knowledge and skills to your company.

I have enclosed my resumé for your review. I would appreciate the opportunity to meet with you to discuss this position further. I can be reached at (555) 555-5555 or johndoe@internet.com. I look forward to hearing from you at your earliest convenience. Thank you for your time and consideration.

Sincerely,

John Doe

Understanding Cover Letters

Directions: Answer the questions below.

1. In what kind of industry is John Doe applying for a job?

   _____

2. What is the name of the company John is applying to?

   _____

3. What specific skills does John list in his cover letter?

   _____

   _____

   _____

4. What work experience does John mention in his cover letter?

   _____

   _____

   _____

5. What details does John include to show his knowledge about the company?

   _____

   _____

   _____

6. What useful information does John give in his concluding paragraph?

   _____

   _____

   _____

The Qualities Employers Want

As you have learned, the job you get will depend on your interests, skills, and training. A person who is a good fit for one job may not be a good fit for another job. That's OK, because people are needed to do all types of jobs!

However, there are a few personal qualities that most employers look for in a new employee. Employees who display these qualities may be given a chance even if they don't have the exact experience the employer is looking for. Showing that you have these qualities may also help the employer overcome any hesitation about hiring you because of your incarceration.

During a job interview, the employer will probably be looking for signs that you are the following:

- Honest
- Responsible
- Respectful
- Professional
- Hardworking
- Motivated to Take Initiative

- Willing
- A Team Player
- Enthusiastic
- Positive
- Self-Confident

You probably have many of these qualities already. However, you can work on developing them if you don't have them naturally. Most of them simply require you to be aware of your actions and change your behaviors accordingly. Think before you speak or act. Ask yourself if what you are about to say or do is honest, respectful, positive, etc. If not, decide to say or do something else that is.

Group Discussion: As a group, define each of the qualities above. Then discuss the following questions.

Which quality do you think would be easiest to develop?

Which quality do you think would be hardest to develop?

What other qualities besides those listed above do you think employers will be looking for?

Talking About Your Qualities

If an employer is impressed with your resumé and cover letter, you will likely be asked to interview for the job for which you have applied. In the interview, you may be asked questions meant to determine which of the basic qualities listed on page 121 you have. If you prepare for these questions now, your interview will go much more smoothly.

Directions: Complete the items below as best you can.

1. Describe a time you proved that you were a team player.

   _____

   _____

   _____

   _____

2. Describe a time you showed initiative in a work setting.

   _____

   _____

   _____

   _____

3. Describe a time you were willing to go above and beyond expectations in a work setting.

   _____

   _____

   _____

   _____

Finding Available Jobs

Finding a job after you are released may be challenging. Your options may be limited, and you may feel like it is never going to happen. However, it will happen if you are patient and you keep trying. Remember, getting a job is simply a numbers game: The more jobs you apply for, the more likely you are to get one. There are plenty of companies willing to hire ex-inmates. There are also federal programs that give employers incentives to hire you.

You will need access to the Internet to do a full job search. Many public libraries offer free use of their computers. Your local YMCA may also offer free computer use or free computer literacy classes. The following is a list of places you can look for open jobs.

Community Assistance Programs and Career Centers. There are many local and national programs that offer job placement services. Here are a few services that can either help you directly or connect you to a program in your community:

- Hire Network, http://www.hirenetwork.org (focuses specifically on people with criminal records)
- CareerOneStop, http://www.careeronestop.org

One-Stop Workforce Centers. Many states have created one-stop workforce centers that offer job training, education, and employment services. For example, the Louisiana Workforce Commission's website (www.LAworks.net) offers many useful services for job hunters, including job searches and information about unemployment benefits.

For a national map of one-stop workforce centers, go to http://www.doleta.gov/usworkforce/onestop/onestopmap.cfm

Local Newspaper (print or online version). Check the classified ads in your local newspaper for open jobs. The jobs are usually organized by category, such as Clerical/Administrative or Food Service.

Internet Job Search Engines. There are many websites that help you find jobs in your area based on job title or keyword. Some good ones include the following:

- www.indeed.com
- www.job.com
- www.monster.com
- www.jobfox.com
- www.vetjob.com (service for veterans)

Company Websites. If you know you'd like to work for a specific company or organization, check its website for its current job openings. You may be able to apply online through the website. Otherwise, use the company website to find an email address or physical address to send your resumé and cover letter to.

Finding Available Jobs

Directions: Answer the questions below.

1. Which of the methods listed on the previous page are you most likely to use to look for a job? Why?

   _____

   _____

   _____

2. What do you think are some pros and cons of using community career services, looking in the newspaper, and searching online to find a job?

   _____

   _____

   _____

   _____

   _____

   _____

   _____

3. What would you do if you didn't find a job after a month of looking? How would you avoid making the same mistakes you have made in the past?

   _____

   _____

   _____

   _____

   _____

Group Discussion: Discuss your answers with a partner. Does talking to another person make you think differently about your answers? Explain.

Reaching Out to Employers

Once you have your career goals set, resumé and cover letter written, and some jobs in mind to apply for, you are ready to make contact with employers. The following are some ways to reach out to employers.

Submitting your resumé and cover letter to the Human Resources Department or hiring manager in response to a job posting:

- You may send your materials through the mail, via email, or through the company's website. You may also submit them in person. The job posting will specify which method the company prefers.
  - If you send your materials through the mail, make sure you print them on clean paper. Print an address label with a computer if possible. If you handwrite the envelope, make sure you write the company name and address correctly and legibly.
  - If you send your materials via email, you should copy your cover letter into the body of the email. The subject line should clearly state the job title for which you are applying. Attach both the cover letter and resumé documents to the email.
  - If you send your materials through the company's website, follow the directions exactly. You will either copy the text of your resumé and cover letter into an online form or upload the original documents.
  - If you submit your materials in person, dress as you would for an interview. This means wear conservative, professional clothing and have a well-groomed appearance. Ask for the hiring manager and be ready to answer a few questions about your background.
- Even if an employer is not hiring for the job you want right now, it doesn't hurt to submit your resumé and cover letter anyway. The hiring manager will be impressed with your initiative, and he or she can keep you in mind for new jobs that become available.

Cold calling companies to ask about open positions:

- You can make phone calls to companies in your chosen industry to ask whether they have open positions that meet your qualifications.
- If they do, ask how they would like you to submit your resumé and cover letter. Also ask for the name of the person to whom you should address your cover letter.

Walking in and filling out an application:

- Going around to companies or establishments in your chosen industry and asking if you can leave a resumé with them is a good way to make a good first impression.
- Some companies do not require a resumé and cover letter from applicants. These companies usually have their own application for you to fill out. Be prepared to answer application questions by bringing specific information about your past jobs and education. You may also be asked to show identification.
- Make sure you are well-groomed and dressed professionally before entering a company or establishment to leave a resumé or fill out an application.

Reaching Out to Employers

Directions: For each statement below, circle whether it is "true" or "false."

1. You should submit your resumé and cover letter to a company's Human Resources department or a specific hiring manager.
   True   False

2. You are applying to a job posting via email. You should leave the body of the email blank and attach your resumé and cover letter.
   True   False

3. Cold calling means to call companies and ask whether they are hiring for positions that match your qualifications.
   True   False

4. If a company is not hiring for the position you want right now, you should forget about it and move on to other job postings.
   True   False

5. Unexpectedly walking into companies or establishments in your industry to submit a resumé is rude.
   True   False

6. You walk by a place where you want to apply for a job, but you're wearing jogging pants and a T-shirt. You should go inside and apply anyway because you're there.
   True   False

7. Address your cover letter to a specific person, if at all possible.
   True   False

8. You are going to a company today to fill out its application for a job. You should bring proper identification and information about your work history with you.
   True   False

Job Placement Assistance Review

Directions: Circle the letter for each correct answer

1. The difference between a job and a career is:
   A. A job is temporary and a career is long-term.
   B. A career is temporary and a job is long-term.
   C. A job may include several careers.

2. If you go the extra mile beyond your minimum job description, you will be:
   A. Wasting your time.
   B. Gaining the respect and appreciation of your employer.
   C. Making lots more money.

3. Research shows that the more your personality traits match up with your chosen career:
   A. The more likely you are to stay in your jobs longer.
   B. The more likely you are to enjoy your job.
   C. Both of the Above

4. What is a career interest inventory?
   A. A test that predicts careers you might enjoy based on your interests.
   B. A list of all of your interests.
   C. A list of careers that other people enjoy.

5. A career goal can be a specific job or a general field you want to work in.
   A. True
   B. False

6. A career plan is:
   A. A list of all the jobs you have had in the past.
   B. A picture you draw of your office.
   C. A plan for your professional future.

7. Through which of the following can you gain valuable skills and experience?
   A. Volunteering.
   B. Working as an intern or apprentice.
   C. Both of the Above.

8. It's okay to lie about your skills on a resumé.
   A. True
   B. False

9. The more jobs you apply for, the less likely you are to get one.
   A. True
   B. False

10. Why is it important to have someone else read your resumé?
    A. To proofread it for errors.
    B. To give you ideas for skills and experience you could add to it.
    C. Both of the Above

11. Using "active voice" in a resumé means:
    A. Including sports you can play.
    B. Stating what you did directly.
    C. Speaking as though you are someone else.

12. You should explain why you were incarcerated in your cover letter.
    A. True
    B. False

13. How many cover letters should you write?
    A. One for each job.
    B. Seven.
    C. One.

14. Your cover letter should refer directly to:
    A. Your resumé and the job posting.
    B. Your physical appearance and your favorite hobbies.
    C. Neither of the Above

15. Why should you do research about the company you are applying to work for?
    A. To be sure you want to work there.
    B. To stand out from other applicants.
    C. Both of the Above

16. You can get free Internet access at many public libraries.
    A. True
    B. B. False

17. What is a non-tangible skill?
    A. A mental skill rather than a physical skill.
    B. A skill that involves your sense of taste.
    C. A physical skill rather than a mental skill.

17. Which one of the following is a website that specifically helps people with criminal records get a job?
    A. Indeed.
    B. Hire Network.
    C. Vet Job.

18. The Louisiana Workforce Commission is an example of:
    A. A one-stop workforce center.
    B. A company website.
    C. A job-search engine.

19. When you submit a resumé and cover letter via email, you should:
    A. Paste the text of your cover letter and resumé in the subject line.
    B. Clearly state the job you are applying for
    C. In the subject line.
    D. Use no subject line.

Money Management Skills

This page intentionally left blank

Money Management Skills

Course Goal: Upon completion of this course, student will develop a realistic financial plan for post-release by means of understanding and managing the basics of credit, banking, and personal budgeting.

I. CREDIT MANAGEMENT

OBJECTIVES

II. BANKING BASICS

OBJECTIVES

III. BUDGETING

OBJECTIVES

Understanding Credit

Credit is the ability to make purchases by borrowing money and promising to pay the money back later. When you pay back the money, you also have to pay interest, the fee for borrowing the money. When you make purchases with credit, you create debt—the amount of money that you owe.

Some examples of credit include the following:

- Credit Cards
- Mortgages
- Auto Loans
- Student Loans
- Personal Loans
- Medical Loans
- Cash Advances

The organizations that give credit are called creditors or lenders. They include the following:

- Banks
- Credit Unions
- Department Stores or Merchants
- Credit Card Companies
- Federal Government

Credit is a useful tool, but it can be dangerous if you don't manage it carefully. The longer you take to pay back a debt, the more interest you will have paid in the end. Also, the higher the interest rate is on the money you borrow, the more interest you will pay. It is important to minimize the interest you have to pay as much as possible.

When you don't pay back your debt based on the schedule in your credit agreement, creditors will charge you late fees and may increase your interest rate. If you continue not to pay, creditors will report you to a debt collector. A debt collector is a third party that collects debts owed to others. This includes collection agencies, lawyers, and companies that buy unpaid debts and then try to collect them. If you don't pay a debt, a creditor or its debt collector can sue you for the money you owe. If creditors or debt collectors win, they can get a court order to take funds directly out of your bank accounts or paychecks.

This section will teach you how to manage your credit responsibly, so that you get the benefits while avoiding the dangers of credit. You will learn how to establish credit and maintain it with good credit habits. You will also learn how to pay off any debt you already have.

What's the Use of Credit?

Credit is important because it allows you buy goods or services when you don't have the cash on hand. Most people need to use credit for a large purchase at least once in their lives.

Establishing a good credit history, also called "good credit," shows lenders that you are responsible and trustworthy. A good credit history means you have proven that you can manage credit well. Having a good credit history will help you negotiate lower interest rates on loans you take out in the future, which will save you money.

But you will need good credit for more than just making purchases. For example, before you can get phone service or electricity hooked up in your home, the utility company will review your credit history to make sure they can trust you to pay your bill.

Other activities you'll need a good credit history for include the following:

- Renting an Apartment or House

- Getting Insurance

- Getting an Auto Loan

- Financing A House

- Signing Up for Cell Phone Service

- Getting Some Jobs

Directions: How do you think you will use credit when you are released? What will you need it for? Write your answer on the lines below.

_____

_____

_____

_____

_____

Group Discussion: Now, discuss your answers as a group. Did others in the group write ways of using credit that you hadn't thought of?

Types of Credit

There are four basic types of credit: secured revolving, secured installment, unsecured revolving, and unsecured installment. All four types of credit include borrowing money and paying it back with interest, but the way you pay it back differs.

Secured and *unsecured* are terms that refer to how the creditor makes sure it will get its money back. All credit is either secured or unsecured credit.

- **Secured Credit:** With secured credit, the creditor puts a lien on something you own to make sure the creditor will get its money back. The lien means the creditor can take this asset from you if you don't pay the money back in the time specified in your agreement. Auto loans, mortgages, and home equity loans are common types of secured credit.
- **Unsecured Credit:** With unsecured credit, the creditor is simply trusting that you will repay what you borrow. Creditors base their decision to loan money to you on your financial history, current income and assets, and current debts. Credit cards, medical bills, and utility bills are common types of unsecured credit.

Revolving and *installment* are terms that refer to how you receive the money and how you have to pay it back. All credit is either revolving or installment credit.

- **Revolving Credit:** With revolving credit, the creditor approves you for a specific credit limit. The credit limit is the total amount of money you can borrow. You can use this credit anytime and as often as you want. In return, you must pay the creditor at least the minimum amount on your balance each month. Examples of revolving credit include credit cards and lines of credit.
- **Installment Credit:** With installment credit, you get a one-time loan for a certain amount of money. You repay the money by making a series of installment payments over a set amount of time. Examples of installment credit include mortgages, auto loans, and student loans.

Directions: Read the scenarios below. Decide which type of credit the person is applying for. Then circle the correct answer.

Scenario 1

Jared applies for a credit card with a $2,000 credit limit. The credit card company approves him based on his financial situation.

Secured Revolving   Secured Installment   Unsecured Revolving   Unsecured Installment

Scenario 2

Anya applies for a loan to help her pay for a new car. The bank offers to loan her the money to purchase the car, but it keeps a lien on the car.

Secured Revolving   Secured Installment   Unsecured Revolving   Unsecured Installment

Establishing Credit

There are several easy ways to start establishing a good credit history. Once you have established a good credit history, you will be able to qualify for the loans you need at low interest rates.

Four basic steps will put you on the road to having good credit. Don't do these steps all at once—start slowly and make sure you know how much you owe. Make sure that you can make the necessary payments at all times. Have patience, and know that a good credit history will open lots of doors for you in the future.

1. **Open a Checking and A Savings Account.**
   - Open the accounts at the same bank or credit union.
   - Deposit all of your income into these accounts, and save as much as you can each month.
   - Many banks will allow you to link your savings account to your checking account for overdraft protection; this is a good safety net.

2. **Apply for A Low-Interest Credit Card.**
   - The interest rate your credit card company charges you is called the annual percentage rate, or APR. The APR you are offered for a credit card can vary depending on several factors. Under 10 percent is generally considered low.
   - If you don't qualify for an unsecured credit card, you can apply for a secured credit card. With a secured credit card, you pay the lender a security deposit to assure the lender that you will pay back your debt.
   - Charge small amounts to the card and pay the balance off each month.

3. **Put Utilities in Your Name.**
   - This applies whether you rent or own your residence.
   - You may have to pay a deposit, but you will get it back later if you pay your balance responsibly.
   - Always pay your bill on time and in full.

4. **Check Your Credit Report Periodically.**
   - You can get a free credit report once a year from www.annualcreditreport.com or by calling 877-322-8228. You can also request a copy of your credit report from one of the credit bureaus described on page 139.
   - Check your report for any errors, and immediately resolve any errors you find.

Responsible Borrowing

Establishing credit is important, but you should be careful to not go overboard. How much you should borrow depends on your income, your credit history, and the interest rates you are offered. Typically, lenders will approve you for up to 28 percent of your monthly salary for a mortgage loan or rent payment. You are allowed to borrow up to 36 percent of your monthly salary on all of your debts combined, including mortgage loans, school loans, auto loans, and credit cards.

Test Your Credit Knowledge

Directions: Answer the questions below. You will learn more about each of these topics later in this book.

1. Why do you think it is important to have both a checking and a savings account?

   _____

   _____

   _____

2. What do you think overdraft protection is, and why do you think it is a good idea?

   _____

   _____

   _____

3. Why do you think it is important to get a low annual percentage rate on your credit card?

   _____

   _____

   _____

4. Why do you think putting utilities in your name helps you establish a good credit history?

   _____

   _____

   _____

5. Why do you think it is important to check your credit report regularly?

   _____

   _____

   _____

Applying for Credit Cards

Almost eighty percent of Americans have credit cards. In 2017, the United States Census Bureau announced that there were almost 3.8 billion credit cards being used in the United States. If you stacked up all those credit cards, they would reach more than 70 miles into space. Credit cards are a part of the American way of life, so it's important to learn how to apply for and manage them responsibly.

Credit card debt, along with school loans, is the biggest source of debt for young adults. Credit card debt may build slowly, without you even noticing how large it has become. And once you've got it, it can be difficult to pay off. But if you are careful when you apply for credit cards, you can reduce your risk of getting trapped in too much debt.

When you are ready to apply, first compare card offers online. The major credit cards you can apply for are Visa, MasterCard, Discover, and American Express. Try to choose one that doesn't charge you any annual fees. Also choose one with a low APR. Cards that offer rewards can also be good, if you know you will use the rewards. For example, a card that gives you airline points is a good deal if you travel a lot.

Finally, don't apply for too many cards. The more cards you have, the more in danger you are of getting into debt that you can't get out of. Apply only for what you need, and charge only what you know you can afford to pay off later.

Credit vs. Debit

Credit is different from debit. Although your credit cards and debit cards may look similar, they work very differently. While credit is borrowing money to pay back later with interest, debit is using money directly from your bank account. So, when you use a debit card to make a purchase, you must be sure that you have the money in the bank and available to use that day.

Group Discussion: What kind of credit card rewards would you use? Would you prefer a travel card that gives you airline points that you can trade in for free flights? A card that gives you discounts at gas stations or grocery stores? A card that gives you a percentage of your charges back in cash?

Understanding Interest Rates

Interest is the fee you pay for borrowing money. An interest rate is that fee given as a percent of the amount borrowed per period of time. The period of time is usually one year. When you borrow money through a credit card or loan, one of the most important factors is the interest rate. It will determine how much more than the initial amount of the loan, or principal, you will have to pay back.

Banks figure out what interest rate to charge you based on the following:

- **The Bank's Costs of Loaning The Money**. If the bank hadn't loaned the money to you, it could be using it for something else. The bank wants to be compensated for this.

- **The Bank's Risk of Not Getting Paid Back.** The bank will look at your credit history to determine how much of a risk it would be to loan to you. If you have made late payments or defaulted, meaning stopped paying on loans in the past, you are more of a risk. The more of a risk you are, the higher your interest rate will be.

- **The Rate of Inflation.** Inflation is the increase in the prices of goods over time. As prices increase, the value of money decreases. So one dollar today will actually be worth less than one dollar a year from now. The bank factors the rate of inflation into your interest rate so that it gets the full amount of its loan back at the end of your loan term.

Depending on the type of loan you take, the lender will calculate the interest you have to pay in one of two ways: simple or compound. Make sure to ask the lender which one it will use. Most credit cards and long-term loans use compound interest.

> **Simple interest** is calculated each period for the term of your loan on the original principal only. The term of your loan is the amount of time you have to pay it back.

> **Compound interest** is calculated each compounding period for the term of your loan on the original principal plus all interest accumulated during past periods. It is important to ask your lender what the compounding period is. Even when the interest is stated as a yearly rate, the compounding periods can be every year, every six months, every three months, every month, or even every day.
>
> Compound interest is basically a series of back-to-back simple interest calculations. The interest earned in each period is added to the principal of the previous period to become the principal for the next period.

You can find loan calculators online to help you figure out how much interest you will pay on simple and compound interest loans. One example is www.interestcalculator.org.

Understanding Your Credit History

Once you have established credit, it is very important to maintain a good credit history. Each activity in your credit history stays on your record for seven years, so pay attention to your credit activity. Your credit history has two parts: a credit report and a credit score.

Your credit report gives potential lenders information about all of your credit accounts. It lists whom you have borrowed from, how much you borrowed, how consistently you have made payments, and how many late payments you have made. Your credit report also lists credit inquiries. A credit inquiry is when a lender or other party looks at your credit report. Each time you apply for a new credit card or loan from a lender, that lender does a credit inquiry. Too many credit inquiries on your credit report looks bad and lowers your credit score.

Lenders use your credit score to decide if you can be trusted to pay back debt in the future. Your credit score is also called a credit rating. Your credit score is based on how consistently you have made payments on your debt, how far back your credit history goes, and what types of credit you have. It is also based on your credit utilization rate. Your credit utilization rate is a comparison of how much you owe to how much credit you have available. In general, the more of your available credit you have borrowed, the lower your credit score. Every time you pay off debt responsibly, your credit score goes up. Every time you are late with a payment or don't live up to a credit agreement that you made, your credit score goes down.

Your credit report and score are generated by credit bureaus. The three major credit bureaus are Experian, Equifax, and Trans Union. These bureaus each use a different system for calculating your credit score, but the bottom line for all three is the same: the maximum score is 850 points. The higher your score is, the better you look to lenders. The higher your score, the more likely lenders will want to lend money to you, and the lower the interest rates they offer you will be.

You can get free copies of your credit report by contacting one of the three credit bureaus at the contact information below or by visiting www.annualcreditreport.com.

- Equifax: (800) 685-1111; www.equifax.com

- Experian: (888) EXPERIAN (397-3742); www.experian.com

- Trans Union: (800) 916-8800; www.transunion.com

Who Has a Better Credit Score?

Directions: Read about Andre's, Jason's, and Max's credit histories below. Then write down who you think has the highest, middle, and lowest credit scores. Explain why on the lines below.

- Andre applied for his first credit card last year. Since then, he has applied for five more cards. One of his credit cards is maxed out right now. He makes the payments, but he was late several months in a row.

- Jason applied for his first credit card five years ago. He uses the card regularly but always keeps his balance low. It's the only credit card he has, but he also has a car loan and a utility bill in his name. He has paid every bill on time.

- Max applied for his first credit card ten years ago. He still has that account open, but he has opened and closed three other credit card accounts since then. He has charged up to near his credit limit on his open credit card account. He is paying it off now, and he always pays his bills on time.

Highest credit score: _____

Middle credit score: _____

Lowest credit score: _____

_____

_____

_____

_____

_____

_____

_____

_____

_____

_____

_____

_____

Paying Off Debt

You now understand about credit history, so what do you do if you already have a bad one? The number-one way to improve your credit history is to pay off debt.

You may already be in debt and have been unable to pay it off consistently. Debt can be a vicious cycle—the more you borrow, the longer it takes to pay off, which means the more interest and/or late fees you pay. Debt can make you feel overwhelmed and depressed. You may want to ignore the credit card or mortgage bills you get in the mail. But if you ignore your debt, it will only get worse and damage your credit score.

Luckily, there are several steps you can take to start paying off your debt. You may have to make some sacrifices, but it will be worth it when you are free of debt in the end.

- **Stop Borrowing Money.** This includes taking out any new loans or using any credit cards. (Debit cards are fine to use.) Put your credit cards away somewhere safe, but don't close the accounts. Closing old accounts may damage your credit score.

- **Figure Out How Much Debt You Have, And What Kind It Is**. Is most or all of your debt from credit cards? Did you take out an auto loan when you bought your last car? You have to know what you are dealing with before you can make a plan to pay it off.

- **Ask Your Credit Card Lender to Reduce Your Annual Percentage Rate.** Often, if you call your credit card company and ask them to give you a lower APR, they will. Try to find offers with lower APRs before you call, so that you can use those as a bargaining tool with your current company.

- **Decide Which Debt to Pay Off First.** Typically, it is best to pay off the loans or credit cards with the highest interest rates first. Pay the minimum amounts on all other debt, and pay as much as you can on the loan or credit card with the highest interest rate. Usually, credit cards have higher interest rates than other types of loans. So, you will probably want to focus on paying off your credit card with the highest APR first. Once you have paid off that balance, move on to the next one. Pay as much as you can while continuing to make minimum payments on all other debt.

- **Set Up Automatic Payments.** The best way to make your debt payments is to have the lender take the payment directly out of your checking account each month. This way, you will never be late with a payment or have to pay late fees. Make sure you have enough money in your account to cover any automatic payments.

- **Reduce Your Expenses.** Try to find ways to spend less money in general. Later in this book, you will learn how to make a budget and stick to it.

More Debt Repayment Options

There are additional options for getting out of debt that may or may not be right for you. There are risks involved with these options, like lowering your credit score. However, the benefits might outweigh the risks in your situation. Be sure to talk to a professional credit advisor before you take action on any of the following options.

- **Transfer Your Balances**. You may be able to find offers for credit cards with 0 percent APRs. It might benefit you to transfer balances from cards with high APRs to a new card with a 0 percent APR. Be very careful and read the fine print on the new card offer. Often, the APR goes up to a high rate after six months or a year. If you don't think you can pay off your balance in that time frame, it is probably not wise to transfer your balance.

- **Consolidate Your Debts.** Debt consolidation is when you take out one big loan with a low interest rate to pay off all of your debts with higher interest rates. This can only be done with unsecured debt (like credit cards or medical bills). It won't work for everyone, and it may damage your credit score.

- **Declare Bankruptcy**. Bankruptcy is a federal court process that helps individuals and businesses wipe out their debts or repay them under the protection of the court. When you declare bankruptcy, you are asking the government to either forgive your debts (Chapter 7 bankruptcy) or help you make a repayment plan based on what you can afford (Chapter 13 bankruptcy). The government protects you from legal action by debt collectors while you are making these payments. Declaring bankruptcy should be a last resort, because it will damage your credit score significantly.

Directions: Do you have debt from before you were incarcerated? If yes, do you think any of the options listed on this page would be a good solution for you? Why? If no, do you know anyone who has used any of these solutions? What effect did it have on his or her life? Write your answers on the lines below.

_____

_____

_____

_____

_____

_____

Developing Good Credit Habits

Once you are on the way to paying off your debt and improving your credit score, you must have good credit habits in order to avoid getting caught in the debt trap again. If you are just establishing credit, learning good credit habits and practicing them regularly are the keys to a healthy financial future. Over time, positive credit habits will lead to a good credit history. A good credit history gives you the freedom to borrow with low interest in the future. It will also help you qualify for a home or car loan and get certain jobs.

Figuring out how to manage your credit can be very confusing, but there are some simple credit habits that will benefit you. These good credit habits may seem difficult to do, but they are just like other habits. Once you have practiced, they will become second nature. Knowing what to do about your credit will help you feel confident and in control of your finances. Try the following positive credit habits:

- **Pay the full balance of your credit card bill each month.** Don't just make minimum payments on your credit cards. It will take too long to pay the full amount off, and you will end up paying a lot in interest.

- **Pay your bills on time, every month.** If you are late with a payment, you will be charged late fees that will add to your total and be subject to interest. The best way to make sure you are not late with a payment is to set up automatic bill pay with your bank or automatic drafts with each lender.

- **Be aware of your credit limit and do not go over it.** Your credit limit is the amount of money a credit card company has approved you to borrow with the card. Do not charge the full amount on the card. You want to have the freedom to make emergency charges.

- **Shop around when you are applying for a new loan or credit card.** The interest rate you agree to will make a big difference in how much you pay in the end if you are not able to pay off the full balance every month.

- **Carry only one credit card with you.** You may not even need to have more than one active credit card. But if you do, carry only the one you use most. If your wallet is lost or stolen, you will still have the use of the other cards. This means there will not be the risk of a thief charging to them.

- **Keep your credit cards open for a long time.** Opening and closing cards frequently lowers your credit score and makes you seem like a risk to lenders.

- **Avoid taking cash advances from your credit cards.** The interest rate on a cash advance is typically much higher than the interest rate for purchases.

- **Check your credit report annually.** You can get your credit report from each of the major credit bureaus. Check the reports carefully, and tell the credit bureau about any errors you find.

Identify Good Credit Habits

Directions: For each credit habit in the left column below, write whether it is "good" or "bad" in the right column.

Credit Habit	Good or Bad
1. Opening credit cards at every department store in the mall.	
2. Paying every bill on time.	
3. Paying more than the required minimum payment each month.	
4. Closing credit card accounts when you haven't used them in a couple of months.	
5. Checking your credit report for errors.	
6. Applying for the first credit card offer you get in the mail.	
7. Not paying attention to your credit limit.	
8. Setting up automatic bill pay.	
9. Never taking cash advances with your credit card.	
10. Carrying all four of your credit cards in your wallet.	

Understanding Bank Accounts

Opening a bank account is the first step on the way to financial success. Bank accounts allow you to keep your money in a convenient, protected place. Keeping your money in the bank is much safer than storing cash, which can be lost or stolen. Bank accounts also let you see exactly how much money you have at any given moment. This will help you to budget. The bank even does the math for you.

Some banks pay you interest on your money. This is because you are basically lending your money to the bank. Your money goes into a big pool that the bank uses to pay loans, withdrawals, and other transactions for other customers. Just like you pay the banks interest on money you borrow from them when you use credit, they pay you interest on the money you let them borrow.

Don't worry—money you keep in a bank account is insured by the federal government for up to $250,000. This means that even though it goes into a pool, you are always guaranteed access to your available balance up to the amount insured by the government.

Here are some of the most common types of bank accounts:

- **Checking Accounts.** A checking account allows you to deposit, or add, money whenever you want. You can also withdraw, or take out, money when you need it. You can even pay your bills electronically from most checking accounts. Most checking accounts don't pay interest, but some pay a small amount.

- **Savings Accounts.** A savings account is a place to save money for the future. You may be saving for a big purchase, your retirement, or your children's college fund. Even if you are not saving for something specific, it is a very good idea to put as much as you can in a savings account each month. You never know when you might need it for an emergency.

- **Money Market Accounts.** A money market account is a type of savings account that typically pays you more in interest than a regular savings account. However, it has more restrictions and possible risks. There will probably be a minimum balance, or the minimum amount of money you must keep in the account at all times. You also may not be able to deposit or withdraw from a money market account as often as you can with other types of accounts.

- **Certificate of Deposit Accounts.** Another type of savings account is a certificate of deposit account, also called a CD. A CD account requires you to put a certain amount of money in the account and leave it there for a certain amount of time. Withdrawing your money early can result in fees, so make sure you can leave your money the entire time before opening a CD. In exchange for agreeing to leave your money in the bank for that amount of time, the bank will pay you more interest than they would for a different type of savings account.

Which Account Is Best?

Directions: For each financial goal on the left, decide whether a checking, savings, money market, or certificate of deposit account would be best. Draw a line to the best account on the right.

Financial Goal	Best Type of Account
1. You want an account that you can deposit your paycheck in and pay your monthly bills from each month.	Money Market Account
2. You want to put some money away and make as much interest as possible on it. You don't care whether you can take the money out any time soon.	Checking Account
3. You want to save to buy a new stereo system. You plan to put a little bit from your paycheck each month into this account until you have enough to buy the system.	Certificate of Deposit Account
4. You just inherited a big sum of money and you want to make good interest off of it. You may need to withdraw some money from this account once or twice, but not often.	Savings Account

Now, write one of your personal financial goals. Which type of account do you think would be best to reach this goal? Why?

_____

_____

_____

_____

_____

_____

_____

Choosing the Right Account for You

Before you decide where to open your accounts, you should decide which accounts will work best for you. Will you have a paycheck to deposit each week or month? Do you want to save for a big purchase? Most people have at least one checking and one savings account, so that is a good place to start.

When deciding which accounts to open, consider the following:

- **Interest Rate.** How much interest do you want to earn on your money? The annual percentage rate (APR) is how much interest your bank will pay you each year. It will vary depending on what type of account you open. It is especially important if you will have a large balance in the account. When you are researching accounts, be sure to pay attention to the APR and how the bank calculates it.

- **Fees.** Banks often charge penalty fees on accounts. For example, you may have to pay a penalty fee when your balance goes below a set minimum or if your account is inactive for a certain length of time. Try to find accounts with no fees. If the account does have fees, make sure you can meet the minimum requirements to avoid the fees.

- **Access to Your Money.** Do you want to be able to withdraw money often or quickly? Do you want to be able to get money orders for free? Think about how you will use your money. Then choose a bank account that gives you the access you want.

- **Overdraft Protection.** Overdraft protection is a service offered by most banks that protects you from overdrawing your account. Overdrawing your account means taking out more money than you have available. With overdraft protection, the bank loans you the money to pay the charge. You then have to pay the bank back with interest, and you may have to pay a fee. If you have overdrawn accounts in the past, ask your bank about overdraft protection.

- **Direct Deposit.** Will your employer offer direct deposit, or the option to have your paycheck electronically deposited into your bank account? Do you like the idea of this, or do you prefer a paper check in your hand?

Directions: What will you look for in a bank account? Write three elements of your ideal bank account in the boxes below.

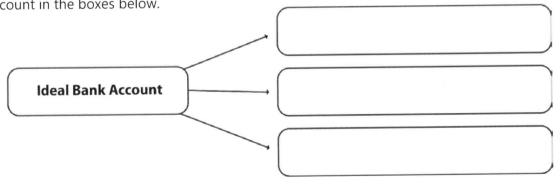

Choosing the Right Bank for You

BANKING BASICS

You have several options for where to open any of the accounts listed on page 145. Each of the following financial institutions has pros and cons. Which one you choose will depend on your situation and financial needs.

A Major Bank Chain. Some of the biggest bank chains are Wells Fargo, Chase, Citibank, and Bank of America. They are the largest and most convenient choices, but they are not always the wisest. While they may have lots of branches and automatic teller machines (ATMs), they may also charge you fees and offer low interest rates.

A Credit Union. Credit unions are cooperatives, meaning they are owned by their account holders. This means that account holders have more say in decisions the credit union makes about their money. Credit unions usually offer accounts with no fees and higher interest rates than major bank chains. However, they may have fewer branches and ATMs than major bank chains. This means they may not be as convenient to use.

An Online Bank. This is a fairly new option. Online banks pay you higher interest on your accounts, but they are not as convenient as bank or credit union chains. For example, it may take several business days to receive money after you have requested a withdrawal. You should also be careful to research the online bank to make sure it is reliable and insured by the federal government.

Good questions to ask about a bank or credit union you are considering include the following:

- How many branch locations does the bank have near me?
- How many ATMs does the bank have near me?
- Does the bank charge ATM fees?
- Does the bank offer online bill pay, or the ability to pay my bills electronically?
- Does the bank have good customer service?
- Is the bank insured by the Federal Deposit Insurance Corporation (FDIC)?

Group Activity: The whole group divides up into three teams. Each team is assigned one of the institutions listed above: major bank chain, credit union, or online bank. Each team has five minutes to prepare an argument about why their institution is the best place to open bank accounts. When the five minutes are up, each team presents to the whole group, trying tb convince them that their institution is the best. At the end, have a whole group discussion about the pros and cons of each institution.

Withdrawing Money from a Bank Account

There are several ways that you can withdraw money from your bank accounts. Sometimes your options will be different with your savings account than with your checking account. Be sure to choose a checking account that gives you the access you want to your money.

Here are some ways you can withdraw money from your checking account at most banks and credit unions.

- **Checks.** When you open a checking account, your bank will usually give you a box of checks for free. These checks can be used to pay bills like rent or utilities, or to make purchases at a store. You write the check to the company or person you are paying, and the recipient deposits it in his or her bank. You can also write checks to yourself to get cash from your account at the bank. This process can take anywhere from a couple of days to several weeks. It is very important to be sure that you have the money in your account to cover the amount of the check when you write it.

- **Debit Card.** Most banks will also give you a debit card when you open a checking account. A debit card works in a very similar way to a check, but it is more immediate. Your purchase gets electronically taken out of your account the day of or day after you use the card. You will choose a secret personal identification number, or PIN, to enter whenever you use the card. This ensures that you (and anyone you have entrusted with your PIN) are the only one who can use it. Try to choose a random number, and don't keep it with your card. Using debit cards is a much more convenient process than writing checks. Many people now use debit cards instead of checks for most purchases.

- **Automatic Teller Machine (ATM) card.** If you have a debit card, it will usually also be your ATM card. An ATM card allows you to get cash from any ATM machine by entering your PIN. The cash comes directly out of your checking account. ATM machines owned by your bank will not charge you fees, but other banks' ATM machines might. Your bank may also charge you fees for using other banks' ATM machines. Pay attention to these fees, because they can add up quickly.

- **Online Bill Pay.** Many banks allow you to pay your monthly bills online. You enter the information about the companies that bill you each month, like the gas company or cell phone company. Then, you tell the bank how much to pay each of those companies each month, and the bank takes the money out of your account and sends it to the companies.

- **Electronic Funds Transfer (EFT).** Many banks allow you to move money between your accounts by logging on to their website or mobile app. It is a good idea to set up automatic EFTS from your checking account to your savings account each month.

If your debit card, ATM card, or checks are lost or stolen, contact your bank immediately. Once someone else has your account information, he or she can pretend to be you and make purchases with it. However, if you let your bank know right away, the bank can cancel the cards or checks before any more charges are made. They will usually also refund any charges made since you last had the card. The bank will then issue you new cards and checks.

Writing Checks

You will most likely need to use checks to make payments from your checking account on occasion. Eventually, paper checks may no longer be used as debit cards replace them. However, for now it is important to know how to fill out a check properly.

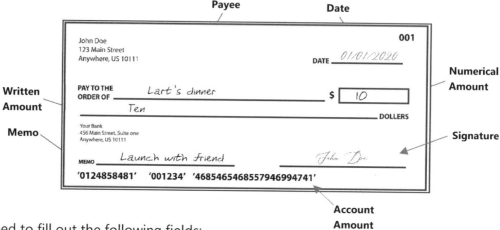

You need to fill out the following fields:

- **Date.** Fill in today's date.
- **Payee.** Fill in the name of the person or business you are paying money to. This is also called the person or business you "make the check out to."
- **Numerical Amount**. Fill in the amount you want to pay.
- **Written Amount.** Write out the dollar amount in words and the cents in numbers. Cents should be written as a fraction over 100. Then draw a line after the cents to make sure that no one can add anything to your check.
- **Memo.** Write what the check is paying for to help you and the payee remember (optional).
- **Signature.** Make sure to sign the check.

Directions: Write the check below to Rick's Cleaners for $22.50 for dry cleaning several pairs of pants and shirts.

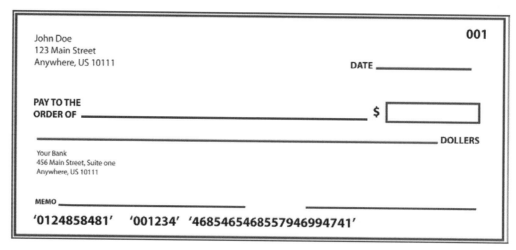

Depositing Money to a Bank Account

There are also several ways that you can deposit money to your bank accounts. Again, make sure the bank you choose offers the services that you want before you open your accounts.

The most common ways of making deposits include the following:

- **Direct Deposit.** Many employers offer a paycheck direct deposit service. This means that your employer automatically deposits your paycheck into your checking account. This saves you both the time it takes to deposit a paper check and the fees you would pay to cash a paper check.

- **In Person at The Bank**. If you do have paper checks to deposit, you can always go into one of your bank's branch offices. They have bank tellers at a counter who will help you fill out a deposit slip and deposit your money into your account. You can also deposit cash this way.

- **Motor Bank.** Your bank or credit union may have at least one drive-through motor bank you can use to deposit checks or cash. This means you drive up to a station and send your check or cash, and deposit slip, to the bank tellers through an air tube.

- **ATM.** You may be able to deposit cash or checks directly into one of your bank's ATM machines. You may or may not need a deposit slip. Depending on your bank and type of account, an ATM deposit may take longer to process than an in-person deposit. That means you won't have access to the money for a day or two after you make the deposit.

- **EFTs.** As described on page 149, your bank may allow you to transfer money from one account to another electronically. This is the easiest way to make regular deposits into your savings account.

Reconciling Your Accounts

Reconciling your bank account means to compare the bank's record of your deposits and withdrawals with your own record. Good ways to keep your own record are to keep all of your receipts and to write down all of your account activity in a log.

It can be easy to overdraw your account if you do not keep track of how much money is going in and coming out. Your bank may charge you hefty fees for overdrawing your account.

It is also very important to check your monthly account statement for errors. Some banks even have a website where you can check your account activity any time. This is a good way catch mistakes the bank has made or possible illegal account activity by someone who has learned your account information without your approval

Filling Out Deposit Slips

When you deposit check(s) or cash into your checking or savings account using a bank branch, motor bank, or ATM, you may have to use a deposit slip. Here is an example of how to fill out a deposit slip properly.

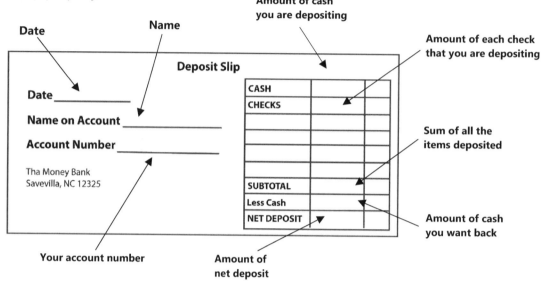

You need to fill out the following fields:

- **Date.** Fill in today's date.
- **Name.** Fill in the name of the bank account holder.
- **Account Number.** Fill in your account number. You can find this at the bottom of one of your checks.
- **Cash.** Fill in the amount of cash you are depositing, if any.
- **Checks.** Fill in the amount of each check you are depositing, if any. List each check separately.
- **Subtotal.** Fill in the sum of all of your deposits.
- **Less Cash.** Fill in the amount of cash you would like to get back, if any.
- **Net Deposit.** Subtract the cash you want from the sum of the deposits to get the total, or net deposit.

Directions: Fill out the slip below for a deposit of $20 cash, one $100 check, and one $300 check.

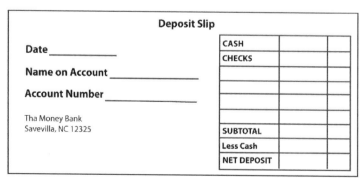

Understanding Withdrawals and Deposits

Directions: Circle the letter for each correct answer.

1. Using a debit card is similar to writing a check, but it is more:
   A. Expensive.
   B. Immediate.
   C. Inconvenient.

2. You can use your debit card to:
   A. Make purchases.
   B. Get cash from an ATM machine.
   C. Both of the above.

3. Your PIN number is:
   A. The number you enter when you want to use your debit or ATM card.
   B. The same as your account number.
   C. Both of the above

4. You can get cash by:
   A. Using your ATM card at an ATM machine.
   B. Getting cash back from a deposit.
   C. Both of the above.

5. "Direct deposit" means:
   A. Your employer deposits your paycheck directly into your checking account.
   B. You deposit a check into your checking account.
   C. You go directly to the bank after you receive your paycheck and deposit it.

6. You can find your checking account number:
   A. On your ATM card.
   B. On your debit card.
   C. At the bottom of one of your checks.

7. If your debit card is lost or stolen, you should:
   A. Contact your bank immediately to let them know.
   B. Not worry about it.
   C. Just use checks until it turns up.

8. Reconciling your bank account means:
   A. Depositing money in it.
   B. Comparing the bank's record of your account activity to your own record.
   C. Hoping that you didn't overdraw it.

9. If you overdraw your account, your bank might:
   A. Charge you fees.
   B. Close your account.
   C. Neither of the above.

10. When writing a check, the "payee" is:
    A. You.
    B. The person you make the check out to.
    C. The bank.

Understanding Investments

You have learned how to save the money you have in savings, money market, and certificate of deposit accounts. You even know how to make it grow a little through interest. But there are options that could make your money grow faster. These options can also cause you to lose money, so there is risk.

Investing money means to buy something because you expect it to earn money in the future. When you invest your money, you expect to spend a certain amount now but end up with a higher amount later. Here are a few of the most common ways to invest money:

- **Buying Stocks.** Stock is the amount of money a company is worth. Some companies sell shares of their stock to individual investors. This is called "going public," or being traded in the stock market. A person who buys shares of a company's stock is called a shareholder. Shareholders own a bit of that company. When the company makes money, its shareholders get some of that profit. However, when it loses money, so do its shareholders.

- **Buying Bonds.** A bond is a loan made to an institution, such as the government or a company, that it promises to repay with interest. The institution gets the cash it needs right away, and the investor gets regular interest payments on top of the original sum in the end. The safest type of bond is a United States Savings Bond. Typically, bonds that pay higher interest-rates are riskier.

- **Buying Real Estate Property.** Some people like to invest their money in land or property. If the investor chooses the right location, he or she can make a profit when the value of the land goes up. However, the investor has to maintain the land in the meantime, and its value may not go up as expected.

Risks of Investing

No matter what you do with your money, there is risk involved. If you stash it all in cash under your mattress, you are risking that it will be stolen or destroyed. If you keep all of your money in a checking or savings account, you are risking that you won't make as much interest as you could on it.

When you invest your money, you always take a risk that your hope of making money may not come true. You may even lose your original investment. But if you invest wisely, the benefits will usually outweigh the risks.

Talk to a financial advisor before you invest any money. Find out which options are riskier than others. For example, stocks are usually riskier investments than bonds. The more risk of losing money you are willing to take, the more money you can potentially make. Decide how much risk you are willing to take. This will depend on your age, income, family situation, and other factors.

What Would You Invest In?

Deciding how to invest your money takes some thought. You have to weigh how willing your are to lose your money against how confident you are that you will make money. Everyone is different, and you should only make investments that you are comfortable with.

Directions: Think about what you would like to invest money in. Would it be stocks, bonds, or real estate? If it is stocks, which company would you buy stock in? If it is real estate, what kind and where? Describe your ideal investment on the lines below.

_____

_____

_____

_____

_____

_____

Now, think about the risk involved in that investment. Are you comfortable with taking that risk? Explain your answer on the lines below.

_____

_____

_____

_____

_____

Understanding Loans

BANKING BASICS

Taking out a loan means borrowing money and promising to pay it back with interest. Remember the types of credit you learned about on page 134? Any loan you take out will be either secured or unsecured.

With a secured loan, you agree to put up something you own as collateral for the loan amount. The bank has a lien on this collateral. That means that if you don't pay your loan back according to the terms of your agreement, the lender can take the collateral to recoup the money they lost.

Secured loans include the following:

- **Auto Loans.** If you can't pay the entire cost of a car upfront, you can get an auto loan through a bank or financing company to pay for the car. It is a good idea to make a down payment, or initial payment, of as much as you can. Then get a loan for the rest. The car you buy is the collateral for the loan. Auto loans are typically paid back over three to five years with interest.

- **Mortgage Loans.** Similarly, when you buy a house or piece of land, you take out a mortgage loan to pay for it. The property you buy is usually the collateral. After you make as large of a down payment as you can, you borrow the rest from a bank or credit union. Typically, mortgage loans are paid back over fifteen to thirty years with interest.

- **Home Equity Loans.** With a home equity loan, you borrow money and use the equity in your house for collateral. Equity is the difference between the current market value of your house and the amount you still owe on the mortgage.

With an unsecured loan, you do not have to offer collateral to the lender. The lender decides whether to trust you to pay the loan back based on your credit history. If you appear trustworthy, the lender will give you the loan. The more trustworthy you appear, the lower the interest rate the lender will offer you for the loan. However, an unsecured loan will almost always have a higher interest rate than a secured loan.

Unsecured loans include the following:

- **Credit Cards.** Explained previously, credit cards are a type of revolving credit that allow you to borrow money anytime and pay back at least a percentage of it monthly. You can borrow up to your credit limit, the maximum loan amount you were approved for.
- **Student Loans.** Student loans are loans you take out to pay for tuition, books, or living expenses while you are enrolled in a college or university. You can get student loans from either the federal government or a bank. The interest rates for student loans are usually lower than for other types of loans. Depending on the loan you get, you may not be charged interest on the loan while you are still in school. You may also be able to postpone your payments until you have the income necessary to make your payments.
- **Personal Loans.** Taking out a personal loan means borrowing money for your personal use. This is a one-time loan that you pay back with interest, usually within 12 to 48 months. The interest rates for personal loans are usually higher than for other loans.

Understanding Loans

Directions: Circle "true" or "false" for each statement below. For false statements, explain your reasoning.

1. With an unsecured loan, you offer a piece of your property that the bank can take if you don't pay back the loan.   ***True   False***

2. With an unsecured loan, the bank bases your interest rate on how much they trust you to pay back the loan. ***True   False***

3. Credit cards are a type of revolving credit. ***True   False***

4. Student loan interest rates are usually higher than other loans' interest rates.
    True   False

5. With an auto loan, the bank has a lien on the car you buy. ***True   False***

6. A down payment is the final payment you make on a loan. ***True   False***

7. A mortgage loan is used for buying real estate property. ***True   False***

8. You may be able to wait until you are out of school to start paying back school loans.
    True   False

9. Equity is the difference between the amount you borrowed and the amount you have left to pay on the loan. ***True   False***

10. Personal loans usually have a lower interest rate than other types of loans. ***True   False***

11. You should make the largest down payment you can on a large purchase. ***True   False***

12. Mortgage loans are usually paid back within ten years. ***True   False***

Group Discussion: Now, compare your answers to a partner's answers. Then discuss the following questions.

What kinds of loans have you taken out in the past, if any?

What kinds of loans do you expect to take out in the future?

What do you think the pros and cons of secured and unsecured loans are?

Making a Budget

A budget is an overview of the way you use money. It is a plan for spending, saving, borrowing, and investing. Making a budget is necessary to make sure you reach your financial goals. Setting clear goals, as well as knowing your income and expenses, are the first steps to creating a realistic budget that you can stick to.

Directions: On the next several pages, you will learn how to make a budget. To prepare, read the steps listed below. Then write your answers to the questions on the lines.

1. **Set Goals.** Think about what you want in life. Do you want to go back to school? Do you want to buy a house? How much money do you think you will need to reach each of these goals?

_____

_____

_____

_____

1. **Figure Out Your Income**. Income is the money you have coming in. You may have income from one or more jobs, side work, or investments you have made. Where will your money come from? Can you think of any other sources of income you might be able to use?

_____

_____

_____

_____

2. **Figure Out Your Expenses.** Expenses make up the money you have going out. What will you spend money on? What will your bills be each month? Will you support other people in your life financially? What will you do for fun? Are all of these expenses necessary? Can you cut any of them out?

_____

_____

_____

_____

Knowing Your Income

In order to reach the goals you listed in the previous activity, you will need a plan to save money. You may be able to get loans to help you reach some goals, but you will need a plan for paying those loans back. Either way, you must know your income before you can plan.

In order to figure out what you can afford to pay for something, you must know exactly how much income you have. When you accept a job, you and your employer agree on a specific hourly, monthly, or yearly pay rate. This is your salary. After you begin working, your employer then gives you a paycheck on a regular schedule. Your paycheck will be for the amount you made for that period based on your salary, minus taxes and other payments the employer took out.

Your paycheck will come with a pay stub. The pay stub shows you the breakdown of what you made and what the employer took out. The following are typical deductions your employer may take out of your paycheck.

- **Federal Income Taxes.** Everyone with a job in the United States is expected to pay federal income taxes. How much you pay will depend on your salary and situation, like whether or not you have children.

- **State Taxes**. Most states take state income taxes from employees' pay. The taxes go toward state programs, such as new roads.

- **Social Security Taxes.** Social Security is a federal program that provides assistance to people in need in the U.S., such as the elderly and disabled. Every working American must give a portion of each paycheck to this program. Your employer also gives a portion on your behalf.

- **Medicare Taxes.** Medicare is a federal insurance plan that provides hospital, medical, and surgical benefits for the elderly and disabled. Every working American must give a portion of each paycheck to this program.

- **Insurance Fees.** Your employer may offer medical, dental, or life insurance to its employees. If you signed up for one or more of these plans, you will probably pay for the plan(s) with a portion of each paycheck. Your employer may also pay a portion.

- **401(k) Plans.** You may be able to sign up for a 401(k) plan through your employer. A 401(k) is a savings account for retirement. You choose a certain percentage of your salary to be put in the account. It is taken out of each paycheck before taxes.

- **Flexible Spending and Health Savings Accounts**. Your employer may offer these accounts to allow you to save money from each paycheck for medical expenses. The money is taken out of your paycheck before taxes.

Knowing Your Income

Let's pretend the pay stub below is from a paycheck at your new job. It shows your earnings, or gross pay, and all the deductions your employer took out. The money you have left over when you subtract the deductions from your gross pay is called your net pay. This is the amount your paycheck is for.

Directions: Calculate your net pay from the weekly pay stub shown below. Hint: Add up the amounts in the Earnings column to get your total gross pay for the week.

Description		Hours	Earnings	Year to Date
Regular Earnings	10.00	32.00	320.00	1200.00
Overtime Earnings				
Back Pay				
Holiday Earnings	10.00	8.00	80.00	80.00
Vacation Earnings				
Gross Pay			$_____	

	Deductions	Year to Date
Federal Tax	45.07	135.21
State Tax	9.14	27.42
Social Security Tax	24.80	74.40
Medicare Tax	5.80	17.40
Medical Insurance	12.50	37.50
401(k)	20.00	60.00
Health Savings Account	10.00	30.00
Total Deductions	_____	

Net Pay $ _____

Knowing Your Expenses

Once you know how much money you have coming in, you should get to know how much money you have going out. You will need to calculate your expenses: Exactly how much you spend each month and on what. Typical expenses include rent, utilities, cell phone bills, and gas money. Your expenses will be unique to your lifestyle and situation.

Expenses can be either fixed or variable. Fixed expenses are the same every month. They don't vary between months and are easy to plan for. Fixed expenses include income deductions (listed on page 159), rent, and car payments. Variable expenses change each month. If you go on a long road trip next month, your monthly gas expense would be much higher than this month's. In the summer, your electricity bill will probably be higher than in the spring. Other variable expenses might include credit card bills, groceries, and entertainment costs. Variable expenses are harder to plan for, but you can estimate them based on how much you know you have spent in the past.

Needs vs. Wants

An important thing to consider as you look at your expenses is that things you want are not always things you need. Most of us want lots of things: an ice cream cone, a new outfit, maybe a boat. But we don't need many of those things. And you might be surprised at how quickly their costs add up.

When you are making a budget, think about the things you don't actually need, and be willing to sacrifice some of them. Try to find as many ways as possible to reduce your expenses. It will be worth it in the end when you have saved enough money to reach your goals.

Directions: List four needs and four wants you have today in the bubbles below.

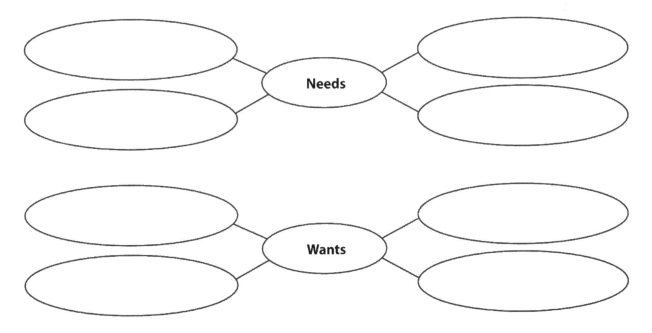

Creating a Budget

When you have 1) set your financial goals, 2) calculated your income, and 3) calculated your expenses, you will be ready to create a budget. This will be a specific plan for how much you can spend and save each month. Once your budget is set, you should do your best to stick to it.

The number-one rule of budgets is that your expenses must not be greater than your income. You want to have some money left to save after you have paid your basic household and living expenses. If your expenses equal your income, you will not be able to save at all. That means you won't reach your financial goals. Worse, it means that you won't have money saved to use in an emergency, such as a trip to the hospital or unexpected car repairs. If your expenses are greater than your income, then you will be in danger of going deep into debt and possibly losing your home or possessions.

The 60% Solution

One approach to making a budget is to use the 60% Solution. The 60% Solution is a system created by financial expert Richard Jenkins. Its name comes from the idea that you should spend 60 percent of your income on regular expenses. These expenses include income deductions, debt payments, household bills, and living expenses.

The 40 percent you have left should then go to the following expenses. Each expense listed below gets 10 percent of your income.

- **Long-Term Savings:** This is money you save to reach your financial goals.

- **Retirement Savings:** This is the money you put into a 401(k) or other retirement account.

- **Irregular Expenses:** These are unexpected expenses that come up each month or things you only have to pay for once in a while. They include things like emergencies and house repairs.

- **Fun Money:** This is money you use for entertainment. You will probably eat out once in while or want to go to a concert sometimes. These are paid for with your fun money.

Note: If you are deep in debt, it is wise to use the 20 percent of your income that would typically go toward long-term savings and retirement savings to pay down your debt. When your debt is paid off, that 20 percent goes back into long-term savings and retirement savings.

Whether you use the 60% Solution or not, the next step is to make a chart that clearly shows each source of income and each expense. You may want to put your expenses into categories, such as "Income Deductions," "Household Expenses," "Food," and "Transportation Expenses." Then, fill in the amount that you expect to spend for each of those categories next to it in the chart.

Creating a Budget

Directions: In the sample budget below, the income information is provided. Fill in typical expenses to complete the budget. Include at least one expense for each category.

Category	Monthly Budget Amount
INCOME	
Salary	
Other Income	
*Total Income	
EXPENSES	
Income Deductions	
Federal Income Tax	
State and Local Income Tax	
Social Security Tax	
Medicare Tax	
Health Insurance	
Health Savings Flexible Spending Account	
Total Income Deductions	
Household Expenses	
Rent/Mortgage	
Homeowners/Renters Insurance	
Property Taxes	
Electricity	
Water and Sewer	
Natural Gas	
Telephone (Land Line, Cell)	
Total Household Expenses	
Food Expenses	
Groceries	
Eating Out, Lunches, Snacks	
Pet Food and Supplies	
Total Food Expenses	

Category	Monthly Budget Amount
(Expenses Continued)	
Family Expenses	
Child Support	
Alimony	
Day Care, Babysitting	
Total Family Expenses	
Transportation Expenses	
Car Loan	
Gas	
Car Insurance	
Other Transportation (tolls, bus, subway, taxis)	
Total Transportation Expenses	
Debt Payments	
Credit Cards	
Student Loans	
Other Loans	
Total Debt Payments	
Savings	
Other Expenses	
*Total Expenses	

Balance_____

(balance = total income — total expenses

Money Management Skills Review

Directions: Circle the letter for each correct answer.

1. Which one of the following is a benefit of credit?
   A. Credit makes you look cool.
   B. Credit lets you spend someone else's money without paying it back.
   C. Credit allows you to borrow money when you need it and pay it back over a period of time.

2. Which one of the following is a danger of credit?
   A. Credit can add up without you noticing how much it's become.
   B. If you don't pay your credit bills on time, you will get charged late fees and higher interest.
   C. Both of the above.

3. What is the main difference between secured and unsecured credit?
   A. With secured credit, you can borrow up to a million dollars.
   B. With secured credit, you use something you own as collateral for the money you borrow.
   C. With unsecured credit, the lender doesn't care whether you pay back the money you borrow.

4. What is the main difference between revolving and installment credit?
   A. With revolving credit, you can use your credit anytime up to a certain credit limit.
   B. With revolving credit, you pay however much you want each month.
   C. With installment credit, you get small
   D. Amounts from the lender each month.

5. What can good credit history help you do Besides make purchases?
   A. Rent an apartment.
   B. Qualify for lower interest rates.
   C. Both of the above.

6. What does "having good credit" mean?
   A. Owing a lot of debt.
   B. Proving that you can manage credit responsibly.
   C. Borrowing from nice lenders.

7. Which one of the following is a step to establishing credit?
   A. Opening a checking and savings account.
   B. Putting utilities in your name.
   C. Both of the above.

8. What does APR stand for?
   A. Annual prorate rent.
   B. Actual price rate.
   C. Annual percentage rate.

9. What is "interest" on a loan?
   A. The lender's trust that you will pay back the loan.
   B. The amount of time you have to pay back the loan.
   C. The fee you pay for getting the loan.

10. An interest rate is calculated as a percent of:
   A. the amount borrowed per period of time.
   B. the amount borrowed per people in your household.
   C. the amount borrowed compared to your credit limit.

11. What is inflation?
   A. The increase in your debt over time.
   B. The increase in the value of goods over time.
   C. The increase in your savings over time.

12. How is debit different from credit?
   A. Debit is a l9an from a credit union instead of a bank.
   B. Debit is taken directly from a checking account instead of borrowed from a Lender.
   C. Debit is a promise that you will pay back the money with interest.

13. What are the two parts of a credit history?
   A. Credit report and credit score.
   B. Credit report and credit rank.
   C. Credit rank and credit listing.

14. What is the number-one way to improve your credit history?
   A. Declare bankruptcy.
   B. Only open new credit card accounts with low APRs.
   C. Pay off your debt.

15. How much of your credit card bill should you ideally pay each month?
   A. The minimum payment required by the lender.
   B. Nothing- the lender doesn't care if you pay it back.
   C. The full balance.

16. When you keep your money in bank accounts:
   A. The bank may pay you interest on it.
   B. Your money is insured by the government.
   C. Both of the above.

17. What does "overdrawing" your checking account mean?
    A. Making too many withdrawals in one month.
    B. Withdrawing more than the available balance of the account.
    C. Telling your friends you have more money than you do in the account.

18. Which one of the following is a drawback of opening an account at a credit union?
    A. It may not have as many branches and ATMs as a major bank chain.
    B. It only offers accounts with fees.
    C. Both of the above.

19. What is the basic risk of investing?
    A. That someone will steal your money.
    B. That you will forget about the money you invested.
    C. That you will not make money the way you expected to.

20. What type of loan is a car loan?
    A. An unsecured loan.
    B. A secured loan.
    C. A personal loan.

21. "Net pay" is:
    A. The amount of money you make per hour.
    B. The amount you pay on a loan.
    C. The amount you take home after income deductions.

22. What is the first step to making a budget?
    A. Setting goals.
    B. Paying down debt.
    C. Trying to get another job.

23. What type of account is a 401(k)?
    A. Checking.
    B. Certificate of deposit.
    C. Retirement savings.

24. What is the difference between fixed and variable expenses?
    A. Fixed expenses change from month to month; variable expenses don't.
    B. Variable expenses change from month to month; fixed expenses don't.
    C. You can budget for fixed expenses, but not for variable expenses.

25. What is the number-one rule of budgets?
    A. Overestimate everything.
    B. Your expenses should not be greater than your income.
    C. Don't set aside money for fun or entertainment.

REENTRY
ESSENTIALS, INC.

Personal Growth & Development

This page intentionally left blank

Personal Growth & Development

Course Goal: Upon completion of this course, student will develop critical skills in order to effectively attain physical, mental, and emotional well-being through positive communication and healthy lifestyle choices.

The Four Communication Styles

One way of thinking about communication is to divide it into four main styles: Passive, Aggressive, Passive-Aggressive, and Assertive. As you read the descriptions and behaviors of the four styles below, think about which style you identify with most.

Passive: I do not directly say what I need, want, or think. I put others' needs above my own. I want to avoid conflict, but I often end up feeling upset with other people for not giving me what I want. Passive behaviors:

- Not looking other people in the eyes.
- Apologizing a lot.
- Often using words and phrases such as "maybe," "probably," "kind of," and "I guess."
- Feeling powerless or unworthy.

Aggressive: I demand what I want and need, with no concern for anyone else. I often end up in fights with other people. Aggressive behaviors:

- Staring and pointing at others when I talk to them.
- Interrupting other people often.
- Blaming others for problems
- Feeling impatient or angry when speaking with people.

Passive-Aggressive: I manipulate others to get what I want. I communicate indirectly. I seem easy to get along with, but I believe my needs are more important than others'. Passive-Aggressive behaviors:

- Lying to get what I want.
- Using sarcasm to make other people feel bad.
- Having trouble connecting with other people.
- Feeling stuck or powerless.

Assertive: I know what I need and want, and I request it in a clear, respectful way. Assertive behaviors:

- Making good eye contact in conversation.
- Listening and caring about what others need and want.
- Having lots of good connections with people.
- Feeling in control of myself and my situation.

Example: You are reaching for the salt at a lunch counter, and the man next to you grabs it right before you do.

- Passive Response: You say nothing at all and eat your bland food without salt.
- Aggressive Response: "Give me that salt, or I'll pour it on your head."
- Passive-Aggressive Response: "I sure do hope there's enough salt in there to go around... some of us were just about to use it."
- Assertive Response: "I'd like the salt, too. Would you please give it to me when you're done using it?"

Recognizing Your Main Communication Style

Most people use every one of the four communication styles at times, depending on the situation and the people involved. However, most people use one style most of the time. This style is a person's main communication style.

Directions: Identify the communication style you use most often (Passive, Aggressive, Passive-Aggressive, or Assertive). Think about a time that you used your main style of communicating to express something you wanted. Write a brief summary of the situation and answer the following questions: How did you feel when the conversation was over? Did you get what you wanted in the end? How did the conversation affect your relationship with the other person?

My Main Communication Style and Situation I Used It In:

_____

_____

_____

_____

Directions: Now, make a list of people you know who use the other three styles most of the time (one person per style). How do you usually feel after talking with each person?

Person #1: _____

Style: _____

I feel: _____

Person #2: _____

Style: _____

I feel: _____

Person #3: _____

Style: _____

I feel: _____

Being More Assertive

You have probably figured out that the Assertive style of communicating is the most effective for most situations. Assertive communicators often use "I" messages to state opinions or ask for what they want. When you use "I" messages, you take responsibility for your feelings and actions without blaming the other person. This makes the other person more willing to listen, and it can help you understand each other better.

One way to learn the Assertive style is to practice the **Assertiveness Formula:**
I feel. . . when you . . . because . . . I want/need....

Step 1: I feel ...
Feelings can usually be described by one word, such as happy, nervous, worried, or excited.

> **Example:** "I feel sad." Not, "You made me feel bad."

Step 2: When you...
State the action you want to talk about instead of making general statements.

> **Example:** "When you say I'm lazy." Not, "When you're being a jerk."

Step 3: Because...
Focus on the effect of the action on the relationship instead of blaming the other person.

> **Example:** "Because I don't feel respected." Not, "Because I hate you."

Step 4: I want/need...
State what you want or need. Use "I" messages and talk about the behavior in Step 2.

> **Example:** "I need you to stop insulting me." Not, "You never say nice things."

Directions: Think of the last time you were upset with a friend. Write down how you could have communicated with that person using the Assertiveness Formula.

_____

_____

_____

_____

_____

_____

Verbal and Nonverbal Communication

Along with the four main styles of communication, there are two main types of communication: verbal and nonverbal.

Verbal

Verbal communication is sending messages to others by speaking or writing. You use verbal communication when you:

- Talk with friends.
- Instructor train others.
- Ask questions.

It is important to know what message you want to get across and to state it clearly when speaking. There is always the chance of confusion, but speaking with a loud, clear voice and using proper grammar will help others understand what you are saying.

Nonverbal Communication

Nonverbal communication is everything that is not spoken aloud. It includes nonverbal cues such as:

- Sign language.
- Facial expressions: smiling, frowning, blushing.
- Body movement and posture: looking at your watch, standing up straight.
- Gestures: crossing your arms, pointing.
- Eye contact: looking at the person, looking down or away.
- Personal space: standing too close, backing away.

When trying to understand someone else's nonverbal communication, remember the following:

- The other person may not be aware of his or her nonverbal cues. Nonverbal cues should match what a person is saying out loud. If your gut feeling tells you that something isn't quite right, you may be picking up on a difference between verbal and nonverbal communication.
- Different cultures or individuals may read nonverbal cues differently than you do.
- Never assume your understanding of a situation is the only "right" understanding.
- The best way to understand what a person is trying to communicate is to ask. "Am I right in thinking you want ..." or "Can you tell me more about what you are feeling right now?"

Being aware of both your verbal and nonverbal cues when communicating with others will help you get your message across in the way you want.

Nonverbal Communication Cues

Understanding nonverbal cues can be tricky. They can mean different things in different situations. You must think about their context (who, where, when) before you decide what they communicate.

Directions: For each nonverbal cue given below, fill in the connected bubbles with two possible meanings.

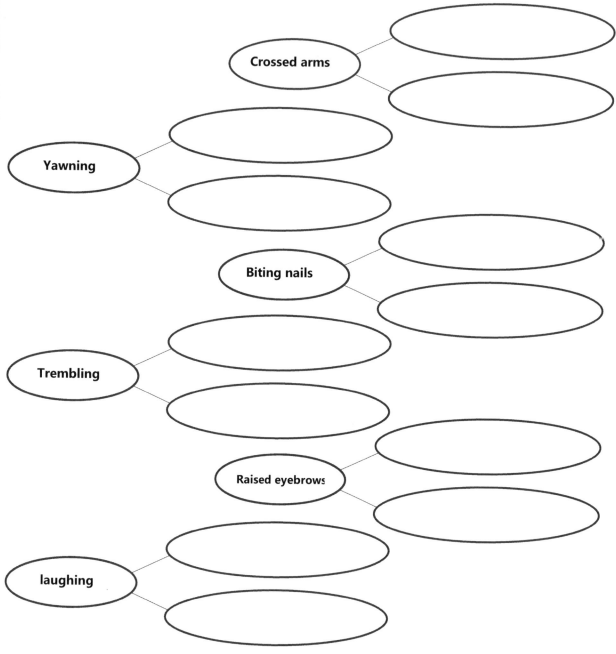

Group Discussion: Now, compare your answers to a partner's answers. Explain the situation you were thinking of for each meaning you wrote. Do you and your partner disagree about any of the meanings? Why?

Listening vs. Hearing

Listening involves paying attention to both verbal and nonverbal communication. It is the most common form of communication—most people spend more time listening than speaking. But listening and hearing are not the same thing. You can hear the words people are saying without processing their meaning. Listening means actively reading verbal and nonverbal cues.

Have you ever had the feeling that the person you were talking to wasn't really listening to you? For example, you tell your best friend you just got paroled, and he says, "Oh well, you'll get 'em next time." He heard the words but didn't listen to their meaning. Listening shows that you respect other people. It can also help you get along with them better.

These Active Listening Guidelines can help you make sure you're listening well:

- Get Ready to Listen.
    - Look directly at the speaker.
    - Use open body language (no crossed arms or legs).

- Focus on The Message.
    - Concentrate on what the speaker is saying.
    - Ignore background noise and other distractions.
    - Determine the speaker's main point.
    - What ideas does the speaker give to support the main idea?

- Look at Body Language.
    - What are the speaker's facial expressions and body language telling you?
    - Does the speaker's body language match his or her verbal message?

- Show You are Listening.
    - Smile or nod occasionally.
    - Use short verbal comments like "yes" or "uh-huh."

- Ask Questions and Respond Appropriately.
    - Ask questions to make sure you understand.
    - Paraphrase or summarize the speaker's comments.
    - Voice concerns or give your opinion respectfully.

Listening or Controlling?

Actively listening includes making verbal responses that encourage communication. During a conversation, it is okay to make short verbal comments like "yes." But, you should wait until the speaker is finished making a point before asking questions or offering your opinion.

As you listen, try not to make judgments or decide what that person should or should not do. Your responses should show the other person that you care and want to better understand. Keep your comments and questions open and neutral. Otherwise, it may seem that you are trying to control the other person. This shuts down communication and is not helpful to either of you.

Directions: Next to each response, write whether it shows listening or controlling.

Verbal Response	Listening or Controlling?
"You have to ..."	
"You should have ..."	
"Am I understanding you ..."	
"Let's not talk about ..."	
"That's interesting ..."	
"How do you feel about ..."	
"Your problem is ... "	
"Tell me more about ..."	
"You'd better ..."	

Making Relationships Better with Communication

Families, friends, and co-workers are important, as is keeping up good communication with them. Talking or writing on a regular basis can make your relationships stronger.

Effective communication is about understanding the other person and building mutual respect and trust. It is a "two-way street." You share your news, thoughts, and feelings, and so does the other person. Conflicts will arise, but you can learn to communicate in a way that leads to more peaceful and healthy relationships.

What do you do if that "two-way street" is blocked by hurt feelings or conflicts? Here are some guidelines that can help you improve communication.

Establishing Positive Communication

- Don't hold grudges.

- Think before you speak, especially if you're about to say something critical or negative. Will your comment help the situation or make it worse?

- Think of positive things to say to help rebuild the relationship.

Working Through Conflict

- Only argue about one thing at a time.

- Use "I" messages rather than "You" messages.

- Try to see the other person's point of view, even if you do not agree with it.

- Don't think about what you're going to say next while the other person is talking.

- Accept criticism thoughtfully instead of being defensive.

- Admit when you are wrong.

- Look for compromise instead of trying to win.

Communicating with Different Types of People

Think about how you communicate differently with different people. How you talk to your friends is different from how you talk to your boss or co-workers. At work, you may need to be more reserved than you are at home with your family and friends. When speaking at work, remember to be professional—avoid swearing, gossiping, and making jokes or comments that stereotype or single out any group of people.

Remember your training on assertive communication and always try to be clear and respectful with all people. You can also be an active listener and try to understand the other person's message and point of view before you respond.

Directions: Read the situations below. With a partner, act out how you would communicate about each of them, first as co-workers and then as friends. Practice the assertive communication and good listening skills you learned from the previous pages.

Situation 1: Your co-worker borrowed something from you without asking.

Situation 2: Your friend borrowed something from you without asking.

Situation 3: You accidentally broke something that belonged to your co-worker.

Situation 4: You accidentally broke something that belonged to your friend.

Situation 5: You thought you were going to meet your co-worker for lunch at 12:30 p.m., but he didn't show up.

Situation 6: You thought you were going to meet your friend for lunch at 12:30 p.m., but he didn't show up.

Group Discussion: Now, discuss how what you said to the co-worker differed from what you said to the friend. Did you and your partner agree on how to communicate respectfully in each situation? If not, why?

Seeing Yourself Clearly

What do you notice first about other people? How do you think others see you? Who do you think has the most influence on the way you present yourself: your friends, your family, your co-workers, the people on TV?

These are all questions we can ask to begin seeing ourselves more clearly. Both your external traits and internal traits affect the way you see yourself and how others see you. External traits are parts of your physical appearance, like height, skin color, haircut, and clothing. Internal traits are parts of your personality, like whether you are shy, kind, or logical.

Our society has some standards for what are "good" external and internal traits. It is important to know yourself and to find a balance between meeting society's standards and being true to yourself.

For example, our society has certain expectations for cleanliness and hygiene. Whether or not you meet those expectations will affect what other people think of you. If you are at home or with family, you may not care as much about meeting those expectations. But showing up to a job interview showered and dressed in clean clothing will make you much more likely to get the job.

Directions: Think about what society expects of you. What are considered positive traits? In the circles below, write down a few internal traits and a few external traits that are considered good. Then, compare your list with a partner's list. Do you agree that the items on your partner's list are considered positive in our society? Why or why not?

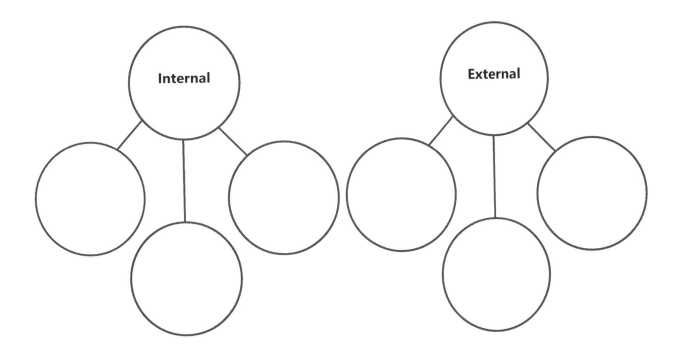

Seeing Yourself Clearly

Getting to know yourself is the first step to becoming the person you want to be.

Directions: Make a list of five external traits and five internal traits that you have today. Next to each trait, write whether it is a trait you like or don't like. Then, next to each trait you like, write one way you could make that trait even stronger. Next to each trait you don't like, write one way you could try to make that trait better.

Example:

my bad temper	don't like	go to an anger management class

External Trait	**Like or Dislike?**	**How to Make It Better**

Internal Trait	**Like or Dislike?**	**How to Make It Better**

Eating a Healthy Diet

It can be hard to make healthy food choices in today's society. Fast-food restaurants are everywhere, and the food they serve is relatively cheap. However, fast-food restaurants do not usually offer the variety needed for a balanced diet. Eating a balanced diet will give you the best chance of reentering society with success. Making healthy food choices can improve your, mental and physical well-being and help you meet life's challenges.

The United States Department of Agriculture names five food groups: fruits, vegetables, grains, protein, and dairy. A nutritious diet includes all of them (except dairy if you are lactose intolerant). Carbohydrates are very important for energy and digestive health. They include grains, fruit, and vegetables. You need protein to build muscle. You also need some fat to absorb certain vitamins and minerals.

Lean meats, whole grains, and fresh fruits and vegetables are the healthiest foods to eat. Foods that are fried, high in calories, or full of sugar are considered junk food.

The image below shows the proportions you should eat of each food group. You can see that vegetables and grains are the biggest pieces.

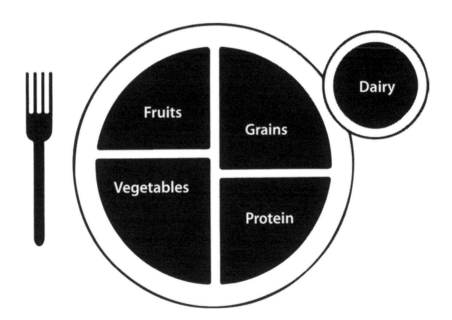

Since our bodies are made up mostly of water, drinking water is very important. You should stay hydrated by drinking water when you are thirsty. If you drink fruit juice, make sure it is 100 percent juice. Try to avoid sugar-sweetened drinks, like soda.

A healthy diet depends on balance—not too much of any one thing. This includes alcohol. Remember that alcohol is a sedative and can damage your health if you drink too much.

Buying Food for a Healthy Diet

When you go grocery shopping, remember to make healthy food choices. Avoid junk food, which is high in sugar and fat. Choose foods from the five main food groups:

Fruits: apples, bananas, grapes, tomatoes

Vegetables: lettuce, zucchini, sweet potatoes

Grains: cereal, rice, popcorn

Protein: beef, chicken, fish, nuts

Dairy: milk, cheese, yogurt

Directions: Read the list of foods in the first grocery list below. Next, cross out the junk food items from the list. Then, fill in the blank grocery list using the remaining foods, placing each food in the correct food group.

Grocery List

Pears
Wheat Bread
Eggs
Collard Greens
Cheddar Cheese
Potato Chips
Almonds
Muffins
Carrots
Pineapple
Granola
Lemons
Milk
Ice Cream
Cookies
Pork Chops
Onions
Spinach
Brown Rice
Potatoes
Plums
Oatmeal

Grocery List

Fruits

_____

_____

_____

_____

_____

_____

Grains

_____

_____

_____

_____

_____

_____

Vegetables

_____

_____

_____

_____

_____

_____

Protein

_____

_____

Dairy

_____

_____

_____

Physical Activity and Exercise

Benefits of Exercise

Exercise has many physical and mental health benefits. It helps reduce stress, blood pressure, and cholesterol levels. It reduces your risk of becoming overweight and getting heart disease or diabetes. It makes you stronger, more confident, and more able to fight off disease.

Exercise also:

- Keeps joints flexible, which makes it easier to move around.
- Helps treat depression.
- Helps relieve stress and anxiety.
- Increases your energy and endurance.
- Helps you sleep better.
- Increases your metabolism (the rate at which you burn calories).

Making Exercise a Habit

It is important to have a regular exercise routine and stick to it. Make sure you discuss any new exercise routine with a doctor before you start. Most doctors recommend 30 minutes of activity five times a week.

The most difficult part of having a routine is getting started. You will be most likely to keep to your routine if the exercise is fun, so choose activities that you enjoy. If you like being with a group of people, try a team sport. If you like to exercise alone, make a personal workout routine. It is also helpful to do different types of exercise on different days so that you don't get bored.

Here are some ways to help you stick to your exercise routine:

- Exercise at a regular time every day.
- Sign a contract with yourself in which you commit to exercise.
- Put "exercise appointments" on your calendar.
- Keep a daily log or diary of your exercise activities.
- Check your progress. Can you walk a certain distance faster now than when you began exercising? Or is your heart rate slower now?
- Ask your doctor to recommend an exercise program. This might include what type of exercise to do, how often to exercise, and for how long.

What Kind of Exercise Is Right for You?

Directions: Rate each activity below on a scale of 1 to 5, with 1 being that you don't like to do it at all, and 5 being that you love to do it. If you can think of an activity that is not on this list, add it to the list.

_____ Lifting Weights

_____ Running

_____ Riding A Bike

_____ Walking

_____ Playing Baseball/Softball

_____ Playing Basketball

_____ Playing Soccer

_____ Playing Football (Touch, Flag, Or Contact)

_____ Playing Tennis

_____ Throwing A Frisbee

_____ Doing Sit-Ups and Pushups

_____ Dancing

_____ Other Physical Activity: _____

_____ Other Physical Activity: _____

What Kind of Exercise Is Right for You?

Planning your exercise routine before you start is the best way to make sure you keep to it.

Directions: Look at the list on the previous page. On which two activities did you score the highest?

Think about how you could make a regular exercise routine with these two activities. Then, fill in the calendar below with exercise appointments for next week. Use both of your favorite activities and try to schedule five appointments for the week.

	Monday	Tuesday	Wednesday	Thursday	Friday	Saturday	Sunday
8:00 a.m.							
9:00 a.m.							
10:00 a.m.							
11:00 a.m.							
12:00 p.m.							
1:00 p.m.							
2:00 p.m.							
3:00 p.m.							
4:00 p.m.							
5:00 p.m.							
6:00 p.m.							
7:00 p.m.							
8:00 p.m.							
9:00 p.m.							
10:00 p.m.							

Communicable and Infectious Diseases

Communicable diseases, also called **infectious diseases,** are illnesses that pass from person to person. Having good health and hygiene habits will keep your immune system working and help you fight off these diseases.

If you get a bacterial infection, a doctor will prescribe antibiotic medicine to help you get better. It is very important to take all of any antibiotic that is prescribed to you. Even though you may feel better after a few days of medicine, there may be remaining bacteria that will cause problems later. Taking all of the antibiotic makes sure you kill all of the harmful bacteria.

Some of the most common communicable diseases are listed below.

HIV/AIDS:

HIV (human immunodeficiency virus) is the virus that causes AIDS. This virus may be passed from one person to another when blood, semen, or vaginal fluid touch another person's broken skin or mucous membranes. Pregnant women can also pass HIV to their baby during pregnancy, delivery, or breastfeeding. HIV lowers the infected person's immune system, putting the person at risk for other deadly infections. There is no cure for HIV/AIDS, but there are medications that extend the life of people who are infected.

Chlamydia:

Chlamydia is a very common sexually transmitted disease (STD). It is a bacterial infection that can be cured with antibiotics if treated early. There are usually no symptoms. When there are symptoms, they appear within 7 to 21 days. Symptoms in women include bleeding between menstrual cycles, painful urination, discharge from the vagina, pain in the lower abdomen, and fever. Symptoms in men include a watery white discharge from the penis and burning during urination.

Genital Warts/HPV:

Genital warts are caused by the human papillomavirus (HPV). HPV is the most common sexually transmitted disease. There are usually no symptoms. When there are symptoms, they appear in 1 to 6 months. The symptoms are small, hard warts, or bumps, around the genitals or anus. There is no cure for the virus, but the warts can be removed. A different strain of I-IPV can cause cervical and other cancers. It is important to get vaccinated for the virus.

Gonorrhea:

Gonorrhea is a sexually transmitted bacterial infection of the reproductive tract, mouth, throat, eyes, and anus. It is the second most commonly reported STD in the United States. There are usually no symptoms, but they can appear within 2 to 21 days after infection. The symptoms in women are a thick, yellow discharge from the vagina, burning during urination, a more painful menstrual cycle, and pain in the lower abdomen. Symptoms in men include a yellow or white discharge from the penis and burning and pain during urination. If not treated, gonorrhea can lead to sterility, arthritis and joint damage, or pelvic inflammatory disease. It can be treated with antibiotics.

Genital Herpes:

Genital herpes is a sexually transmitted viral infection that has no cure. Nationwide, 1 out of 5 adolescents and adults have herpes. There may be no symptoms, but they can appear 2 to 30 days after initial infection. Symptoms include small, painful blisters on the genitals or mouth, painful and frequent urination, and flu-like feelings. Genital herpes may be passed to babies during delivery. In babies, it can cause brain damage or death if not treated. Antiviral medications can reduce the symptoms and risk of transmitting herpes.

Syphilis:

Syphilis is a sexually transmitted bacterial infection. There are usually no symptoms, but they may occur 1 to 12 weeks after infection. Symptoms include a sore or rash on or near the genitals and flu-like feelings. If not treated, sores or a skin rash may appear. Syphilis may also cause heart damage, paralysis, and mental illness. It can easily be treated with antibiotics in its early stages.

Hepatitis:

Hepatitis is a disease that causes inflammation of the liver. It is most often caused by a virus, but it can also be caused by other things, including alcohol abuse, medications, or chemicals. There are three types of hepatitis.

Hepatitis A (HAV) is transmitted through personal contact, or through food or water contaminated by fecal matter. Symptoms may include nausea and vomiting, jaundice (yellowing of the eyes and skin), dark urine and light colored stools, fatigue, fever, and abdominal pain. Most people recover without treatment within a year and are then immune to the virus. There is a vaccine for HAV that is taken in two doses.

Hepatitis B (HBV) is spread through contact with infected body fluids. HBV can be spread sexually and through needles, including tattoo needles. HBV is 100 times more contagious than HIV. Symptoms may include flulike feelings, swelling and pain in the joints, jaundice, and dark urine and light colored stools. Chronic FIBV is one of the main causes of death in the world. There is a vaccine for 1-1B V that is considered safe and effective. There is no treatment for HBV.

Hepatitis C (HCV) is the most common bloodborne infection in the United States. It is spread through contact with blood and less commonly through sexual contact. Symptoms of HCV almost never appear. A small percentage of people with HCV will develop symptoms similar to those of HAV or FIBV, but milder. More than half of infected people will develop chronic HCV, which may lead to extreme tiredness, liver damage, cirrhosis, liver failure, or liver cancer. Chronic HCV can be managed with medication. There is no vaccine for Hepatitis C, so prevention is important.

Tuberculosis:

Tuberculosis (TB) is an infection caused by a bacteria that usually attacks the lungs but can affect other parts of the body. There are two different stages of tuberculosis—TB infection and TB disease. A person who has TB infection has the bacteria in his or her body but cannot spread TB to others. In a person who has TB disease, the bacteria are active and can be spread to others. TB is spread when people who have TB disease cough, sneeze, or speak and then another person breathes in the germs. Most TB infections never develop into TB disease. Some symptoms of TB disease are a persistent cough, chest pain, coughing up blood or phlegm, weakness and fatigue, weight loss, loss of appetite, fever or chills, and night sweats. TB disease can be treated through medication.

Staph Infection:

A staph infection is any infection caused by the family of Staphylococcus bacteria. These bacteria live on the skin around your nose, mouth, genitals, and anus. They usually do not cause problems unless they enter the body through a break in the skin. Most staph infections produce pus-filled pockets called abscesses, which usually appear just beneath the surface of the skin. But abscesses can also form deep within the body. If untreated, staph can be life threatening. It is usually easily treated with an antibiotic.

Understanding Communicable and Infectious Diseases

In order to keep yourself and the people around you healthy, you must understand how communicable diseases are passed from person to person and how they can be treated.

Directions: For each of the diseases below, fill in the blank with the way(s) the disease can be transmitted.

Example: Hepatitis C _____Contact with blood._____

1. HIV _____

2. Gonorrhea _____

3. Syphilis _____

4. Hepatitis B _____

5. Genital Herpes _____

6. Chlamydia _____

7. Tuberculosis _____

8. Genital Warts/HPV _____

Now, list the treatments for the diseases listed below.

1. HIV/AIDS _____

2. Gonorrhea _____

3. Syphilis _____

4. Hepatitis B _____

5. Genital Herpes _____

6. Chlamydia _____

7. Tuberculosis _____

8. Genital Warts/HPV _____

Understanding Communicable and Infectious Diseases

You need to be able to recognize the symptoms and health effects of communicable diseases so you can get treated if you are already infected.

Directions: Draw a line from the disease in the left column to its symptom/health effect in the right column.

Disease	Symptom / Health Effect
Hepatitis C	Rash Near Genitals
Staph Infection	Lowered Immune System
HIV/AIDS	Inflammation Of The Liver
Gonorrhea	Blisters On Genitals Or Mouth
Syphilis	Bleeding Between Menstrual Cycles
Genital Herpes	Abscesses
Chlamydia	Burning During Urination
Hepatitis A	Cough And Chest Pain
Genital Warts/HPV	Swollen, Painful Joints
Tuberculosis	Bumps Around Genitals Or Anus
Hepatitis B	Nausea And Vomiting

Group Discussion: Now, as a whole group, discuss the stereotypes you have heard about the diseases explained on pages 186-188. Is each stereotype correct or incorrect?

Protecting Yourself Against Disease

It is important to protect yourself against communicable disease, because your health also affects the health of your family, co-workers, and community. If you have good hygiene and make smart decisions, staying healthy is easy. The following are good health habits to practice.

Always Practice Safe Sex

Not having sex at all is called abstinence. This is the only way to completely protect yourself from pregnancy and sexually transmitted diseases. Having sex with only one partner is called monogamy. If your partner has been tested and is known to be uninfected, and if he or she is not having sex with anyone but you, then monogamy is safe.

Another way to protect yourself against sexually transmitted diseases is to use condoms. Condoms are not 100 percent effective, but they can provide protection from disease. Keep in mind that condoms provide less protection for genital herpes and HPV because they may not cover the infected area of skin. Always use a new latex condom for each act of vaginal, anal, and oral sex. Remember to change the condom after each sexual act—condoms should be used only once. You should also never use an oil based lubricant or condoms with oil-based products on them. Use only water-based lubricant.

Get Immunizations/Vaccinations

Vaccines have reduced or wiped out many communicable diseases. We must all be sure to keep getting them, or else some of these diseases can reappear. Your doctor or local clinic will have an immunization schedule that you should follow. You will need proof that you got these immunizations to start at some jobs and schools or to travel abroad. If you have children, you will need proof that they got their vaccines before they can enter the school system.

Maintain Good Personal Hygiene

You can kill most germs with just soap and water. Showering regularly and wearing clean clothes is important to reduce the growth and spread of germs. Washing your hands is another easy way to stop germs in their tracks. Wash your hands well with soap and water:

- Before eating and preparing food.
- After using the toilet.
- After changing a diaper.
- After cleaning the toilet.
- After sneezing, coughing, or blowing your nose.

Protecting Yourself Against Disease

Directions: Circle the letter for each correct answer. Then, answer the questions that follow.

1. I should wash my hands:
   A. After sneezing into them.
   B. Before touching food.
   C. After changing a diaper.
   D. All of the Above

2. "Abstinence" means:
   A. Having sex only once a week.
   B. Having sex with only one partner.
   C. Not having any sex at all.
   D. None of the Above

3. If I don't get vaccinated for communicable diseases:
   A. I might get infected with a disease.
   B. I might infect others with a disease.
   C. I may not be able to get some jobs.
   D. All of the Above

4. A condom should be used:
   A. Only once.
   B. However, many times you have sex that night.
   C. Only if it's convenient.
   D. None of the Above

5. You can get a vaccination schedule from:
   A. The grocery stores.
   B. The doctor.
   C. The TV news.
   D. All of the Above

6. Condoms protect against every sexually transmitted disease.
   A. True
   B. False

7. Can you think of any other ways to protect yourself from communicable diseases that aren't listed on page 191? Write at least one below.

   _____

8. Why do you think it is so important for everyone to get vaccinated against diseases? What do you think would happen if people stopped?

   _____

   _____

   _____

Recognizing Abuse

Abuse means doing harm or injury to another person. Abuse also includes using a chemical or drug, like alcohol, too much or illegally. Abuse can happen anywhere: in the home, at school, at work, or in the community. The major types of abuse are listed below.

Physical:

Physical abuse occurs when one person causes pain, injury, or other physical suffering or bodily harm to another person. This includes physical violence and also restraining someone against his or her will.

Emotional/Mental:

Emotional abuse occurs when one person uses manipulation or brainwashing to lower another person's self-confidence and sense of self worth. This includes efforts to frighten, control, isolate, or intimidate another person. Sometimes it can be committed under the guise of "guidance" or "teaching." Emotional/mental abuse leads the victim to lose all trust in himself or herself.

Verbal:

Verbal abuse occurs when one person insults another aloud, including criticizing, screaming, threatening, blaming, or calling names. This abuse also includes using sarcasm and humiliation to make someone feel bad. Similar to emotional/mental abuse, verbal abuse lowers victims' self-confidence and trust in themselves.

Sexual:

Sexual abuse occurs when one person commits unwanted sexual behavior upon another. This includes non-consensual sex, forced sexual acts, and verbal sexual behavior, such as threats. Even if someone seems to be willing at first, if that person says "no" at any point and you still have sex, you are committing sexual abuse. It is also abuse if the other person is underage or unable to consent for any reason.

Chemical:

Chemical abuse occurs when someone habitually uses or has a need for a mood-altering drug, alcoholic beverage, or other substance. Often, chemical abuse can lead people to commit other types of abuse.

The Different Types of Abuse

Directions: Working with a partner, read the situations below aloud. Then, decide which type of abuse they are. Fill in the blanks using the answer choice box.

Physical	Emotional/Mental	Verbal
Sexual	Chemical	

Example: A father punches his teenage son if his son disobeys him. _____Physical_____

1. A mother calls her son a "lazy, no-good deadbeat." _____

2. A boss threatens to fire an assistant if she does not have sex with him. _____

3. A classmate beats up a boy for his lunch money once a week. _____

4. A husband convinces his wife that she isn't smart enough to get a job so that she will stay

   home. _____

5. A student takes pills he got from a friend to stay awake all night studying for exams.

   _____

6. A man has forcible sex with a woman who went home with him from a bar, but then said no.

   _____

7. A jealous husband shoves his wife into a wall. _____

8. A woman drinks so much on the weekends that she often has to call in sick to work on

   Mondays. _____

Chemical Use, Abuse, and Dependency

What is the difference among using, abusing, and being dependent on alcohol or drugs? People have used mind-altering substances for centuries. In small doses, they may not be a problem. But if you make a habit of abusing or you depend on drugs and alcohol, they can cause a lot of harm.

Use is defined as the choice to take in a substance, in a reasonable amount and with reasonable frequency. When you are using your free will and you are not being harmed by the alcohol or drug, you are simply using it. However, remember that using any amount of illegal drugs is a criminal act and can lead to arrest.

Abuse happens when you use a substance in unreasonable amounts or with unreasonable frequency. This leads to significant problems, such as not showing up to work or school, getting into dangerous situations, having legal problems, or damaging friendships or family relationships.

Dependency is continued drug or alcohol use that leads to three or more of the conditions below within a twelve-month period. It is also called **addiction.**

- Developing a tolerance, as larger amounts of the substance are needed to achieve the same effect. Tolerance also means that the same amount of the substance has less effect over time.

- Having withdrawal symptoms when you stop taking the substance. Alcohol withdrawal symptoms include sweating or pulse rate greater than 100, hand tremors, nausea or vomiting, anxiety, seizures, and hallucinations. This condition also includes taking the same substance to avoid the symptoms of withdrawal.

- Taking a substance in large amounts or over a longer period than was intended.

- Having the desire to quit, or trying and failing to cut down or control substance use.

- Spending a lot of time getting the substance (like driving long distances), using the substance (like chain smoking), or recovering from its effects (like frequent hangovers).

- Giving up important social, work-related, or fun activities because of substance use.

- Continuing the substance use even though you know you have a physical or mental problem that was caused or made worse by the substance. An example of this is continuing to drink alcohol even though it's making your ulcer worse.

What Do You Know About Drug and Alcohol Abuse?

Directions: Test your knowledge about substance abuse by circling True or False after each fact below.

1. Alcohol is a stimulant.   **True   False**

2. Men are twice as likely to abuse drugs than women. **True   False**

3. Drug overdoses kill as many people as car accidents every year in the United States.
   True   False

4. The heroin addict spends between $50 and $100 per day in order to maintain a heroin addiction.
   True   False

5. Meth is a highly addictive drug that can be made from over-the-counter products available anywhere in the United States. **True   False**

6. Cocaine can be detected in hair follicle tests for several months after use. **True   False**

7. Alcohol stays in an unborn baby's system longer than it stays in the mother's. **True   False**

8. One hundred people die from drug overdoses in the U.S. every day. **True   False**

9. Nearly one quarter of all drug-related emergency room visits are due to cocaine abuse.
   True   False

10. Mixing prescription drugs is never dangerous. **True   False**

11. Prescription drugs are not as addictive as illegal drugs. **True   False**

12. One side effect of taking meth is teeth rot. **True   False**

13. Withdrawal from a long-term addiction can potentially be fatal. **True   False**

14. Even if you end up in the hospital, if you take a drug just once then you are simply using it.
    True   False

15. Having friends who don't want to hang out with you anymore because of your drinking is a sign that you are abusing alcohol. **True   False**

What Do You Know About Drug and Alcohol Abuse?

Here are the answers to the questions on the previous page. How many did you get right?

1. False - Alcohol is a sedative.

2. True

3. True

4. False - The heroin addict spends between $150 and $200 per day in order to maintain a heroin addiction.

5. True

6. True

7. True

8. True

9. False - Nearly half of all drug-related emergency room visits are due to cocaine abuse.

10. False - Mixing prescription drugs can be very dangerous, even fatal.

11. False - Prescription drugs can be just as addictive as illegal drugs.

12. True

13. True

14. False - If you end up in the hospital from taking a drug, then you have abused the drug.

15. True

Group Discussion: Discuss the correct answers as a group. Which answers surprised you? Why?

Is It Addiction?

Addiction is habitual use of or need for a substance (such as heroin, nicotine, or alcohol) or activity (such as gambling or stealing). The three major symptoms of addiction include the following:

- **Tolerance** is developed when you need more and more of a substance over time to get the same effect from it. You can develop a tolerance to any substance, from aspirin to heroin. You can also develop a tolerance to a behavior like gambling.

- **Compulsive use** is when you need to use a substance or engage in a behavior over and over again. This can lead to very bad consequences. People who are controlled by a compulsion can lose everything in their lives that they care about, including their job, family, and health.

- **Withdrawal** is a set of symptoms that occur when you stop taking the substance or engaging in the behavior. Withdrawal symptoms can range from anxiety to vomiting to headaches. In extreme cases, they can even include seizures or death.

Other signs of addiction include the following:

- Sudden weight loss or gain.
- Being extremely hyper or talkative.
- Change in friends.
- Losing interest in things that were important before.
- Drop in school or work performance.
- Being late or not showing up to appointments.
- Losing interest in family activities.
- Lack of motivation, energy, or discipline.
- Being moody, irritable, or nervous.
- Violent temper or odd behavior.
- Paranoia or extreme anxiety.
- Secretive or suspicious behavior.
- Car accidents, fender benders, household accidents.
- Lying, stealing, trouble with police.
- Being unable to explain where money goes.
- Change in personal hygiene.
- Having drug paraphernalia.

People do recover from addiction and go on to live healthy lives. If you have an addiction, you can recover—but you must first recognize that you are addicted.

Do You Have Symptoms of Chemical Dependency?

The American Psychiatric Association uses seven symptoms to diagnose dependency on alcohol, drugs, or other substances. You are considered dependent if you experience three of these seven symptoms.

Directions: Check the box next to any symptom you have experienced.

☐ You have developed a tolerance to the substance over time.

☐ You have withdrawal symptoms when you stop or reduce the amount of the substance.

☐ You have taken the substance in a larger amount or over a longer period of time than you intended to.

☐ You spend a lot of time preparing to use, using, or recovering from use of the substance.

☐ You have stopped or reduced social, professional, or other fun activities because of using the substance.

☐ You continue to use the substance even though you know it has caused problems or made existing problems worse.

☐ You have tried to cut down, control, or stop using the substance but failed to do so.

Look at the list above. Did you check more than three boxes? Do you think you have an addiction? Why or why not? Write your answer on the lines below.

_____

_____

_____

_____

_____

_____

The Effects of Addiction

The first step of recovering from an addiction is recognizing that you have one. Addictions are very harmful to your own physical and mental health, but they can be even more harmful to your family, friends, and loved ones. Addictions can lead to abuse situations and destroy relationships.

If you checked more than three of the boxes in the previous activity, it is time to think about how an addiction may be affecting your life.

There are many consequences of addiction. They affect every part of your life.

- **Health:** Alcohol or drug addiction harms your health. There are a wide range of effects, from depression and anxiety, to heart disease and cancer, to contracting HIV from risky behavior.

- **Family:** Drug addiction can also cause health problems for your family. Secondhand smoke affects everyone near you, and it can lead to birth defects and asthma in children, or cancer and stroke in adults. Family relationships suffer as you spend more time using the drug or trying to get the drug. If abuse is involved, your children could be taken from you.

- **Finances:** Most addictions are expensive. The money used for buying drugs or gambling is money that could have been spent feeding your family or improving your life.

- **Work:** When you are addicted, the drug clouds your judgment. Not showing up to work, or worse—getting caught using at work—can get you suspended or fired.

Getting Help with Addiction

Loved ones are important in helping you change addiction behaviors. Therapy or addiction counseling and recovery programs, like Alcoholics Anonymous (AA) and Narcotics Anonymous (NA), can also help you take control of your addiction and your life.

Don't try to do it alone; it's too easy to relapse. Remember that support is necessary and available. Recovering from drug addiction is much easier when you have people you can lean on for encouragement, comfort, and guidance.

Here are some options that can help you recover from addiction and stay in control.

- Attending therapy or addiction counseling.
- Getting involved in a community of other recovering addicts (AA).
- Joining church or faith programs.
- Spending time with close friends and family.
- Exercising or playing a team sport.
- Meditating.
- Talking to a doctor.

The Effects of Addiction

Directions: For each area of your life listed below, write one example of how an addiction has affected it. If you don't have examples from your own life, you can use examples from a friend or family member.

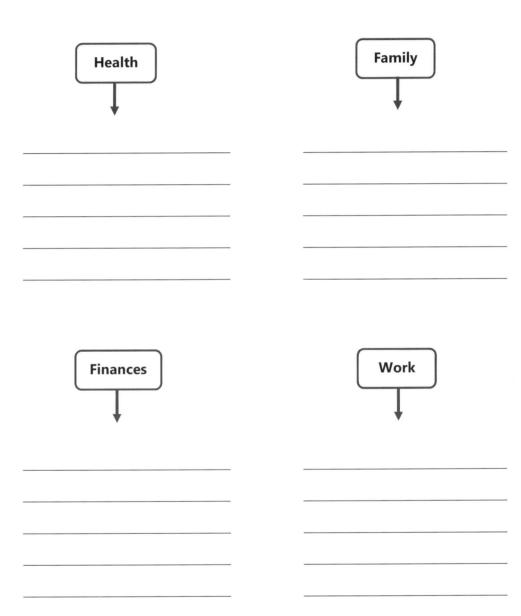

Setting Goals

Directions: Look at the list of possible support options for recovering from addiction on page 200. Which ones could you use for help? Choose two from the list and write one in each box below, along with why you chose it. Then, on the lines underneath each box, write two recovery goals you could work on with that option.

Example:

Support:

> Program at my church because I know those people care about me.

↓

Recovery Goals:

Stop partying so much with friends.

Get involved in church activities in the evenings.

[ ]

↓

_____

_____

[ ]

↓

_____

_____

Personal Growth & Development Review

Directions: Circle the letter for each correct answer.

1. Which communication style is the most effective?
   A. Aggressive.
   B. Passive.
   C. Assertive.

2. What communication style am I using if I'm lying to get what I want?
   A. Passive-Aggressive.
   B. Passive.
   C. Aggressive.

3. What is the best type of message to use in a conflict situation?
   A. "You" message.
   B. "We" message.
   C. "I" message.

4. Facial expressions are what type of communication?
   A. Verbal.
   B. Nonverbal.

5. What is a good way to show you are listening?
   A. Asking questions.
   B. Not making eye contact.
   C. Getting distracted by background noise.

6. Which of the following are parts of respectful communication?
   A. Admitting when you are wrong.
   B. Trying to see the other person's point of view.
   C. Both of the Above.

7. When your boss asks you to do something, the most appropriate response is:
   A. "Sure, man."
   B. "Yes, sir."
   C. "Gotcha."

8. When you are going to a job interview, which external trait is NOT appropriate to have?
   A. A clean shave or trimmed beard.
   B. A tie.
   C. Dirty jeans.

9. Which two food groups should you eat the most of?
   A. Vegetables and grains.
   B. Grains and protein.
   C. Fruits and dairy.

10. It is important to drink enough water because:
    A. Water helps you float.
    B. Our bodies are made mostly of water.
    C. Water can take the place of food when you're hungry.

11. Alcohol is:
    A. A sedative.
    B. A stimulant.
    C. Completely harmless.

12. The purpose of carbohydrates is:
    A. To absorb vitamins.
    B. To build muscle.
    C. To make energy.

13. How often do most doctors recommend you exercise?
    A. Every single day.
    B. Twice per week.
    C. Five times per week.

14. Exercise has which of the following benefits?
    A. It helps you sleep better.
    B. It prevents heart disease and diabetes.
    C. Both of the Above

15. Chlamydia is a sexually transmitted disease.
    A. True.
    B. False.

16. There is no cure for genital herpes.
    A. True.
    B. False.

17. HIV can be passed through:
    A. Blood.
    B. Saliva.
    C. Urine.

18. The only 100 percent effective way to prevent sexually transmitted diseases is:
    A. Using condoms.
    B. Monogamy.
    C. Abstinence.

19. The definition of "monogamy" is:
    A. Having sex with multiple partners.
    B. Having sex with only one partner.
    C. Not having sex with anyone.

20. Holding someone down against his or her will is what type of abuse?
    A. Verbal
    B. Physical
    C. Chemical

21. How do you know when someone is abusing a drug instead of just using it?
    A. He or she is choosing to use the drug on occasion.
    B. It has started to cause problems in his or her life.
    C. He or she tried it once.

22. "Dependency" is also called:
    A. Addiction.
    B. Abuse.
    C. Using.

23. Failing when you try to quit using a substance is a sign of dependency.
    A. True.
    B. False.

24. Withdrawal symptoms can include:
    A. Nausea.
    B. Seizures.
    C. Both of the Above

25. "Tolerance" to a substance means:
    A. You like it.
    B. You stopped taking it.
    C. You need more and more of it to get the same effect.

Problem Solving & Decision Making

This page intentionally left blank

Problem Solving & Decision Making

Course Goal: Upon completion of this course, student will develop valuable conflict resolution skills and make subsequent constructive decisions.

I. PROBLEM SOLVING

OBJECTIVES

II. DECISION-MAKING

OBJECTIVES

Using Compromise to Resolve Conflicts

Conflict is inevitable. Conflicts happen for lots of different reasons. One thing is for certain: everyone is going to be involved in a conflict at one time or another. Compromise is a good way to resolve conflict.

Compromise means agreeing to a solution that both parties can live with. It means both sides win a little and lose a little. You get some of what you want but not everything. Does this sound easy? It is, and it isn't. Sometimes during conflicts, our minds get so worked up it is hard to even think about compromise.

Think about a time you felt really angry with someone else about a conflict you were having.

Was compromise the first thing that came to your mind? Probably not. Sometimes before we can even think about compromise, we need to "cool down" and come up with a plan. "Cooling down" just means taking a minute or two to regroup and get calm.

Then, you need a plan.

Compromise involves being flexible. Talk to the other parties involved. Think about different solutions. Negotiate something that will work for both sides. Be ready to G-R-I-N!

G - Good listening. Listen to what everyone has to say.

R- Respect others' ideas. Think about other people's point of view; use good body language.

I - Investigate your options. Brainstorm different things that might work; eliminate solutions you can't live with.

N - Negotiate. Come up with a plan that is workable for both parties.

Compromise is not always easy, but figuring out a workable solution is a good outcome!

Creative Compromising

Directions: Working with a partner, think of at least three possible compromises to solve each conflict. Then, on your own, circle the compromise you would choose in each situation. Compare your answers with your partner's answers.

Did you both select the same compromises to each solution? Why or why not?

Talk with you partner about why you selected each specific compromise.

Conflict 1

Sarah, Liz, and Kia rent a three-bedroom apartment. The master bedroom is much bigger than the other two bedrooms. They are having trouble deciding who gets the master bedroom for their 12-month lease. Sarah, Liz, and Kia need to figure out a workable solution. Think of three compromises. Write them on the lines below.

Compromise # 1: _____

Compromise # 2: _____

Compromise # 3: _____

Which option would you choose? Why? Talk about this with your partner.

Conflict 2

Max and Ron have been roommates and close friends for five years. Recently, Ron lost his job. He is using his savings to pay the rent evey month. He has also been cleaning, painting, and doing all sorts of helpful things to fix up their apartment. Max is grateful to Ron for his help, but he has been so busy at work he hasn't been able to help around the apartment at all. He is so tired after work that he doesn't even do his own dishes after dinner. Ron is not happy with the current situation. Max and Ron need to figure out a workable solution. Think of three compromises. Write them on the lines below.

Compromise # 1: _____

Compromise # 2: _____

Compromise # 3: _____

Which option would you choose? Why? Talk about this with your partner.

Smiling Through Compromise

Remember, compromise involves being flexible. It is not always easy. It is important to be ready to G-R-I-N and compromise! Figuring out a workable solution is a good outcome.

> **G- Good listening.** Listen to what everyone has to say.
>
> **R - Respect others' ideas.** Think about other people's point of view; use good body language.
>
> **I - Investigate your options.** Brainstorm different things that might work; eliminate solutions you can't live with.
>
> **N - Negotiate.** Come up with a plan that is workable for both parties.

Directions: Read each situation. Reread G-R-I-N. Write the letter that best explains what letter of G-R-I-N is represented.

Note: Some sentences may have more than one correct answer. Be ready to explain why you selected your specific answer.

Example:

___N___ Leslie and Shea are close friends. They both want to have a party Saturday night. Their guest list is almost identical. They decide to combine the parties and split the cost.

_____ 1. Evan tells Karen that he is tired of cooking and cleaning up dinner every night while Karen watches television. He thinks they need to come up with some ideas to divide the work fairly.

_____ 2. Charlie and Coretta cannot agree on what to name their new pet puppy. They decide on two names that they both like and ask a friend to choose.

_____ 3. Selina asks Matt a question about his idea. She wants to make sure she understands what he is saying.

_____ 4. Gino explains how he will pay Liam back. Liam has to think about it a little bit because he had not even considered Gino's idea.

_____ 5. Julia really wants to apply for a job at the mall. Her best friend wants to apply, too. There is only one job available. They talk about why each of them wants the job.

Summing Up Compromise

Group Discussion:

1. Why do you think good listening, good body language, and the ability to respect other people's ideas are so important in compromise?
2. What do you think the hardest part of compromising is? Why?
3. What do you think the easiest part of compromising is? Why?

Final Evaluation: Answer the following questions in your own words.

1. Why is being able to compromise important?

   _____

   _____

2. Give one example of what being a good listener might look like.

   _____

   _____

3. Why is it so important to respect other people's ideas when you are trying to compromise?

   _____

   _____

4. What does "investigate your options" mean?

   _____

   _____

5. Define the word "negotiate."

   _____

   _____

Recognizing Alternatives to Settling Conflict

Solving conflicts can be hard. Sometimes figuring out a solution can seem almost impossible. It is important to think about as many different alternatives as you possibly can to settle your conflict.

Before you can start thinking about your options, though, what you need most is a positive attitude. A positive attitude can go a long way toward helping you solve problems.

What does a positive attitude look like? Posture and tone of voice are two key components. Your posture and body language offer clues about what you are thinking and how you are feeling. They can mean the difference between being able to settle a conflict and having a conflict reach the point where it is much more difficult to solve.

Tone of voice is a good indicator of how someone is feeling. Tone of voice offers clues that can help you figure out if it is going to be easy or difficult to work with someone to resolve a conflict. Often, your tone of voice matters as much as the words you say.

Directions: Look at the behaviors below. Circle the behaviors that show a positive attitude.

Slumping Over	Making Eye Contact	Smiling	Avoiding Eye Contact
Shrugging Shoulders	Frowning	Active Listening	Ignoring
Using A Friendly Tone Of Voice	Yelling	Walking Away	Being Sarcastic

Group Activity: Practice reading each sentence in two different tones of voice. Notice how the same words mean different things depending on your tone of voice and the words you emphasize.

1. "I have been here several times before." *Try a voice that sounds* _superior_.
   "I have been here several times before." *Try a voice that sounds* _sympathetic_.

2. "Do you realize what time it is?" *Try a voice that sounds* _surprised_.
   "Do you realize what time it is?" *Try a voice that sounds* _angry_.

3. "Did you see the way the cashier looked at you?" *Try a voice that sounds* _suspicious_.
   "Did you see the way the cashier looked at you?" *Try a voice that sounds* _amused_.

4. "We could go to the movies." *Try a voice that sounds* _enthusiastic._
   "We could go to the movies." *Try a voice that sounds* _reluctant._

Bandage Solutions

Once you have your positive attitude in place, it is time to recognize specific alternatives that might help you settle your conflict.

Some conflicts can be fixed by Bandage Solutions. Are you having a fight with your friend about directions or where to go out to dinner? These are the types of conflicts that can often be solved with Bandage Solutions. They are conflicts that are not likely to matter too much for the long term. They are irritating, like all conflicts, but should not take too much time to solve.

1. **Flip a Coin**. Leave it to chance. For example, you and your brother can't agree on a TV show. You flip a coin, and the winner selects the show this time.

2. **Split the Difference**. Come up with a compromise. For example, you don't want to go to dinner and a movie with your parents. You decide to go to dinner and not the movie.

3. **Laugh it Off.** Smile and don't worry about it. For example, someone makes a rude comment about your new shirt. Laugh it off. It really doesn't matter.

4. **Let it Go.** Some things just aren't worth worrying about. For example, you are sure you know the best way to get to the store. Your best friend disagrees. Let it go.

5. **Apologize.** Sometimes saying you're sorry is the right thing to do. Admit your mistake and move on. For example, you forgot to invite a close friend to your party. Admit your mistake and apologize.

Directions: Read each conflict. Draw a line from each conflict to the Bandage Solution that you think you could use to settle the conflict. You may connect each conflict to more than one Bandage Solution.

<u>**Conflicts:**</u>

You forget to call your friend when you said you would.

You and your brother want to listen to different songs on the radio.
You and your friend both want to drive Saturday night.

Someone bumps into you and makes you spill some of your soda at the movies.

Someone tells you your new haircut makes you look like an elf.

You want to go out with Jeff on Friday night, but you are supposed to drive your brother to work.

<u>**Bandage Solution:**</u>

Flip A Coin

Split the Difference

Laugh It Off

Let It Go

Apologize

Group Discussion: Which Bandage Solutions did you use the most? The least? How did you decide which Bandage Solution(s) would best help you solve each conflict?

Brainstorming Additional Alternatives

If the problem is too serious to be handled with a Bandage Solution, you need to figure out something else. First, be sure to keep a positive attitude. Then, once you have your positive attitude in place and have decided that a Bandage Solution will not solve your problem, you must figure out something else. Now, it is time to try to think of other options that could help you solve your conflict.

Keep in mind that everyone solves problems differently. As you think of new options, try to keep an open mind. There may be an unexpected way to solve your problem. Think of as many alternatives as you can to settle your conflict.

Directions: Read each conflict. Read the three alternatives suggested for each conflict. Work with a partner to try to come up with two more alternatives to solve the conflict.

1. Someone in your automotive technology class has stolen a copy of the final exam answer key. He is selling copies to your classmates. Passing the exam will mean you earn a certificate that could help you get a job. The test is being graded on a curve, so only a certain number of students will get As, Bs, Cs, etc. What should you do?
   A. Do nothing.

   B. Tell the teacher.

   C. Memorize the answer key.

   D. _____

   E. _____

2. You just met someone at a party whom you really like. You know it is the same woman your friend has been talking to on the phone and emailing after work. He has been talking about her and plans to ask her out soon. What should you do?
   A. Give the woman your number and see whom she calls next.

   B. Talk to your friend about the situation.

   C. Tell the woman how wonderful your friend is and then walk away.

   D. _____

   E. _____

Group Discussion: Now, talk with your partner about the alternative(s) you think would be best to solve each conflict. Why do you think these alternatives are best?

_____

_____

Figuring It Out

Directions: Read each sentence and fill in the blanks, using the answer choice box. Use the word that best completes each sentence.

Flip a Coin	Alternatives	Positive Attitude	Conflicts	Yelling
Tone of Voice	Bandage Solution	Avoiding Eye Contact	Apologize	

1. Posture and tone of voice are two key parts of a _____.

2. The Bandage Solution that leaves things to chance is _____.

3. Sometimes your _____ matters more than the words that you say.

4. Conflicts that are not likely to matter too much for the long term can sometimes be solved by a _____.

5. For more complicated conflicts, brainstorming different _____ is a good idea.

6. Solving _____ can be hard.

7. _____ and _____ do NOT show a positive attitude.

8. If you make a mistake, you should _____.

Personal Assessment

Directions: Write about a conflict you have had or something you are having difficulty with right now.

_____

_____

_____

_____

_____

_____

_____

_____

_____

_____

Write three different ways you might be able to solve this conflict.

1. _____

_____

_____

2. _____

_____

_____

3. _____

_____

_____

Being H-O-N-E-S-T

Power struggles happen in conflicts when two people both want to be in control of the situation. These conflicts can be very difficult. Sometimes in conflicts where there are power struggles, neither party is willing to compromise. Both parties involved in a power struggle want to "win" the conflict. They might think that by "winning" the conflict, they are proving that they are more powerful and that they are in charge. This may matter more to them than how or if the conflict is actually solved.

To prevent power struggles in conflicts, it is important that you avoid the following:

- Name-Calling
- Attitude
- Sarcasm
- Threatening

You must also be H-O-N-E-S-T.

> **H- Have The Right Attitude.** Try to stay positive!
>
> **O - Open Mind.** Keep an open mind.
>
> **N - Name Your Need.**
>
> **E- Empathy.** Listen to the other person's needs and position.
>
> **S - Say Exactly How You Feel.**
>
> **T- Turn It Around.** Get out of the power struggle-work toward a compromise!

Always start with a positive attitude. Keep an open mind. Remember, there is more than one way to solve every conflict. Clearly name what you need. Be patient as you listen to the other person's needs and position. State how you feel. Explain that you are willing to work together to figure out a good compromise. Work toward resolving the conflict rather than wasting time on a power struggle. A power struggle will not help you resolve your conflict!

The Power Struggle Breakfast

PROBLEM SOLVING

Directions: Act out the situations below. In which situation did the people follow the H-O-N-E-S-T guidelines? In which situations did they let their power struggle get the best of them? Talk about each situation. Have you ever found yourself in a similar situation? Discuss this with your classmates.

Juan and Eric work together at Meetings and More. With company cutbacks, their boss needs to save money. He announces that the company will no longer take its employees out to breakfast each month for the meetings. Instead, the meetings—and breakfast—will occur at the office. Their boss assigns Juan and Eric the task of "catering" these monthly meetings.

SITUATION A

Juan: I'm excited about being in charge of the food at our breakfast meetings! I'll pick up two dozen bagels and cream cheese from the bakery across from my apartment. My girlfriend works there, and it's the best! I'll pick up juice, too—that way I can get all of my favorite flavors. You bring the paper goods and get to the office early. You can set up the office and get it ready while I am picking up the food.

Eric: I hate bagels and cream cheese!

Juan: Well, eat breakfast before you come to work, then. Most people love bagels and cream cheese.

Eric: Breakfast tacos are a much better idea. I'll pick up two trays of them on my way to the office. I'll get lots of different types, and everyone will love it. You get to the office early to set up and make the coffee.

Juan: I don't know why you think everyone wants breakfast tacos! Plus, I can barely get to work by 8 o'clock. There is no way I am getting to the office early—you are in charge of setting up breakfast, too!

Eric: What makes you think I can get to the office early? There is no way I am going to get to the office early while you hang out with your girlfriend and pick up bagels for breakfast.

Juan: I hate working with you!

Eric: I hate working with you!

Group Discussion: How do you think Juan is feeling in Situation A? How do you think Eric is feeling in Situation A? How do you think they feel about each other? What is their power struggle?

SITUATION B

Juan: I'm excited about being in charge of the food at our breakfast meetings! I'll pick up two dozen bagels and cream cheese from the bakery across from my apartment. My girlfriend works there, and it's the best! I'll pick up juice, too—that way I can get all of my favorite flavors. You bring the paper goods and get to the office early. You can set up the office and get it ready while I am picking up the food.

Eric: That sounds like a thoughtful idea. I know you really like bagels, but I'm not a big fan of bagels. I do love breakfast, though. I would like to help with some of the breakfast food ideas, too. To be honest, I'm a little worried about the getting to the office early part of this assignment. I know we are going to have fun doing this task together and need to do a good job. Maybe we can talk about exactly how breakfast is going to work? What do you think?

Juan: Oh, I forgot. We are always both racing up to our building at 8:01! The setting up part is going to be hard! Maybe we should alternate being in charge of setup? I forgot how much you like breakfast!

Eric: I like your idea about rotating the setup. It would be easier for me if I only have to get to the office early every other month for setup. What about the food? Maybe we could do a rotation on that, too?

Juan: Oh! That is a great idea. What about if I pick up bagels and drinks this month and you do the setup. Next month, I'll do the setup and you pick up whatever you think would be good for breakfast?

Eric: That is a great idea! I'm really looking forward to working with you on this. It is going to be a lot of fun!

Juan: Yes! I'm excited.

Group Discussion: What things were done in Situation B to help turn the power struggle between two co-workers into two co-workers looking forward to working together?

Clearly Stating Your Needs

PROBLEM SOLVING

Sometimes power struggles happen because people involved in a conflict choose to get defensive rather than clearly stating what they really want. "I feel" statements can help you tell people what you are really feeling without blaming or accusing anyone of anything. Clearly stating what you need makes it less likely that one or both parties will feel the need to get defensive.

Example: Clara comes home past curfew on Saturday night, and her mom is furious.

Her mom's first thought is to yell at Clara and tell her that she can never go out again. Instead, her mom decides to use an "I feel" statement to clearly state her needs to Clara. Her mom hopes that by clearly stating her feelings that Clara will understand how she feels. She also hopes this will prevent the conflict from happening again.

Clara's mother says, "I feel <u>worried</u> when you stay out <u>past your curfew</u>. I want you to <u>call me the next time you are going to be late, so I don't stay up worrying</u>.'

Her mother's statement starts by telling Clara her <u>feeling</u> (worried) when Clara <u>does a certain behavior</u> (stays out past her curfew). Then, she states <u>what would make her feel better</u> (having Clara call her the next time she is going to be late). Clearly stating your needs is a good way to avoid power struggles in conflict situations.

Identify your <u>real</u> needs and talk about them. Use an "I feel" statement.

I feel (<u>feeling</u>) when you (<u>behavior</u>). I want (<u>what would make you feel better</u>).

Directions: Write "I feel" statements for the two situations below.

Your friend borrowed $20 from you. She promised to pay you back as soon as she got paid. Two weeks later, you see her at the movies with some friends, buying popcorn. You are really mad. Write an "I feel" statement to say to your friend.

I feel _____ when you _____.

I want _____.

Your brother sits in the front seat and controls the radio every time you drive with a relative or friend. If you request a different song, he ignores you. When you tell him you don't like a song, he turns the volume up. You are really mad. Write an "I feel" statement to say to your brother.

I feel _____ when you _____.

I want _____.

Restating Your Needs

Remember, conflicts often happen because two people do not communicate about how or why they are feeling a certain way. "I feel" statements help you tell people what you are really feeling without blaming or accusing anyone of anything.

Directions: Working with a partner, take turns making an "I feel" statement based on each situation below. Then, talk about your "I feel" statements with your partner.

SITUATION 1

Marta has repeatedly asked her roommate, Pete, to turn off the lights when he leaves for work. Each evening when she returns home, every light in the apartment is on. When Marta opens the new electricity bill, it is $20 more than the previous month.

I feel (feeling) when you (behavior). I want (what would make you feel better).

SITUATION 2

Tim has been looking forward to his Tuesday evening basketball game all week. He promised his friends he would be there. On Tuesday afternoon, his girlfriend tells him that she wants him to skip the game to help her babysit.

I feel (feeling) when you (behavior). I want (what would make you feel better).

SITUATION 3

Mark loans his close friend, Sam, his favorite tie to wear to an important company dinner. The next day, Mark calls Sam several times hoping to stop by and pick up his tie. Sam doesn't return Mark's calls. Two months later, Mark runs into Sam at a restaurant. Sam is wearing his tie.

I feel (feeling) when you (behavior). I want (what would make you feel better).

Passing on Power Struggles

Directions: Think about the information you have just learned about avoiding power struggles in conflict situations. Answer the questions using what you have learned. Go back and reread the previous pages as needed.

1. Power struggles happen in conflicts when _____.

2. Write the part(s) of H-O-N-E-S-T that you think might be the most helpful to you when trying to avoid power struggles in conflict situations.

   _____

   _____

   _____

3. Look back at pages 218—219, where you read about the Power Struggle Breakfast. In the two situations, who was the power struggle between?

   _____

4. Why do you think Juan and Eric were having a power struggle?

   _____

   _____

5. Think about a power struggle you had in a conflict situation in the past. Write an "I feel" statement that clearly states your needs and what you think might have helped you resolve your conflict.

   I feel _____ when you _____.

   I want _____.

Active Listening

Active listening means to be a deliberate listener. It means to concentrate on what other people are saying without interrupting or making judgment. The symbol below is the Chinese symbol for "to listen."

On the left of the symbol, there is an ear. On the right of the symbol, there is "you"—actively listening. The two most important parts of active listening are shown below "you." These two things are eyes and undivided attention. Your eyes should be on the person who is talking to you. The speaker should have your undivided attention while he or she is speaking.

The heart at the bottom is important, too. The heart represents the most important thing that active listening shows. Active listening shows that you care. Active listening shows that you value the speaker and that you know that what he or she has to say is important.

"To Listen"

Ear

You

Eyes

Undivided Attention

Heart

Listening

Activity 1

Directions: With your classmates, form a circle or several circles. Circle size can vary but should not exceed 10 to 12 people. The oldest person in each circle will start the listening/storytelling game. He or she will start the story with two to three sentences. The next person in the circle will continue the story with two to three more sentences. The story needs to make sense, and the sentences need to build on each other. When the story reaches the end of the circle, the person who started the story will give a brief summary of your group's story.

Group Discussion: Did your group's story make sense? Did your group's sentences build on each other? Did you feel like you had to be an active listener in this game? Why or why not?

Activity 2

Directions: Find a partner. Each of you will select one of the topics below and talk about it for five minutes. Remember to be active listeners by making eye contact and giving your partner undivided attention. Don't interrupt.

- If I had a million dollars...
- My favorite meal...
- My most embarrassing...
- My favorite hobby...
- A place I would like to travel to...
- I like to listen to...
- Someone I look up to...

Group Discussion: Was it easy or hard to listen? Did anything in particular help you be a more active listener? Was it difficult to stay quiet and not interrupt?

Personal Assessment

1. During Activity 1 on page 224, did you find it hard or easy to listen? Why?

   _____

   _____

   _____

2. During Activity 1 on page 224, were you a better listener to the story before or after your turn in the circle? Why?

   _____

   _____

   _____

3. During Activity 2 on page 224, on what topic did you find it easiest to be an active listener? Why?

   _____

   _____

   _____

4. During Activity 2 on page 224, on what topic did you find it the most difficult to be an active listener? Why?

   _____

   _____

   _____

5. What do you think your strengths as a listener are?

   _____

   _____

Being an Active Listener

Directions: Answer the following questions using the information you just learned about active listening.

1. What are two important things to do to be an active listener?

   _____

2. According to the Chinese symbol for "to listen," what is one thing active listening shows?

   _____

3. What is the hardest part of active listening for you?

   _____

4. Write about one thing you could work on to help you become a better listener.

   _____

5. Why do you think it is important not to interrupt when you are actively listening?

   _____

6. Why do you think it is important not to immediately make judgments when you are actively listening?

   _____

7. How did you feel when your partner actively listened to you during the game? Why?

   _____

8. Draw a circle around the example of active listening. Put an X on the example that does not show active listening.

PROBLEM SOLVING

The Power to Decide

Every day we make decisions—lots of them. Some of the decisions we make are small.

- What will we eat for breakfast?
- What movie will we go see?
- What should we wear?

Some of the decisions we make are more important.

- What job will we accept?
- Where will we live?
- Whom will we marry?
- Should we go along with the group or do our own thing?

The power to decide is a big responsibility. So how do we D-E-C-I-D-E? What should we do when we have to make hard choices?

D - Define the Problem. What is the problem? What decision has to be made?

E- Explore the Alternative. What are the options? Brainstorm alternatives.

C- Consider Consequences. Think about the future—what are the risks? Give thought to your actions. Will your decision have consequences—good or bad?

I - Identify your Values. Remember to be true to yourself. Peer pressure can sometimes be hard to resist, but it is important to focus on what is best for you. Always make decisions with a clear head—unclouded by drugs and alcohol.

D - Decide. Make your decision.

E- Evaluate your decision. Did you solve your problem? Do you think your decision was the right one?

D-E-C-I-D-E

Directions: Read the scenario. Use D-E-C-I-D-E to help you make a decision about what to do next.

1. Your roommates are going out of town this weekend. Your best friend's birthday is Saturday night. All of your friends are encouraging you to have a party, and you really, really want to host one. You are sure it would be a lot of fun. Your roommates do not want you to have guests over when they are out of town, but you doubt they would find out.

Define the problem: _____

Explore your alternatives *(try to name at least three):*

- _____
- _____
- _____

Consider the consequences *(try to name at least three):*

- _____
- _____
- _____

Identify your values: _____

Decide: _____

Evaluate your decision: _____

Group Discussion: Talk about the different decisions people in your class made. What things did people consider when they made their decisions? Did the D-E-C-I-D-E strategy help you make a decision or not?

Thinking Things Through

Directions: Think about a decision you need to make. Use the D-E-C-I-D-E strategy to figure out the right decision for you.

Define the problem: _____

Explore your alternatives *(try to name at least three):*

- _____

- _____

- _____

Consider the consequences *(try to name at least three):*

- _____

- _____

- _____

Identify your values: _____

Decide: _____

Evaluate your decision: _____

Good Decisions for YOU

One important thing to consider when making decisions is your personal goals. Think about the things that you want to achieve. Think about if the decision you make is going to help <u>you</u> get to where you want to be. Remember to keep your values in mind. Also, think about how people around you are going to be harmed or helped. Think about how you are going to feel after you make your decision. What effects will your decision have? Will they be good or bad? Is your decision going to help you get closer to your goals or farther away from them?

Making decisions is much easier if you are able to keep your goals in mind. Having clear goals can help you keep yourself on track. Goals can serve as a reminder of the things that are really important. Visualizing your personal goals can help you stay on track even when you face a really difficult decision.

Directions: Think about your personal goals. Write about them below.

1. List three **goals** you have for yourself.

    - _____
    - _____
    - _____

2. List two <u>decisions</u> that you can make to help you achieve your **goals**.

    _____
    _____
    _____

3. Write about one <u>decision</u> you have made that has NOT helped you get closer to your **goals.**

    _____
    _____

4. Write about one <u>decision</u> that you have made that HAS helped you get closer to your **goals.**

    _____
    _____

Would You Rather?

Many people have a hard time making decisions. Sometimes you have plenty of time to think about and make a decision. Other times you have to make a decision very quickly.

This fun game will give you practice making silly decisions/choices quickly. Think about what you would rather do and then decide!

Directions: Read each of the *Would You Rather?* questions listed below. Make a quick decision and circle your answer.

1. Would you rather go to bed really early or really late?

2. Would you rather be two feet tall or ten feet tall?

3. Would you rather live in the frozen tundra or in the desert?

4. Would you rather have both your arms in a cast for one year or lose your pinkie toe forever?

5. Would you rather be a dog or a cat?

6. Would you rather only be able to speak in a whisper or only be able to yell?

7. Would you rather be able to only eat your favorite food or never be able to eat your favorite food again?

8. Would you rather be stuck on an island alone for a year or stuck on an island with someone you really dislike for a year?

Challenge: Think of a *Would You Rather?* question of your own. Ask your partner your question. Answer your partner's *Would You Rather?* question.

Considering the Consequences

When you are faced with a serious decision, you need to take the time to analyze the problem. Before you make a decision, you should think about your options and values and consider the consequences of each possible option. Then, you can choose the best option for the situation.

Directions: Read the *Would You Rather?* questions listed below. Think carefully about each situation before you make a decision. Write down the possible consequences of each option. Then, circle the answer you think is best.

1. Would you rather have to talk all day or have to listen all day?

   _____

   _____

2. Would you rather lose your sight or lose your hearing?

   _____

   _____

3. Would you rather lose your memory or lose your voice?

   _____

   _____

4. Would you rather find the cure to a disease or win the lottery?

   _____

   _____

5. Would you rather be able to stop time or live forever?

   _____

   _____

Group Discussion: With a partner, review your decisions and talk about how and why you made each decision. Were some of the questions harder to answer than others? Why?

DECISION-MAKING

Problem Solving & Decision Making Review

Directions: Circle the letter for each correct answer. Write answers for the last three items.

1. Which of the following is a good way to resolve conflict?
   A. Engaging in a power struggle.
   B. Making a compromise.
   C. Avoiding the situation.

2. "Cooling down" means:
   A. Going swimming.
   B. Stating your feelings right away.
   C. Taking a minute or two to get calm.

3. The "N" in G-R-I-N stands for:
   A. Negotiate.
   B. Neutralize.
   C. Nag.

4. "Investigate your options" means!
   A. Use your original plan.
   B. Look for alternatives.
   C. Ignore others' ideas.

5. A positive attitude does NOT include:
   A. Friendly tone of voice.
   B. Active listening.
   C. Avoiding eye contact.

6. Tone of voice is a good indicator of:
   A. What someone is wearing.
   B. How someone is feeling.
   C. How tall someone is.

7. "Split the difference" means you:
   A. Leave it to chance.
   B. Come up with a compromise.
   C. Say you're sorry.

8. "Let it go" means:
   A. Don't worry about it.
   B. Apologize.
   C. Leave it to chance.

9. To avoid power struggles in conflict situations, make sure you do NOT:
   A. Threaten.
   B. Compromise.
   C. Compliment.

10. Power struggles happen because:
    A. Two people want to be in control.
    B. Nobody wants to be in control.
    C. People want to get along with others.

11. In "I feel" statements you:
    A. State how you feel.
    B. Hide how you feel.
    C. Ask how the other person feels.

12. Active listening shows that you:
    A. Are disinterested.
    B. Care.
    C. Like to interrupt frequently.

continued on next page

13. Active listeners show they are listening by:
    A. Making eye contact and giving undivided attention.
    B. Avoiding eye contact and walking away.
    C. Interrupting and asking lots of questions.

14. In D-E-C-I-D-E, the "C" means:
    A. Be courteous.
    B. Consider the consequences.
    C. Compromise.

15. What should you do when you evaluate a decision?
    A. Think about peer pressure.
    B. Think about whether the decision was successful or not.
    C. Think of other ways you could solve the problem.

16. Write about how being an active listener could help you solve problems more successfully.

    _____

    _____

    _____

17. Why do you think a positive attitude can go a long way toward helping you solve problems?

    _____

    _____

    _____

18. Write about one thing you learned about problem solving and decision-making during this class.

    _____

    _____

    _____

REENTRY
ESSENTIALS, INC.

Reentry
Support
Resources

This page intentionally left blank

Reentry Support Resources

Course Goal: Upon completion of this course, student will obtain release documentation and utilize the available resources provided by federal, state, and local agencies as well as other service providers.

Available Programs

Figuring out which programs are available to you and finding a job after your release from prison can seem like overwhelming tasks. Where will you work after your release? Why should an employer hire you? What programs are available to help you adjust to supporting yourself again? Learning about the specific programs available to you after your release is critical to your future.

Plan on spending some time on the computer and on the telephone to learn additional information about some of the programs discussed in this section.

U.S. Department of Labor: Good news! The U.S. Department of Labor wants you to get a job! The Federal Bonding Program insures employers who hire ex-offenders free of charge. The bonds can be issued to your employer as soon as you are hired and have a start date.

There is no special application or papers for your employer. Your employer will not even need to pay a deductible. Call 1-877-872-5627 to contact your state bonding coordinator and to find out specific details about the Federal Bonding Program.

The Work Opportunity Tax Credit (WOTC) is designed to help ex-felons move into gainful employment and get job experience. The WOTC encourages employers to hire ex-felons and other harder to place applicants. After you are hired, your employer can receive a $1,200—$9,600 tax credit based on your qualified wages. Employers are eligible for this Work Opportunity Tax Credit when they hire you during your first year after release.

For employers to get this tax credit, they will need to contact your state's Workforce Agency no later than 28 days after your initial start date. More specific details about this program can be found on the United States Department of Labor website at http://www.doleta.gov/wotc.

Knowing Your Educational Goals

Education can improve your chances of finding a job, keeping a job, and creating a more stable life for yourself after your release.

Start by thinking about your educational goals.

- If you didn't graduate from high school, do you want to take the GED® tests?

- Are you interested in attending a technical school to learn a specific skill?

- Do you hope to attend a community college or a university?

Directions: List three jobs that you might like to have.

1. _____

2. _____

3. _____

Now, write some of the education/training/skills you think you might need for each of the jobs that you listed.

1. _____

_____

_____

2. _____

_____

_____

3. _____

_____

_____

Educational Options

There are many different educational paths. Thinking about the path that is right for you is important. Getting an education will cost you both money and time. Since both of these things are very valuable, you will need to be thoughtful when choosing the path that is right for you. Will the education you receive really help you get the job you want? After you spend money on your education, will your paycheck provide you with enough income to cover the cost of your student loans?

Education will offer you something very valuable— a set of skills that will increase your value to an employer. Hopefully, your education will also enable you to get a job that you enjoy.

- **Adult Education:** Adult education—also called continuing education—can help you successfully complete Adult Basic Education (ABE) and/or work toward passing the tests of General Educational Development (GED®). Adult education courses vary and can be taken at many colleges throughout the United States. It is also possible to take both ABE and GED® classes online. Adult education can give you the basic literacy and math skills you will need to find a job. It can also prepare you to be admitted to a technical or community college or university.

- **Technical College:** Technical college can provide you with certification or job training to enter a specific field. Many mechanics, electricians, plumbers, welders, chefs, and computer programmers have attended technical school to learn specific skills and obtain the certification needed to qualify for their jobs.

- **Community College:** There are over 1,600 community colleges in the United States. Since community colleges cost less to attend than four-year colleges, they are an excellent place to begin your education. There are many advantages to attending a community college. You can earn many of the "basic" college course credits you will need for a four-year degree. Since community colleges cost less, the cost of taking these courses will be lower than the costs at a four-year university. If you are unsure about what field you want to pursue, a community college might be a good place to start. Taking several classes in fields you think you might be interested in could help you make your decision. Also, since many people attending community colleges also work full-time jobs, most community colleges offer flexible class scheduling with classes at night and on the weekends.

- **College/University:** Four-year colleges offer many different degrees. Two excellent reasons to pursue your college degree are job satisfaction and earning power. Workers with college degrees usually have pursued a degree in a field they were interested in and therefore end up liking jobs in that field. Also, workers with college degrees tend to have higher earning power than workers with no degree. The ability to earn more money in a job you like is a good reason to pursue a college education. Most four-year colleges will require you to have an SAT or ACT score, have a high school diploma, or have passed the GED® tests.

The Right Path

Directions: Read each situation. Fill in the blank with the educational choice (adult education, technical college, community college, or college/university) that you think would help—or helped—the person in each situation to be successful.

1. Jeff struggled with reading throughout high school and didn't complete the courses he needed to graduate. After his release from prison, he attends _____ classes to get the reading skills he needs to work at the front desk of a hotel.

2. Mary is a chef at a popular downtown restaurant. Mary's training at _____ taught her the skills she needed to work in a large kitchen.

3. Javier was promoted quickly to Master Electrician after he received advanced certification at his local _____.

4. Kent completed all of his "basics" at his local community college. He transferred to a _____ to complete his four-year degree and earn his teaching certificate.

5. Leslie earned specific training about how to work on large diesel engines. Classes she took at her local _____ allowed her to receive the certification she needed for her job.

6. Tony had to pass the tests of General Educational Development (GED®) before he was eligible to enroll in community college classes. He enrolled in _____ classes so that he could prepare for the GED® tests.

Figuring Out Funding

You know that getting an education is a smart idea. There is only one problem—the cost! How can you afford to get yourself the education you want? Start by being confident. You can do whatever you set your mind to. You will need to have a plan. It may take you some time to figure out your financial options and what is right for you.

Plan to spend some time researching all of your options for financial assistance. Make sure to note application deadlines on your calendar so that you do not miss any deadlines. Here are some ways to fund your education:

- **Student Loans:** Student loans have to be paid back after graduation. Taking out student loans and completing a degree could give you long-term earning power, job happiness, and job stability. Student loans usually have very low interest rates. Student loans do not need to be repaid until a student graduates—or is no longer enrolled—in school. You usually have to start paying back your loan six to nine months after you get out of school. You have between ten and twenty-five years to repay your student loan. Public loans are guaranteed by the government and can be subsidized or unsubsidized. Private loans usually have a higher interest rate. Obtaining a private loan through your bank or other private institution will usually require you to have good credit.

- **Grants:** Grants do not have to be repaid. They are awarded to people pursuing additional education who complete their education obligation for which the grant was awarded. State and federal grants (PELL, SEOG, etc.) are available to students who qualify, usually based on their financial need during the tax year before enrollment. (Example: If a student plans to enroll during the Fall 2020 semester, his or her 2019 income would determine his or her grant eligibility). Getting this type of financial assistance takes time. Make sure to check for application deadline information for each grant you apply for. In many cases, the fewer financial resources you have available, the more likely you are to be awarded a grant.

- **Financial Aid:** The United States Department of Education is an excellent resource for finding out about both state and federal programs that can offer you financial assistance. Information can be found online at http://studentaid.ed.gov.

  The National Association of Student Financial Aid Administrators has information about state financial aid programs. Information can be found online at http://www.nasfaa.org. You must complete the Free Application for Federal Student Aid (FAFSA) to determine your eligibility for loans. This application can be completed online at www.fafsa.ed.gov. You can request a paper FAFSA by calling 1-800-4-FED-AID (1-800-433-3243). The application process is free. You can check your status and find answers to many of your questions online.

Social Security Disability

Do you qualify for Social Security Disability Insurance (SSDI) or Supplemental Security Income (SSI)? If you think you may qualify, what do you need to do to receive the benefits you qualify for? Social Security Disability Insurance (SSDI) and Supplemental Security Income (SSI) are two of the largest programs offered by the Federal Government to provide assistance to people with disabilities. To qualify for either of these two programs, you must have a disability that meets specific medical criteria and is documented by a doctor.

Your application will include an interview and medical documentation about your disability. You do not automatically qualify for Social Security Disability Insurance and/or Supplemental Security Income just because a doctor states that you are disabled or because you are receiving disability from a current or previous job. You still must go through the application process to qualify. The application process to receive this assistance usually takes between three and five months.

The following questions may help you determine if you qualify for either program. For additional information, go to www.socialsecurity.gov/applyfordisability or call 1-800-772-1213. You may not apply online, but you can learn specifics about each program and determine if you are eligible for either one.

Social Security Disability Insurance (SSDI)

- Have you previously held a job where you paid into Social Security? (Look online for specific details about how long you need to have worked.)

- Have you been unemployed for a year or more because of your disability?

- Are you unable to return to your previous job or do a different job because of your disability? Your "disability" must be a documented medical condition.

Supplemental Security Income (SSI)

- Are you 65 or older with limited financial resources?

- Are you blind?

- Will your disability prevent you working for the next year?

- Will your disability most likely result in your death?

Healthy Living

Healthy food and nutrition are important parts of a healthy, stable lifestyle. There are several state and federal programs that can help you lower your food costs. These programs include the following:

The **Supplemental Nutrition Assistance Program (SNAP)** provides basic food for low-income families. It provides money to supplement your monthly grocery bill. This extra grocery money each month may allow you to make healthier choices at the grocery store. Fruits, vegetables, and non-processed foods are often more expensive than processed foods. To be eligible for this program, you must apply and meet certain requirements. Additional information about this program can be found by visiting www.fns.usda.gov/snap.

The **Combined Application Projects (CAP)**: Seven states have CAP programs to increase Food Stamp Program participation. These programs target low-income and disabled seniors. The United States Department of Agriculture has information on eligibility at
http://www.fns.usda.gov/snap/government/promising-practices/CAPsDevelopmentGuidance.pdf

The **United States Department of Health and Human Services** offers many social service programs to support individuals in need. For example, the Office of Child Care (OCC) provides access to childcare through the Child Care Assistance Program (CCAP) so you can work, go to school, or get job training. Additional information about the Child Care and Development Fund can be found by visiting http://www.acf.hhs.gov/programs/occ.

Social Service Smarts

Directions: For each situation below, decide which social service(s) might be helpful. Fill in the blanks using the answer choice box.

> Combined Application Projects (CAP)
>
> Child Care Assistance Program (CCAP)
>
> Supplemental Nutrition Assistance Program (SNAP)
>
> Supplemental Security Income (SSI)/Social Security Disability Insurance (SSDI)

1. Felix lives alone. He is 65 years old and needs help purchasing food each month.

   _____

2. Peggy wants to accept a job at a local museum but needs help with childcare for her two young children.

   _____

3. Max has a limited income and needs help with grocery money every month so that he can afford to make healthier choices at the grocery store.

   _____

4. David is blind and needs additional money each month.

   _____

5. Susan spent ten years working and putting money into Social Security. Recently, she was seriously injured on her job and will not be able to work again for several years.

   _____

Personal Assessment: Which of the social services explained on pages 243 and 244 do you think might help you? Why do you think they would be helpful?

_____

_____

_____

_____

Primary Identification

Obtaining proper identification is important. You'll need proper identification to do the following:

- Get a job
- Cash A Check
- Open A Bank Account
- Apply for Social Services (SNAP, SSDI, SSI)
- Take The GED® Tests or Other Certification Tests
- Apply to College
- Board an Airplane
- Enter Some Government Buildings

Primary forms of identification confirm who you are. Primary forms of identification generally include your name and signature or your name and photograph and are issued by trusted federal or state sources. Having two forms of primary identification will be critical to your success after release. Here are some examples of primary forms of identification.

- Current States-issued photo driver's license or photo ID card. If your driver's license expired 60+ days ago, you will need a letter from the state that issued it.
- Original or certified birth certificate with state seal
- Military identification
- Valid, unexpired United States passport
- Valid, unexpired foreign passport
- United States citizenship and immigration service documentation
- Marriage license/certificate
- Merchant Marine identification card
- Native American tribal document
- Any confirmation of date of birth as recorded with a judge's signature and seal

Directions: Review the list of primary forms of identification. What primary forms of identification do you already have? What forms do you plan to obtain before or shortly after your release from prison?

Already Have	Plan to Obtain
_____	_____
_____	_____
_____	_____

Secondary Identification

It is also helpful to have secondary forms of identification. Many federal, state, and local programs, as well as employers, may require you to present both primary and secondary forms of identification. Secondary forms of identification help confirm your identity and current place of residence. Here are some examples of secondary forms of identification.

- Computerized check stubs with the applicant's full name printed on the stub
- Work identification (identification that includes a photo is best)
- Social Security card or proof of Social Security benefits
- Health insurance card
- Internal Revenue Service tax forms or state tax forms
- Military records
- School records or college identification
- Vehicle registration or car title
- Original adoption documents
- Library card
- Financial statements (checking account statements, savings account statements, loan statements)
- Deed or title to property

Directions: Answer each question below.

1. What is the difference between primary and secondary forms of identification?

   _____

   _____

2. Which type of identification is more trusted—primary or secondary? Why?

   _____

   _____

Obtaining a Driver's License

A driver's license is one of the most common types of primary identification. Ask yourself the following questions to figure out how to get or renew your driver's license:

- Are you getting your driver's license for the first time?

- Do you need to renew an expired driver's license?

- Do you need to renew an expired driver's license that has revocations or has been suspended?

- Do you need to renew an unexpired driver's license that has revocations or has been suspended?

Start by visiting http://www.usa.gov/TopicsíMotor-Vehicles.shtml to find out specific details about obtaining or renewing your driver's license.

If you are attempting to get your driver's license for the first time, you must visit the licensing agency in your state. States vary in their requirements, but you will be required to show some form of identification. Here are some common documents required to get a. driver's license.

- Proof of Identity

- Proof of Residence: A utility statement, lease agreement or mortgage payment, cable TV statement, or voter registration card will prove your residency. Military personnel can bring a letter from their supervisor confirming their residency.

- Social Security Number

Contact your states licensing agency directly if you have specific questions about the documents you will be required to show.

Before you can obtain your driver's license for the first time, you may be required to do the following:

- Pass A Vision Test

- Pass A Written Test

- Show Proof of Automobile Insurance

- Pass A Driving Test

Understanding Your Situation

If you previously had a driver's license, but it has been lost or expired, you will need to follow steps to update your identification. If you have revocations or suspensions, you will need to clear your revocations or suspensions so that you are eligible for a driver's license in your state of residence.

If you are an inmate in California, Oregon, or Minnesota, you may already be working to obtain your driver's license. These three states have innovative programs to help inmates obtain their driver's license prior to release. In other states, you will have to work directly with your state's licensing agency to obtain your driver's license. Getting your driver's license will require planning and effort on your part. Obtaining this primary form of identification will help you secure a job, housing, and other necessities.

Directions: Answer each question. Then, write down your specific plan for obtaining your driver's license.

1. What is the status of your driver's license?

   _____

   _____

2. What documents will you need to obtain your driver's license?

   _____

   _____

3. What specific steps do you need to complete to obtain your driver's license?

   _____

   _____

   _____

   _____

   _____

   _____

Obtaining a Social Security Card

You'll need a Social Security card for many things—getting a job, applying for Social Security Disability Insurance (SSDI), and applying for Supplemental Security Income (SSI).

The first step to getting a new Social Security card or replacing an old Social Security card is to complete Form SS-5. You will also need to have one of the following valid documents to verify your identity:

- Driver's License

- Marriage or Divorce Record

- Military Records

- Adoption Record

- Life Insurance Policy

- Passport

- Health Insurance Card (Not A Medicare Card)

- School ID Card

- Alien Green Card (Form 1-551, 1-94, 1-688B or 1-766)

Visit http://www.socialsecurity.gov for additional information about obtaining your Social Security card. There is no cost for obtaining a Social Security card.

Directions: Write about the specific steps you need to take to obtain your Social Security card.

_____

_____

_____

_____

_____

_____

_____

_____

SS-5 Form

Directions: Practice filling in this sample SS-5 form. Follow the directions carefully. Ask questions if you need help.

SOCIAL SECURITY ADMINISTRATION
Application for a Social Security Card

Form Approved
OMB No. 0960-0066

1

NAME TO BE SHOWN ON CARD	First	Full Middle Name	Last
FULL NAME AT BIRTH IF OTHER THAN ABOVE	First	Full Middle Name	Last
OTHER NAMES USED			

2 Social Security number previously assigned to the person listed in item 1 ☐☐☐ – ☐☐ – ☐☐☐☐

3 PLACE OF BIRTH _____ (Do Not Abbreviate) City _____ State or Foreign Country

Office Use Only — FCI

4 DATE OF BIRTH _____ MM/DD/YYYY

5 CITIZENSHIP (Check One)
☐ U.S. Citizen ☐ Legal Alien Allowed To Work ☐ Legal Alien Not Allowed To Work (See Instructions On Page 3) ☐ Other (See Instructions On Page 3)

6 ETHNICITY Are You Hispanic or Latino? (Your Response is Voluntary) ☐ Yes ☐ No

7 RACE Select One or More (Your Response is Voluntary)
☐ Native Hawaiian ☐ Alaska Native ☐ Asian ☐ American Indian ☐ Black/African American ☐ Other Pacific Islander ☐ White

8 SEX ☐ Male ☐ Female

9

A. PARENT/ MOTHER'S NAME AT HER BIRTH	First	Full Middle Name	Last

B. PARENT/ MOTHER'S SOCIAL SECURITY NUMBER (See instructions for 9 B on Page 3) ☐☐☐ – ☐☐ – ☐☐☐☐ ☐ Unknown

10

A. PARENT/ FATHER'S NAME	First	Full Middle Name	Last

B. PARENT/ FATHER'S SOCIAL SECURITY NUMBER (See instructions for 10B on Page 3) ☐☐☐ – ☐☐ – ☐☐☐☐ ☐ Unknown

11 Has the person listed in item 1 or anyone acting on his/her behalf ever filed for or received a Social Security number card before?
☐ Yes (If "yes" answer questions 12-13) ☐ No ☐ Don't Know (If "don't know," skip to question 14.)

12 Name shown on the most recent Social Security card issued for the person listed in item 1
First _____ Full Middle Name _____ Last

13 Enter any different date of birth if used on an earlier application for a card _____ MM/DD/YYYY

14 TODAY'S DATE _____ MM/DD/YYYY

15 DAYTIME PHONE NUMBER _____ Area Code _____ Number

16 MAILING ADDRESS (Do Not Abbreviate)
Street Address, Apt. No., PO Box, Rural Route No.
City _____ State/Foreign Country _____ ZIP Code

I declare under penalty of perjury that I have examined all the information on this form, and on any accompanying statements or forms, and it is true and correct to the best to my knowledge.

17 YOUR SIGNATURE

18 YOUR RELATIONSHIP TO THE PERSON IN ITEM 1 IS:
☐ Self ☐ Natural Or Adoptive Parent ☐ Legal Guardian ☐ Other Specify _____

DO NOT WRITE BELOW THIS LINE (FOR SSA USE ONLY)

NPN			DOC	NTI	CAN		ITV
PBC	EVI	EVA	EVC	PRA	NWR	DNR	UNIT
EVIDENCE SUBMITTED					SIGNATURE AND TITLE OF EMPLOYEE(S) REVIEWING EVIDENCE AND/OR CONDUCTING INTERVIEW		
							DATE
					DCL		DATE

Form **SS-5** (08-2011) ef (08-2011)   Destroy Prior Editions   Page 5

Obtaining a Copy of Your Birth Certificate

A certified copy of your birth certificate is another good primary form of identification. A certified copy is a copy of an original document that has an endorsement proving that it is a copy of the primary identification source. A certified copy also has an original signature of someone verifying its authenticity.

A copy of your birth certificate may be required when you apply for certain jobs. It is required if you want to obtain a United States passport. In the future, your birth certificate may even be required when you apply for a driver's license or for Social Security benefits.

Some states are "closed record" states. In closed record states, birth and death records are not available to the general public. In these states, you must provide proper identification to receive a certified copy of your birth certificate. The federal government does not distribute birth certificates, but the Center for Disease Control and Prevention maintains a website with information about obtaining vital records in each state. Visit http://www.cdc.gov/nchs/w2w.htm for state specific information on how you can obtain a copy of your birth certificate.

Directions: To obtain a certified birth certificate, you usually have to provide information about yourself and your parents. Fill in the information below.

Your Full Name At Birth: _____

Date Of Birth: _____

Place Of Birth: _____

Mother's Full Maiden Name: _____

Father's Full Name: _____

Your Identification

Every individual is in a different situation with regard to primary and secondary identification documents. Obtaining proper primary and secondary identification is important. You will need proper identification to drive, locate housing, find a job, and get paid. Use this page to write about your plans for getting your personal situation in order after your release.

ID Documents I Have   **ID Documents I Need**

Identification Documents

Directions: On the lines below, write some notes about specific things you will need to do to obtain necessary primary and secondary identification documents for yourself.

Getting Informed About Identification

Directions: Circle the correct forms of identification listed in the answer choice boxes. Then write your answer on the lines provided.

1. Circle the primary forms of identification.

> Current Driver's License   Merchant Marine Identification Card
>
> Unexpired Passport   Certified Birth Certificate with State Seal
>
> Credit Card Without Photo   Library Card
>
> School Identification Card   Expired Driver's License
>
> Grocery Discount Card   Native American Tribal Document

2. Circle the secondary forms of identification.

> Expired Driver's License   Vehicle Registration
>
> Social Security Card   Grocery Discount Card
>
> Health Insurance Card   Certified Birth Certificate
>
> Current Driver's License   Original Adoption Documents
>
> Library Card   Credit Card

3. Write two reasons why having proper primary and secondary identification is important.

_____

_____

_____

_____

_____

_____

Using All of Your Resources

On pages 238-245, you learned about some of the financial governmental assistance programs that might be available to you after your release.

- **Employment Resources:** Federal Bonding Program, Work Opportunity Tax Credit
- **Education Resources:** Student Loans, Grants, and Financial Aid
- **Financial Resources:** Social Security Disability Insurance / Supplemental Security Income
- **Health Resources:** Supplemental Nutrition Assistance Program, Combined Application Projects, and Child Care and Development Fund

Another good place to find reentry resources is the National Reentry Resource Center. The National Reentry Resource Center provides education, training, and technical assistance for ex-offenders. This organization has compiled a list of reentry services available in different states. To access specific information about some of the programs in your state visit http://www.nationalreentryresourcecenter.org/ and go to the Reentry Services Directory.

Here are some other helpful reentry resources.

- **The National-H.I.R.E. Network** (http://hirenetwork.org/clearinghouse) helps ex-offenders find jobs.
- **American's Service Locator** (http://www.servicelocator.org/) provides a list of One-Stop Career Centers that provide job, training, and career resources.
- **The National Directory of Programs for Women with Criminal Justice Involvement** (http://nicic.gov/wodp/) provides information on programs and services for women with criminal records.
- **Reentry Essentials** (https://www.reentryessential.org/) helps connect ex-offenders with employers, property managers, and other community resources.
- **Prison Fellowship** (http://www.out4Life.com) tries to meet the spiritual, physical, and personal needs of newly released prisoners and helps them use resources available through their local churches and nonprofit institutions.

Directions: Write your answers to the following questions on the lines below.

Which of the above mentioned programs interest you? Why?

_____

_____

_____

_____

_____

Taking Care of Yourself

Good health is important. Maintaining your good health by getting regular checkups, eating healthy, and exercising will make you feel and look your best. This kind of self-care is called preventive medical care. Preventive care will help you stay healthier longer. Visiting your doctor regularly can help detect medical problems before they get serious.

Health insurance is something you need to think about when you are released. Health insurance can help protect you and your family. Even though health insurance can be expensive, it is important to have. If you do not have health insurance and get injured or sick, you could put yourself—and your family—in a difficult situation.

Ideally, you will obtain health insurance through your job. Unfortunately, many jobs do not offer health insurance.

Medicaid is a state and federal program that provides health coverage for people with lower incomes and disabilities. It also provides coverage for older people. Each state has different Medicaid requirements.

You might qualify for Medicaid if you:

- Are Disabled
- Are Vision Impaired
- Are A Low-Income Parent Of Children Under Age 19
- Are Under Age 19
- Are Pregnant
- Have No Health Insurance and Need To Be Treated For Breast Or Cervical Cancer
- Receive Medicare And Are Low Income

Visit http://www.medicaid.gov to find out specific information about eligibility requirements in your state.

Applying for Medicaid

Since Medicaid is a state and federal partnership, each state has different eligibility requirements. In all states, Medicaid provides health coverage for people with lower incomes, elderly people, people with disabilities, and some families with children.

Visit http://medicaid.gov to find out about the specific requirements for qualifying for Medicaid in your state. Also, visit http://CMS.gov to obtain additional state specific information about your eligibility for Medicaid programs.

Filling out your Medicaid application will take time. Most Medicaid applications require you to provide information about members of your household, your income and assets, and your expenses. Contact your state Medicaid provider to find out exactly what information you will need to provide.

The list below gives examples of types of information often required on Medicaid applications. To make your application process easier, you should gather the following pieces of information before you start filling out your application:

- ☐ **Proof of Identity:** Social Security number, driver's license, proof of residence, etc.
- ☐ **Income:** paycheck stubs, checking account statements, savings account statements, investment income statements, child support income, etc.
- ☐ **Assets:** Life insurance policies, stocks, bonds, cars, boats, campers, etc.
- ☐ **Expenses:** Rent/mortgage, utilities, child support payments, childcare expenses, medical expenses, etc.
- ☐ **Other Health Insurance Coverage** (if any)

Many states require that you submit applications online. You may need an email address and a computer with Adobe Reader® to access your Medicaid application and to receive verification that your application has been accepted or denied.

Beginning in 2014, most adults with incomes under $15,000 per year will qualify for Medicaid in every state.

Other Health Programs

Even if your employer does not offer health insurance and you do not qualify for Medicaid, you still have options. Other health care options include the following:

- **CHIP:** Children's Health Insurance Program provides health care to uninsured children up to 19 years old. Eligibility and benefits vary by state. For more information about CHIP in your state, visit http://insurekidsnow.gov/state/index.html.

- **Information for Pregnant Women:** Information on health care for pregnant women can be found at http://www.healthcare.gov/law/information-for-you/pregnant-women.html.

- **Private Insurance Options:** Private insurance costs and options vary widely. Visit http://www.healthcare.gov/using-insurance/low-cost-care to investigate low-cost private insurance options.

Directions: On the lines below, write about what type of health insurance you think you will get when you are released. Why do you think you will get that type of health insurance?

_____

_____

_____

_____

_____

_____

_____

_____

_____

_____

Group Discussion: Did you have health insurance before you entered prison? Why or why not?

Substance Abuse

Eighty percent of offenders have substance abuse problems. Often these problems led to the criminal activity that placed them in prison.

Think about the following questions; Did substance abuse problems result in your incarceration? Do you think you will need substance abuse treatment when you are released from prison? If you do want to seek treatment, you have several options.

Alcoholics Anonymous (A.A.) and Narcotics Anonymous (N.A.) are two free programs that hold meetings at churches, synagogues, and other public spaces around the United States. You can find out more information about Alcoholics Anonymous and information about where meetings are held by visiting http://www.aa.org. You can find out more information about Narcotics Anonymous and information about where meetings are held by visiting http://www.na.org.

Supportive Housing and Innovative Partnerships (SHIP) offers a safe, sober place for people to live in a supportive environment. To be considered for this housing, applicants must have been sober for thirty days, completed a detoxication program, applied, and been interviewed. Once you are accepted, you can remain in this housing as long as you want as long as you pay your rent and stay clean and sober. Learn more about this program at http://www.shipinc.org/re-entry-services

Visit http://findtreatment.samhsa.gov/ to learn about additional programs to end substance abuse.

Directions: Which of these programs would be helpful to you? Why?

_____

_____

_____

_____

_____

_____

_____

_____

Work Programs

In some states, Transitional Work Programs offer offenders the opportunity to start working one to three years prior to their release in an approved job setting. Probation and parole officers monitor the transitional work program. The goal of transitional programs is to help offenders successfully make the transition between prisons and into the work force. Your state's department of corrections may have additional information on Transitional Work Programs.

If you did not participate in a transitional work program, there are many resources available to help you find a job after your release. Here are some helpful employment resources.

- Unicor Federal Prison Industries has been helping prisoners learn the skills they need to successfully reenter the workforce for over seventy-five years. Jobs are available in many different fields. Job training is available in printing, embroidering, cable assembly, making prescription eyewear, and making signs and promotional items. Unicor's Federal Bonding Program provides theft insurance to employers who hire ex-offenders. For more information on Unicor, visit http://www.unicor.gov/.

- The United States Department of Labor Employment & Training Administration also has a bonding program for ex-offenders without UNICOR work experience. Since eligibility varies by state, visit the Department of Labor's Directory of State Coordinators online at http://www.doleta.gov/usworkforce/onestop/FBPContact.cfm for more information.

- The Federal Bureau of Prisons lists some employment resources for ex-offenders. Visit online at http://www.bop.gov/inmate_programs/itb_references.jsp. One resource is the Employment Information Handbook. This handbook has advice for prisoners preparing for release.

Websites such as https://www.usajobs.gov and http://www.careeronestop.org may help in your search for employment. If you are a veteran, visit the Veterans Affairs jobs website at http://www.va.gov/jobs/.

Directions: Answer the questions below.

1. Do any of the resources on this page interest you? Which ones?

   _____

   _____

   _____

2. Explain why each program interests you.

   _____

   _____

Finding the Right Place to Live

Finding housing is a critical part of being able to lead a stable, productive life.

Visit http://portal.hud.gov/hudportal/HUD to find out about specific programs that may help you through the United States Department of Housing and Urban Development. Some of the options include the following:

- **Subsidized Apartments:** The United States Department of Housing and Urban Development helps apartment owners be able to offer reduced rents to qualifying tenants by paying them part of the rent. You can search for subsidized apartments at http://www.hud.gov/local.

- **Public Housing and Housing Choice Vouchers (Section 8):** Public housing is available to low income individuals or families who qualify. Call 1-800-955-2232 with questions about public housing. Depending on your offense, you may or may not qualify.

- **Halfway Houses:** Some halfway houses are state-sponsored and house people recovering from substance abuse, people recently out of jail, or people suffering from mental illness. Residents usually pay some rent based on what they earn. Halfway houses offer a place to live while you readjust and find permanent housing.

Directions: Answer the following questions on the lines provided.

1. Where do you plan to live when you are released?

   _____

   _____

   _____

   _____

2. What do you need to do before your release to secure your planned housing?

   _____

   _____

   _____

   _____

Locating the Right Resource

Directions: For each need in the left column, write a possible social service program or website that might be a good first step to obtain additional information about the need.

Need	Possible Social Service Program or Website
1. Information for Pregnant Women	
2. Get Help with Alcohol Abuse	
3. Search for A Job Making Signs or Promotional Items	
4. Find Out About Transitional Work Programs	
5. Get Health Insurance	
6. Find Out About Financial Aid for Education	
7. Learn About Renewing an Expired Driver's License	
8. Find A Place to Live	
9. Get Temporary Housing While You Readjust	

Reentry Support Resources Review

Directions: Circle the letter for each correct answer.

1. Education can increase your chances of a stable life.
   A. True
   B. False

2. If you need to learn to read, you can enroll in:
   A. College.
   B. Technical school.
   C. Adult education.

3. If you are seeking a four year degree, you should enroll in:
   A. College/university.
   B. Technical school.
   C. Adult education.

4. Money used for education that does not have to be paid back is called a:
   A. Student loan.
   B. Student grant.
   C. Both A and B

5. The program that provides basic food for low-income families is:
   A. Social Security Disability Insurance (SSDI).
   B. Supplemental Security Income (SSI).
   C. Supplemental Nutrition Assistance Program (SNAP).

6. Secondary identification is as good as primary Identification.
   A. True
   B. False

7. An example of a primary form of Identification is:
   A. Your driver's license.
   B. Your vehicle registration.
   C. Your library card.

8. For over seventy-five years, _____ has been helping prisoners learn the skills they need to successfully reenter the Workforce.
   A. The U.S. Department of Labor
   B. Adult Basic Education
   C. Unicor Federal Prison Industries

9. A certified copy of your birth certificate is a good form of _____ identification.
   A. Primary
   B. Secondary
   C. Neither of the above

10. You are primarily responsible for obtaining the resources that you need after you are released from prison.
    A. True
    B. False

11. Approximately what percent of offenders have substance abuse problems?
    A. 25 percent
    B. 50 percent
    C. 80 percent

REVIEW

12. Getting regular check-ups, eating healthy, and exercising are examples of:
    A. Preventive medical care.
    B. Not having health insurance.
    C. Not listening to your physician.

13. If your doctor states that you are disabled, you automatically qualify for Social Security Disability Insurance.
    A. True
    B. False

14. Which program provides health care for uninsured children up until 19 years of age?
    A. CHIP
    B. SNAP
    C. CAP

15. Transitional Work Programs give offenders the chance to work:
    A. Before they are released.
    B. After they are released.
    C. Both A and B

16. The work Opportunity Tax Credit (WOTC) offers employers:
    A. A tax credit for hiring you.
    B. Money to pay you.
    C. Both A and B

17. If you are attempting to renew your driver's license, you should contact the:
    A. Vital records office in your state.
    B. Licensing agency in your state.
    C. Federal licensing agency.

18. The SS-5 Form will help you obtain your:
    A. Social Security card.
    B. Birth certificate.
    C. Medical insurance.

19. Your library card is a form of:
    A. Primary identification.
    B. Secondary identification.
    C. Both A and B.

20. You might qualify for Medicaid if you:
    A. Are a middle-income parent.
    B. Have health insurance.
    C. Are under age 19.

Values Clarification, Goal Setting, & Achieving

This page intentionally left blank

Values Clarification, Goal Setting, & Achieving

Course Goal: Upon completion of this course, student will learn the value of moral character traits in order to achieve productive personal goals and live as a responsible citizen.

I. AWARENESS OF SELF AND OTHERS

OBJECTIVES

II. SHORT-TERM AND LONG-TERM GOAL SETTING

OBJECTIVES

III. ACHIEVING GOALS

OBJECTIVES

Value Yourself

You must value yourself and your good qualities. Do not let others make you feel bad about yourself. But how do you value yourself and stay positive in today's society? It can be hard. Remember to tell yourself that you are important and valuable. You really can help make the world a better place—by valuing yourself and valuing other people.

- **Accept yourself:** Forgive yourself for any mistakes you have made. You cannot change the things you have done or the mistakes you have made in the past. You can change the things you do in the future. You can make better choices and do things differently. Accept yourself as an individual who is doing the best that you can, and then work hard to do your absolute best.

- **No excuses:** Everyone makes mistakes. Everyone falls short sometimes. Remember, nobody is perfect. Don't make excuses for your own shortcomings. Own your mistakes—the ones that you have made in the past as well as the ones that you will make in the future. Change yourself and your plan—if needed—and carry on.

- **Don't compare yourself to others:** The world is filled with different people with different strengths and weaknesses. Your job is to figure out your strengths and then work hard to be the best that you can possibly be. Keep your eye on yourself—not on others. Do not compare yourself to images you see in the media. These images are not real! Remember, the people in commercials and in magazines are actors and models. Don't waste your time comparing yourself to people you know and/or people the media puts in front of you. Spend your time making yourself better and being proud of who you are.

Directions: Make a list of ten things you like about yourself.

1. _____
2. _____
3. _____
4. _____
5. _____
6. _____
7. _____
8. _____
9. _____
10. _____

Setting Your Priorities

Part of valuing yourself is knowing yourself.

- What do you care about?
- What things and values are important to you?
- What are your priorities?

Priorities are the things that are most important to you. Everyone has different priorities. Figuring out your priorities and using your priorities as a guide will help you make choices based on the things that matter most to you.

Directions: Read each pair of sentences. Circle the one that is more important to you. The sentence that you circle is an example of your priority.

1. Watching your favorite TV show.	Having a long conversation on the phone with a friend.
2. Working in a job that you love.	Working in a job where you make a lot of money.
3. Going on a long walk.	Going on a long bicycle ride.
4. Spending time painting or drawing.	Going shopping with a friend.
5. Having dinner with your family every night.	Picking up extra night shifts so you can have more spending money.
6. Celebrating your birthday with your parents.	Celebrating your birthday with your friends.
7. Reading a good book.	Helping your elderly neighbor mow her lawn.
8. Watching an important football game.	Playing a board game with your neighbors.
9. Going fishing with your friends.	Studying for the GED® tests so you can apply to community college.

Personal Assessment: List three things that you like to do that you hope to make priorities after your release.

_____

_____

_____

Positive Self-Talk

Part of valuing yourself involves being kind to yourself. Being kind to yourself means making sure your self-talk is positive and encouraging. Self-talk is your inner dialogue. It is the things you think to yourself as life goes on all around you.

Self-talk is usually based on your past experiences or things that you heard or felt as a child. For example, imagine that you had a hard time learning to read in the first grade. You didn't feel smart. School was very hard for you. Even twenty years later, when you are faced with a school-like challenge—reading out loud or solving a math problem—your stress level rises. Your mind says things like, "I'm not good at school! I am not a good reader! I can't do this." Negative self-talk creates a roadblock for your confidence.

What should you do? You have to change. You have to retrain your mind to turn your negative self-talk into positive self-talk. You have to change "I can't do this" into "Why can't I do this?" or "Yes! I can do this." You have to change "Nobody ever likes me" into "I am likeable." Your own positive self-talk is part of valuing yourself.

Directions: Read each statement. Circle the statements that are examples of positive self-talk. Cross out examples of self-talk that could create a roadblock for your confidence or make you feel like you couldn't do something well.

1. I can handle this.
2. I'm good at sports.
3. I never can get this right.
4. I'll try my best.
5. I'm so bad at meeting new people.
6. I can do this even if it is a new situation.

7. Nobody ever likes me.
8. I am likeable.
9. I'm not smart.
10. I like trying new things.
11. I'm not good at anything.
12. If I work hard, I'll get better at this.

Personal Assessment: Write down two examples of your negative self-talk. Then, change these negative thoughts into positive self-talk.

_____

_____

_____

_____

_____

_____

Fake It Until You Make It

One of the best ways to portray a positive self-image is to act confident!

"Fake it until you make it" means that the more you act like you have confidence, the more people will believe you actually do have confidence—and the more confident you will appear! What can you do to look more confident? So think HAPPINESS, and remember these important things to "fake it until you make it."

H - Help Others. Look around you. Is someone you know in need of help? Research has shown that helping others actually results in the helper feeling healthier, happier, and more confident! Helping others will increase your positive self-image.

A - Always Dress Well. You never have a second chance to make a first impression. Look the part for the job you want to have and the person you want to be. Keep yourself clean and neat. Overdress instead of underdressing. Dressing well and looking good will portray a positive self-image.

P - Pick Gratitude. Be grateful—for what you have, when other people help you, for the things around you, and for the things that go right in your life. Look closely. There are lots of things to be grateful for. Speak openly and often of your gratitude. Being grateful will portray a positive self-image.

P - Posture. Sit up straight and walk upright. Look confident. Having good posture will portray a positive self-image.

I - In Shape. Get in shape! Take a walk or a bike ride. Go for a swim. Exercising will improve your mood. Getting in shape will portray a positive self-image.

N - Never underestimate the power of your abilities! You are smart. You are capable. You can make the changes you need to get your life on the right track. Believe in yourself. Knowing that you have lots to offer the world will portray a positive self-image.

E - Eye Contact. Make eye contact when you are talking to people. Make eye contact when you are listening to other people. Making eye contact will portray a positive self-image.

S - Smile. Smile at people you know. Smile when you are walking down the street. Smile when you are in the grocery line. Feel positive about the people around you. Expect the best from others. Smiling will portray a positive self-image.

S - Say Something Positive. Be the first to compliment other people. Compliment the people close to you. Compliment people you meet. Notice the best in other people. Help them notice good things about themselves. Saying something positive to people around you will portray a positive self-image.

Selling Yourself

Commercials convince us to buy things. Sometimes they convince us to buy things we need—like toothpaste. Other times, they convince us to buy things we don't need—like donuts. Commercials convince us to buy certain products because they "sell" us on them. They list many good things about the item they are advertising.

Do commercials mention the product's faults? No. Do they mention the times the product has failed? Absolutely not. Commercials mention only the good. They mention the best qualities about a specific product.

Part of portraying a positive self-image involves being comfortable speaking up about your own positive qualities. You must be confident enough to promote yourself.

Directions: Complete the items below.

1. Start by listing five to eight of your best qualities on the lines below.

    _____   _____

    _____   _____

    _____   _____

2. Turn your list into a commercial advertising yourself. What makes you uniquely wonderful? Sell yourself!

    _____

    _____

    _____

    _____

    _____

    _____

    _____

    _____

Group Discussion: Share your commercial with the group. Talk about the importance of being able to "sell" yourself.

Healthy Relationships

Healthy relationships are built around mutual love and respect. Healthy relationships make you feel good, not bad. Healthy relationships exist between two people who care about each other and want the best for each other.

What do you need to be capable of being involved in a healthy relationship?
You need to B-E-L-I-E-V-E that you deserve to be a part of a healthy relationship.

B - Be Independent. You need to be independent to be part of a healthy relationship. You can't depend on someone else for your happiness—find your happiness and self-worth independently and then seek out a person to share it with.

E - Effort. A good relationship takes effort, time, and energy.

L - Laugh. A good sense of humor goes a long way. Be ready to laugh and find humor in everyday situations.

I - Involved. Stay involved and committed to the relationships that are important to you. Problems will arise, but if the relationship is meaningful to you, try to work it out.

E - Everyday Kindness. Healthy relationships involve being kind and compromising. Try not to yell or accuse. Be thoughtful and loving.

V - Value. In a healthy relationship, both partners value each other.

E - Equality. In a healthy relationship, both partners take turns making decisions and compromising.

Healthy Relationship Checklist:

☐ I have things I like to do independently of my partner.

☐ Sometimes I get to pick the movie my partner and I see—sometimes my partner picks the movie.

☐ My partner and I are good at talking things over with each other.

☐ I don't question where my partner was or what my partner was doing every moment of the day.

☐ My partner and I can laugh at funny things that happen to us—even if they sometimes do not seem funny at the time.

☐ My partner and I value each other's ideas.

☐ I like spending time with my partner.

☐ My partner and I believe in each other.

Solving Relationship Problems

Relationships are not always easy. Sometimes partners and friends disagree. Problems will arise. What should you do? There are different ways to solve problems. Some different options are listed below. Remember that healthy relationships are built around mutual love and respect. These two things should always be kept in mind when you are working to solve relationship problems.

Directions: Read each problem-solving option and example. Then think of an example of when you used each problem-solving option successfully. Share your personal examples with a partner and/or with the class.

1. **Compromise.** Compromise involves coming up with a solution that works for both parties. In compromise, you usually get some of what you want but not everything. You come up with a solution that both parties can feel pretty good about.

   Example: Lily and Francesca are roommates. They both really want a pet. Their landlord requires a $500 deposit for each pet. They have only enough money for one pet deposit. Lily really wants a cat. Francesca really wants a dog. They spend a lot of time debating about which pet to get. Finally, they agree to get a rabbit instead. Both of them like rabbits.

   When have you compromised to solve a personal problem?

   _____

   _____

   _____

2. **Focus on one specific issue.** Sometimes fights can get messy. You may be arguing about one thing with your partner when he or she brings up something that happened last week (or even last year!). This often results in the fight escalating. Focus—and try to solve—one specific issue at a time. If you start bringing all sorts of different problems into a disagreement, nothing will be solved and both parties will likely walk away angry.

   Example: Pedro is angry at Maria for being late to their Valentine's Day dinner date. During their discussion about her tardiness, he thinks about how she frequently is late when she picks him up from his college class on Monday nights. Then he remembers he needs to focus on the specific issue. He tells Maria that it hurt his feelings when she was late for their Valentine's Day dinner date and asks if there is anything, he can do to help her be on time the next time they get together.

   When have you successfully solved a problem by focusing on one specific issue during an argument?

   _____

   _____

3. **Respect.** Respecting someone during an argument means hearing his or her side of the story. The best way to do this is by being an attentive listener. Make eye contact, don't interrupt, and listen to what the person has to say without making judgments.

   Example: Manny was furious when Katy didn't come to the office party to celebrate his promotion. When Katy explained to him that she had really wanted to come but had been at the hospital caring for her sick mother, he understood that her not attending had been out of her control.

   When have you chosen respect to solve a problem successfully?

   _____

   _____

   _____

4. **Use "I feel when you" statements when you are trying to solve problems.** The only person you can fully understand and take responsibility for is you. Taking responsibility for how you feel will make the other person feel less defensive. Also, describing how you feel will help the other person understand exactly how you are feeling. An "I feel" statement does not blame or judge the other person. It simply explains to the other person how you are feeling.

   Example: Fred was mad when Lucy forgot his birthday. His first instinct was to say, "You are so thoughtless for forgetting my birthday." Instead, he thought about it and said, "I felt like you didn't care about me when you forgot my birthday." Lucy apologized, and they figured out a time for a belated celebration.

   Name a time you have used an "I feel _____when you_____" statement to successfully solve a problem with a partner.

   _____

   _____

   _____

   Group Discussion: Talk about different things you have done to successfully solve problems in a relationship.

Effective Communication

Healthy relationships involve effective communication. Using an "I feel ___ when you ____"statement, let your partner know how you are feeling without putting your partner on the defensive. "I feel" statements do not accuse; they just explain exactly how you are feeling.

Example: Kelly feels left out when Karen and Marty plan to go to a movie without including her. When Karen asks her if something is bothering her, instead of saying, "You and Marty are mean for going to the movies without me!" she says, "I feel left out when you and Marty go to the movies without me." Karen does not feel like she is being accused. Instead she understands Kelly's feelings and apologizes. She talks to Marty, and they apologize for the oversight and invite Kelly to go to the movies, too.

Directions: Read each situation. Then write an "I feel ____ when you _____" statement to go with each one.

1. Tamara is late to pick up Damien from work every day.

   Damien: I feel _____ when you _____.

2. Matt owes Meghan $20. He promised to pay her back by last Friday but has not paid her back yet.

   Meghan: I feel _____ when you _____.

3. Tom never cleans up his dishes or helps Mary with any of the chores around their apartment.

   Mary: I feel _____ when you _____.

4. Kent makes a joke about what Edward is wearing in front of a large group of people.

   Edward: I feel _____ when you _____.

Personal Assessment: Now, think of something that is bothering you in your own personal life. Write an "I feel ____ when you _____" statement that might be able to help you solve your problem.

_____

_____

_____

_____

_____

Being a Good Friend

Have you ever heard the saying, "You must be a friend to have one"? Research has shown that people who have good, stable friends in their lives are actually happier and healthier people.

What does a good friend look like?

- Good friends are supportive. They are encouraging and want you to succeed. They are not threatened by your success.
- Good friends are loyal. They are not going to gossip or share secrets behind your back. They will stick with you in good times and bad times.
- Good friends are fun to be around. They are positive and upbeat, and you likely share some of the same interests.

How can you be a good friend?

- Listen to your friend. Reach out and hear what he or she has to say. Make sure to keep information he or she shares with you confidential.
- Care about your friends. Be thoughtful. Do nice things for your friends.
- Be supportive. Good news? Bad news? Be supportive of your friends in good times and bad times. Help your friend when he or she needs help.

How can you pick out good friends?

- Take your time. Building a friendship takes time. Don't trust or expect too much from your friends right away. Take time to get to know your friends, and let your trust in each other grow.
- Pick friends who share your interests.
- Pick positive people. You need friends who will support and encourage you. Optimism is good—surround yourself with optimistic people!

Are You a Good Friend?

Directions: Spend some time thinking about each item below. Then complete each one.

1. List three of your own qualities that make you a good friend.

   _____

   _____

   _____

2. List three qualities that you think you could work on to become a better friend.

   _____

   _____

   _____

3. List three friends that you already have that you can count on.

   _____

   _____

   _____

4. List someone you know who might make another good friend for you.

   _____

5. Why did you select this person as a potential friend?

   _____

6. Friends share common interests. Make a list of five things that you like to do that you might be able to share as a common interest with a friend.

   _____   _____

   _____   _____

   _____

Goal Setting

Setting goals for yourself is important. You should set both short-term and long-term goals.

Short-Term Goals

Short-term goals are goals that you are going to achieve in the near future—today, tomorrow, or next week. A short-term goal might be finding a job within four weeks after your release from prison or volunteering once a month at the soup kitchen in your neighborhood.

Long-Term Goals

Long-term goals are goals that you are working toward achieving over a longer period of time. These are goals you want to achieve within a year, a decade, or your lifetime. It is good to set **enabling** goals to help you achieve your long-term goals. Enabling goals are shorter term, attainable goals that "enable" you to successfully achieve your longer-term goals. For example, if earning your college degree is one of your long-term goals, two of your enabling goals might be applying for financial aid or signing up for classes at your local community college. Your enabling goals set you on the path for achieving your long-term goal in the future.

Types of Goals

Since you may have a long list of goals—in many different areas—you may want to group specific goals into different categories.

- Work Goals

- Family Goals

- Physical Goals

- Financial Goals

- Education Goals

- Community Service Goals

Keeping Track of Your Goals

Set up a journal, document, phone application, or spiral notebook where you keep a list of your goals. Write down the steps you take as you work to achieve each goal and the date you complete each step. Writing down your goals and keeping track of them will help make you more accountable and likely to achieve your specific goals.

Realistic vs. Unrealistic Goals

Some goals are more realistic than others. For example, planning to take a space shuttle to the moon within a year of being released from prison is probably an unrealistic goal. Making a plan to take some classes in engineering or about space travel are more realistic goals. Setting realistic goals that you can actually obtain after your release is important. Make sure to set some short-term and some long-term goals.

Your goals should be **R-E-A-L.**

R - Readily measurable. For example, a goal like "I want to earn tons of money" is not as good as "I want to work my way into a job where I make $20 an hour within the first year of my release from prison." A good goal is measurable. It is something you can keep track of and hold yourself accountable for.

E- Exact. A good goal is exact and specific. It sets specific expectations and is clear so that you can actually work to achieve it. It needs to be time bound. For example, "I will find permanent housing within six months of my release from prison" is a more exact goal than "I will find permanent housing." Set up specific steps that will help you achieve your goals in the set time parameters.

A- Attainable. Your goal should be attainable. Setting your sights on being a star on American Idol might happen—it is attainable, but unlikely. Set your goal to be more easily attainable. For example, "I plan to attend open mike night every month for six months" or "I will sign up for a spring voice class at a local recreation center" are goals that are more attainable—and realistic. They are goals that you are more likely to be successful in achieving.

L - Long-term. Set goals that have your long-term interests at heart. Before you set your R-E-A-L goals, spend some time thinking about exactly what it is that you are hoping to achieve during your lifetime. What sort of things do you want to have accomplished at the end of your life? What do you want to be remembered for? Thinking about who you are working to become and what you want to achieve over the course of your lifetime will help you set goals that matter.

Your Goals

Directions: Think about your personal goals. Write a short-term and long-term goal for each category.

	SHORT-TERM GOALS	LONG-TERM GOALS
Work		
Family		
Physical		
Financial		
Education		
Community Service		

Personal Assessment: Review the long-term goals you identified. Choose the one that is the most important to you and write it on the line below.

_____

Next, write three enabling goals that you think could help you achieve the long-term goal you listed.

1. ENABLING GOALS	2. ENABLING GOALS	3. ENABLING GOALS
_____	_____	_____
_____	_____	_____
_____	_____	_____
_____	_____	_____
_____	_____	_____
_____	_____	_____
_____	_____	_____

Getting Your Basic Needs Met

Abraham Maslow was a United States psychologist who created Maslow's hierarchy of needs. Maslow's pyramid shows what you need in order to become the person you want to be. There are five levels on Maslow's hierarchy of needs: physiological, safety, love/belonging, esteem, and self-actualization.

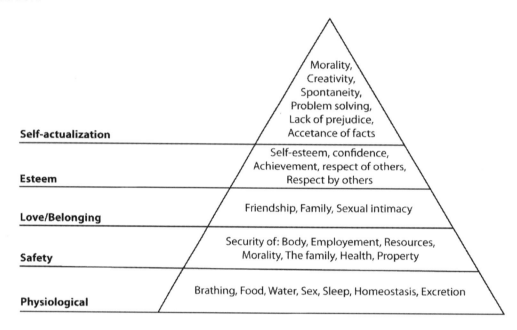

- The bottom layer of the pyramid includes your **basic needs**—things like food and shelter. You have to have these needs met before you can progress to higher levels of self-actualization.

- The second layer of the pyramid involves getting your **safety needs** met. If you are worried about keeping your job or having a safe place to sleep, it will be hard to progress beyond this level of Maslow's hierarchy of needs.

- The third layer of the pyramid is **social needs**. This level requires feeling like you belong and are accepted. You need to have friends who care about you and support you before you can progress beyond this level of the pyramid.

- The fourth level of the pyramid is your **self-esteem** and **self-worth**. To progress beyond this level of Maslow's hierarchy, you must feel confident that people respect you, and you must have a sense of respect for other people.

- **Self-actualization** is at the top of the pyramid. It means being self-aware, not being worried about what other people are thinking, and striving to reach your highest potential. What is your highest potential? It is achieving happiness and making the most of your talents and abilities.

Maslow Matches

Directions: Draw a line from each human need in the left column to the Maslow's hierarchy of needs level in the right column.

1. Reaching one's highest potential	Safety need
2. Dinner	Self-actualization
3. A place to sleep	Basic need
4. A friend to talk to	Self-esteem
5. Clean air to breathe	Safety need
6. A warm hug	Basic need
7. A weekly paycheck	Social need
8. A warm sweater for a cold day	Basic need
9. Confidence in yourself	Basic need
10. Creating an award-winning movie	Social need
11. Six hours of sleep	Self-actualization
12. Being part of a loving family	Basic need
13. Owning a house	Social need

Group Discussion: Think of one example from your own life for each type of need on Maslow's hierarchy. Then discuss your examples with the group.

Food and Shelter

Making plans for two of your basic needs on Maslow's hierarchy of needs—food and shelter—will be a primary goal when you are released from prison.

In prison, your basic needs have been met. You have had both food and shelter provided for you.

When you are released, you will need to start to figure out how to meet these two needs independently. There will be resources and support available to you. You will need to locate these resources and use them effectively.

Directions: Read the basic needs goals below. For each goal, write three steps you will take to meet it.

Goal: Find housing within thirty days after I am released from prison.

Steps I will take to meet this goal:

1. _____

2. _____

3. _____

Goal: Find employment so I can pay for food and shelter within thirty days after I am released from prison.

Steps I will take to meet this goal:

1. _____

2. _____

3. _____

Making Changes and Setting Goals

You will need to make changes when you are released from prison in order to live a crime-free life.

Why were you incarcerated? How are you going to prevent yourself from being incarcerated again? Setting personal post-release goals is important. You will need to make changes in your life to successfully achieve your post-release goals.

Directions: Think about your post-release goals and the changes you will need to make to achieve them. Then write your goals, the changes you will make, and the steps you will take to make those changes.

Example: Post-release goal: Be sober.
Change I want to make: Stop drinking.

Steps I need to take to make this change:

- Attend an Alcoholics Anonymous meeting every day after release.
- Do not purchase any alcohol.
- Find other activities I enjoy to replace drinking.

1. Post-release goal: _____

   Change I want to make: _____

   Steps I need to take to make this change:

   _____

   _____

   _____

2. Post-release goal: _____

   Change I want to make: _____

   Steps I need to take to make this change:

   _____

   _____

   _____

Stages of Change Model

How do people commit to and make a change successfully? Two researchers named James Prochaska and Carlo DiClemente developed a theory of change that they called the "Stages of Change Model." They wrote about change as a process. Everyone knows that change does not happen overnight. The Stages of Change Model considers change a process that progresses through five stages. Each stage takes time. The five stages of change Prochaska and DiClemente wrote about include the following:

- **Precontemplation:** Consider the fact that we need to change a specific behavior.

- **Contemplation:** Actively think about needing to change a specific behavior.

- **Determination:** Start preparing mentally or physically for making a change in our behavior.

- **Action:** Take action. For example, take an hourlong walk if you have decided to implement exercise.

- **Maintenance:** Continuing to take action to make our change.

Directions: Think about a change you need to make. Then answer each question below. Next, discuss your answers with a partner.

Date: _____

Contemplation: What change do you think you need to make?

_____

Determination: What things are you going to do both mentally and physically to make your change?

_____

Action: What action have you taken to make your change happen?

_____

Maintenance: How will you make sure you keep/maintain your change?

_____

Evaluating a Personal Goal

How do you evaluate your personal goals? Start by selecting a target date for achieving your goal. It can be a specific day or a time frame. For example, "I will turn in my paperwork to take the GED® tests by April 30" or "I will pass my driver's license test within 60 days." Then write down three steps you are going to take to meet your goal by your target date.

Directions: Think about a personal goal you want to set. Then complete the items below.

Today's date: _____

Your personal goal: _____

Target date for achieving your personal goal: _____

Three steps you are going to take to reach your goal by your target date:

1. _____

2. _____

3. _____

How will you measure—or evaluate—if you have met your personal goal?

_____

_____

Did you meet your goal? Why?

_____

_____

_____

When Life Gives You Lemons

When life gives you lemons... make lemonade, right? What happens when you are trying to reach certain goals and you just keep falling short? Which obstacles keep getting in your way? What if you are successfully achieving some of your goals and then you start to wonder if you even care about the things you are working toward? Having goals is important—setting your goals in stone is not. You might achieve several of your enabling goals only to realize your original long-term goal no longer matters to you. Should you keep working toward your long-term goal since you have successfully completed some of the short-term goals needed to reach it? Of course not! Just like people, goals can change.

As you evolve, so will your goals. Just as you spent time clearly stating your goals and working toward them, you should also spend time reassessing your goals. When you realize that your goals are not working or need to change, step back and reevaluate. Are the goals you are working toward still relevant? If not, clearly state and start working on new short- and long-term goals.

Directions: Answer the questions below. Discuss your answers with a partner.

1. Have you ever set a goal, become disinterested in it, or decided it was no longer a goal you wanted to achieve? Describe that goal.

   _____

   _____

   _____

2. What did you do about that goal?

   _____

   _____

   _____

3. Why do you think most people's goals change throughout their lives?

   _____

   _____

   _____

Prioritizing Your Goals

Prioritizing your goals is important. Prioritizing means to arrange in order of importance. You should put the most effort and attention into the goals you want to achieve the most.

Directions: Set a stopwatch for three minutes. Quickly brainstorm ten goals you want to achieve. Write the goals below.

1. _____
2. _____
3. _____
4. _____
5. _____
6. _____
7. _____
8. _____
9. _____
10. _____

Personal Assessment: Now, spend time reading through your list of goals. First, cross out the four least important goals that you brainstormed. Second, rank your six remaining goals by writing them in order from 1 to 6. Number 1 will be your most important goal, number 2 your second most important, and so on.

1. _____
2. _____
3. _____
4. _____
5. _____
6. _____

Check on It!

Another good thing about reassessing your goals is it helps you determine where you have made progress. Which goals have you been able to achieve? Which goals are you close to achieving? Are there certain goals where you have gotten off track? What do you need to do to get back on track and successfully achieve this specific goal? Reassessing your goals is an important part of successfully achieving and implementing goals.

When you reassess your goals on a regular basis, you can adjust them and what you need to do to reach them. You can identify areas where you are having a hard time making progress. You can note areas where you are having success.

Directions: Complete the items below.

1. Select one of your top six goals from page 289. Write this goal on the line below.

   _____

2. List three steps you have already taken to achieve this goal.

   _____

   _____

   _____

3. Write two adjustments that you think you could make to more effectively achieve this goal.

   _____

   _____

   _____

4. Do you think you have been effective in working to achieve this goal? Why?

   _____

   _____

   _____

   _____

Change

Have you ever heard the saying that the only thing that is constant throughout life is change itself? Life is always changing. Your life will be very different the first week after you are released from prison compared to six months after your release.

Richard Beckhard and David Gleicher developed the **Change Equation.** The Change Equation shows that you are most likely to make changes if you are very dissatisfied with how something is going in your life, or if you can visualize a better way to do something. Then you will be ready to take the first steps toward change. Your steps toward change may be small. Continue forward even if your change is met with some resistance. Here is what the Change Equation looks like.

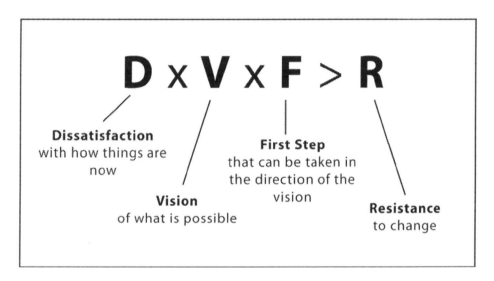

Directions: Use the Change Equation to identify an area of your life that you would like to change.

D - What are your dissatisfied with?

_____

V - How can it be better?

_____

F - What steps can you take to make it better?

_____

R - What are some obstacles you may encounter?

_____

Improving

Change is a process that takes time. People do not change overnight. People change as they work toward their goals, have experiences, gain perspective, and age. Sometimes a dramatic event—such as the loss of a loved one, or a fire—changes us.

People meet change with five common emotions.

- Fear: Change can be scary.

- Anger: Many people are resistant to change.

- Jealousy: People might envy a new leader who wants change.

- Grief: Losing something can be hard.

- Joy: Change is inevitable and can be good for everyone.

If you experience negative emotions when you try to change, remind yourself of why you are trying to change and why the change is important to you. Keep in mind that change can seem very slow at times. Achieving your goals can seem very hard at times. Do not despair. If you are willing to do the work, set your goals, keep a positive attitude, and want to change, you will.

Personal Assessment: What emotions will you need to overcome to make changes and reach your goals?

_____

_____

_____

_____

_____

_____

_____

_____

_____

_____

_____

Values Clarification, Goal Setting, & Achieving Review

Directions: Circle the letter for each correct answer.

1. Priorities are the things that are least important to you.
   A. True
   B. False

2. A good friend is:
   A. Supportive.
   B. Threatened by your success.
   C. Never available.

3. Positive self-talk means making sure your inner dialogue is:
   A. Defeating.
   B. Encouraging.
   C. Quiet.

4. An example of positive self-talk is:
   A. "i'll never get this right."
   B. "I can do anything I set my mind to."
   C. "I wish I was smarter."

5. One of the best ways to portray a positive self-image is to act:
   A. Embarrassed.
   B. Confident.
   C. Both A and B

6. Part of portraying a positive self-image is:
   A. good posture.
   B. A negative attitude.
   C. Not speaking.

7. Healthy relationships are built around mutual love and respect.
   A. True
   B. False

8. Short-term goals are designed to happen:
   A. Over a period of days or weeks.
   B. Over a period of years or decades.
   C. Over a lifetime.

9. What happens when you compromise to solve a problem?
   A. You get your way.
   B. You get some of the things you wanted, but not everything.
   C. You don't get any of the things you want.

10. Unrealistic goals are goals that you are _____ to attain.
    A. Unlikely
    B. Very likely
    C. Neither of the above

11. Your goals should be measurable.
    A. True
    B. False

12. In Maslow's hierarchy of needs, food and shelter are:
    A. Basic needs.
    B. Social needs.
    C. Self-esteem needs.

13. Reassessing your goals helps you see:
    A. Where you have made progress.
    B. Where you have not made progress.
    C. Both of the above

14. Change is inevitable.
    A. True
    B. False

15. Reaching one's highest potential is called:
    A. Self-esteem.
    B. Self-actualization.
    C. Flexibility.

16. _____ goals help you achieve long-term goals in a step-by-step way.
    A. Lifetime.
    B. Resisting.
    C. Enabling.

17. The target date you list next to your goal(s) is:
    A. The date you want to start trying to achieve your goal.
    B. The date you want to complete your goal.
    C. The date you want to reassess you goal.

18. Helping others will make you feel better about yourself.
    A. True
    B. False

19. Change is a process, and it takes time.
    A. True
    B. False

20. It is not important to have a connection between your dreams and bigger goals.
    A. True
    B. False

REENTRY
ESSENTIALS, INC.

Victim Awareness & Restitution

This page intentionally left blank

Victim Awareness & Restitution

Course Goal: Upon completion of this course, student will comprehend and accept the consequences as well as make restitution for the offender's crime and acknowledge that the offense has had a negative impact on the lives of the primary, secondary, and tertiary victims; take responsibility for those impacts; and consider ways of repairing harm done.

I. VICTIMS

OBJECTIVES

II. EFFECTS OF VICTIMIZATION

OBJECTIVES

III. OFFENDER REALIZATION AND RESTITUTION

OBJECTIVES

The True Victims of Crime

There is no such thing as a "victimless crime." Even crimes such as prostitution, drug dealing, and fraud affect multiple people, including you.

Primary Victims: When you use the word "victims," you probably think about the people directly hurt by your crime. These might be the people who were stabbed, murdered, or robbed. These are the "primary" victims of a crime.

Secondary Victims: Your crime indirectly hurts many other people. Secondary victims include the family, friends, co-workers, neighbors, and other people who were close to the primary victim. Witnesses to the crime and emergency responders are also considered secondary victims. This second level of victims also includes your family and friends, who must deal with your incarceration.

Tertiary Victims: Even strangers can be affected by your crime. These are called "tertiary" (pronounced tur-shee-er-ee) victims. "Tertiary" is another word for "third-level." Tertiary victims include people who are not close to the primary victims but are still affected by the crime. For example, survivors of past crimes can be re-traumatized when they hear about similar crimes on the news. Communities and local businesses often suffer from stress and fear in the aftermath of a crime.

The chart below shows the three levels of victims.

Primary Victims
Person(S) Directly Hurt or Killed By Crime

Secondary Victims
Witnesses
Emergency Responders
Victim's Family and Friends
Your Family and Friends

Tertiary Victims
Community Members
Workplace and/or School
People Who Live or Work Near the Crime Scene
Former Victims Who Are Reminded of Their Own Experience
People Who Hear About the Event Through News Media

The True Victims of Crime

Directions: Read the following passage. Then, fill in the primary, secondary, and tertiary victims in the boxes below, using the answer choice box.

Bill and Amanda had a violent marriage, marked by domestic violence arrests and restraining orders. One night, Bill went drinking with workers from the construction company he owned. When Bill came home, he and Amanda started arguing. Bill flew into a rage. He stabbed Amanda, killing her, while their 10-year-old son hid in his bedroom.

Bill was arrested and charged with first degree murder. At his jury trial, he was sentenced to life in prison. His business closed down. Bill's son moved far away to live with his grandparents.

List of Victims		
Amanda The 10-Year-Old Son Workers From Bill's Company	Amanda's Family Bill's Family Neighbors Community Members	Police Responders Court Workers Jail Workers

Primary Victims

_____

Secondary Victims

_____

_____

_____

_____

_____

Tertiary Victims

_____

_____

_____

_____

Victims of Your Crime

You can begin to see how many people are hurt by a crime. In the next activity, you will identify the primary, secondary, and tertiary victims of the crime for which you were incarcerated.

Directions: Think about the details of your crime. Write the details on the lines below.

Your Crime: _____

Time of Day: _____

Location: _____

Think about who was affected by your crime. Use the details to help you complete the boxes below.

Primary Victims
_____
_____
_____

Secondary Victims
_____   _____
_____   _____
_____   _____
_____   _____
_____   _____

Tertiary Victims
_____   _____
_____   _____
_____   _____
_____   _____
_____   _____
_____   _____

How Crime Affects Victims

On the previous pages, we talked about who was hurt by your crime. Now, we are going to look at how your crime hurt victims at each level.

In your mind, picture yourself standing on the side of a pond. The water is smooth and clear. You can see all the way to the bottom, where fish swim between plants. Now, imagine yourself throwing a rock into that pond. See it splashing? The water ripples out from the point where the rock landed.

As this water ripples out, it has other effects. It scares the fish and stirs up mud, making the water cloudy. Fish eggs and delicate roots at the bottom of the pond may be crushed by the rock, too. As you can see, this one simple action can have many effects.

Your crime also has a ripple effect. It not only affects the primary victim, but it also ripples out and creates problems for those connected to the victim, the offender, and the community. Over time, high crime rates can affect entire states and even countries.

The picture below shows some ways that crime ripples out and impacts others.

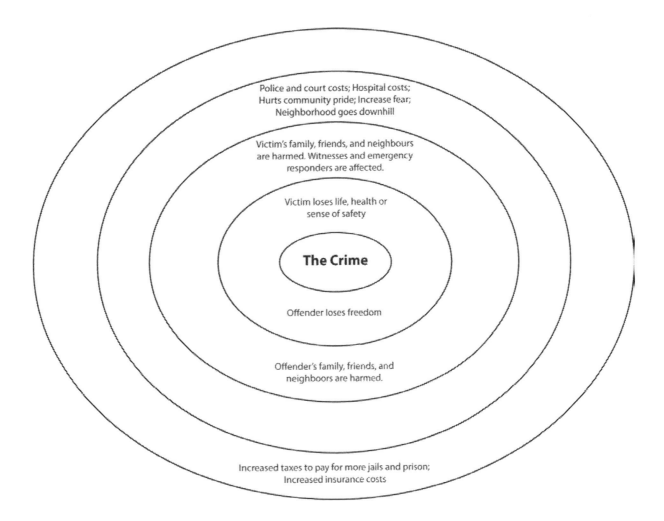

Police and court costs; Hospital costs; Hurts community pride; Increase fear; Neighborhood goes downhill

Victim's family, friends, and neighbours are harmed. Witnesses and emergency responders are affected.

Victim loses life, health or sense of safety

The Crime

Offender loses freedom

Offender's family, friends, and neighboors are harmed.

Increased taxes to pay for more jails and prison; Increased insurance costs

How Crime Affects Victims

Directions: Read the passage below about Mario.

Mario worked in a music store and had big dreams of becoming a music producer. However, when his girlfriend became pregnant, Mario decided that he wasn't making enough money to support a family and changed his plans. He began selling drugs on a corner near an elementary school.

"You gotta do what you gotta do," Mario always said, even though he knew deep down that he was on a bad path. Soon, things grew worse, and there was a gunfight on Mario's corner. Mario was arrested for multiple drug and weapons crimes, even though he did not hurt anyone else. After a costly court case, Mario was sentenced to 10 years in prison, with hard labor and a large fine.

In prison, Mario was unable to support his new family. His girlfriend left him, and Mario never had the chance to meet his son.

Next, fill in the chart with the effects of Mario's crime. Focus on how his crime affected others.

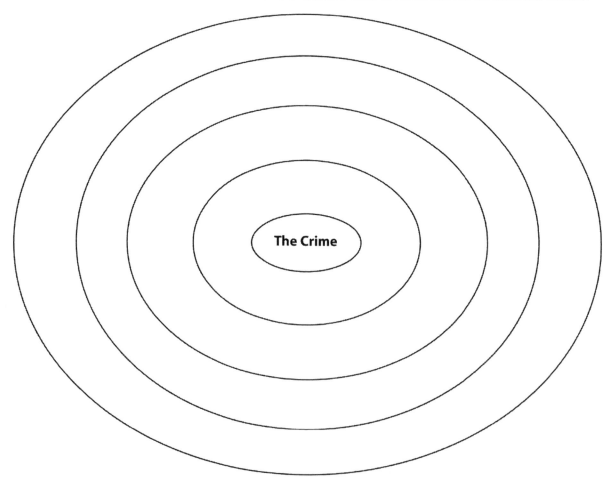

Group Discussion: With a partner, talk about your charts. Discuss what you wrote and why. Were there any effects that you had not thought of?

Empathy: The Strength to Care

Think about a time when someone close to you was hurt. Maybe it was your little brother, heartbroken after his first breakup. Or perhaps it was when a close friend had broken bones after a car accident.

When the other person felt pain, whether physical or emotional, did you hurt, too? That hurt you felt is caused by empathy, the ability to share and understand others' emotions and feelings. It is sometimes called "putting yourself in another person's shoes."

Empathy is recognizing the other person's feelings. It does not mean that you have to agree with the person's actions or decisions. Let's look at an example of an empathetic response compared to an indifferent, uncaring response.

> Your cousin, Albert, is upset because he lost a neighborhood basketball free-throw contest. You know he did not practice at all. How can you be empathetic?
>
> **Empathy:** "Losing is tough. Do you want to go shoot some hoops at the rec center to get ready for next month's contest?"
>
> **Indifferent:** "What did you expect? You are not that good anyway."

Empathy is not a sign of weakness. It takes a strong, confident person to show empathy. It also takes practice. First, you must learn to respect and care for yourself. Then, you can learn to respect and care for others.

What does empathy look like?

- Compassion
- Sympathy for Others' Problems
- Understanding
- Identifying with Others' Feelings and situations

Some attitudes get in the way of empathy.

- Selfishness
- Hostility
- Indifference
- Cynicism
- Distrust
- Negativity
- Blaming the Victim

Showing Empathy

Directions: Read each of the following statements. Circle the ones that show empathy.

1. "That must have really hurt."
2. "She got what she deserved."
3. "Not my problem."
4. "I know how that feels."
5. "Why should I care?"
6. "I can see why you're mad."
7. "How can I help?"
8. "Get over it!"
9. "You are just being dramatic."
10. "He was asking for trouble."

11. "I know where you're coming from."
12. "Well, someone's in a bad mood."
13. "You're just overreacting."
14. "Whatever . . . "
15. "I hear you."
16. "Come on. It couldn't have been that bad."
17. "I understand."
18. "What does that have to do with me?"

Group Activity: Next, compare your answers with those of a partner. Write two other statements that show empathy.

_____

_____

_____

_____

_____

Personal Assessment: Review the list of statements that were not circled. Explain how you feel when others respond to you with these types of comments.

_____

_____

_____

_____

_____

Developing Empathy

Developing empathy takes practice. One of the easiest ways to do it is by looking at how you have responded to situations in the past.

Directions: Spend a few minutes thinking about each of the questions below. Then, answer them as honestly as possible.

1. Think of a time when you showed empathy and put yourself in someone else's shoes. Who was involved?

   _____

   _____

   What was going on?

   _____

   _____

   How did you help?

   _____

   _____

   How did you feel afterward?

   _____

   _____

2. Think of a time when you were indifferent to someone in need. Why do you think you were indifferent? What attitudes prevented you from feeling empathy?

   _____

   _____

   _____

   _____

Effects of Victimization

What happens to victims after a crime? You can use your knowledge of empathy to understand how your criminal actions hurt victims. Every area of their lives may be changed by the event.

Here are some ways that crime may impact victims:

	Primary Victims	Secondary Victims	Tertiary Victims
Spiritual	Question Their Faith	Question Their Faith	Question Faith in Community
Emotional / Psychological	• Inability to trust • Cannot cope • Damaged relationships with others • Depression • Post-traumatic stress • Flashbacks	• Blame themselves • Worry about safety • Grief • Depression • Loneliness	• Loss of community pride • Distrust • Isolation
Physical	• Injuries • Permanent disability • Stress-related illness	• Increased aggression among children of incarcerated	• Empty parks and public spaces
Financial	• Lost wages • Medical bills • Property loss • Court-related costs	• Court-related costs • Attorney fees • Therapy costs • Loss of income	• Increased taxes • Decreased property values • Increased insurance costs • Increased court costs • Increased demand on foster care system

Effects of Victimization

The list below includes common ways that crime impacts victims.

Directions: Read each of the following sentences. Then, decide what kind of impact it shows. Write the letter that is the best match for the kind of impact that is described.

S = Spiritual   E = Emotional/Psychological   P = Physical   F = Financial

Example: ____S____ The primary victim stops attending church.

1. _____ The offender's family worries about how the offender is doing in prison.

2. _____ Cities close parks and public places to reduce crime.

3. _____ The victim's parents meet with their pastor to discuss how the crime affects their faith.

4. _____ The primary victim worries the offender may seek revenge.

5. _____ Children blame themselves, thinking the crime was their fault.

6. _____ Children move in with relatives or enter foster care.

7. _____ Victims and witnesses take time off from work so they can go to the court trial.

8. _____ Neighbors stay inside, afraid to go out.

9. _____ Employers add drug testing to their hiring process.

10. _____ Children begin to have anger issues or depression.

11. _____ The offender's family is searched during visitation at the correctional facility.

12. _____ Cities raise taxes to pay for more jails.

13. _____ Primary victims find it hard to trust their friends anymore.

14. _____ The family loses its main breadwinner.

15. _____ Children do poorly in school and drop out.

Impact of My Crime

Directions: Use the chart below to identify how your crime impacted the lives of others. Start by writing the name or description of a primary victim, a secondary victim, and a tertiary victim in the boxes on the top of the chart.

Then, describe how each victim was impacted by your crime in the four categories.

	Primary Victim _____	Secondary Victim _____	Tertiary Victim _____
Spiritual			
Emotional / Psychological			
Physical			
Financial			

Grief and Loss

Grief is an emotional response that occurs when you lose something important. It can happen to victims and the offender. Below are just a few examples of losses that can bring on grief.

Loss of a Loved One

- Victims' families lose their loved one literally, if the person was killed. If the victim survived, he or she may have been changed physically or emotionally by the crime. "She was never the same after that day," the family might say about how the crime changed their loved one.
- When you are incarcerated, you lose daily contact with your family and friends.

Loss of Material Goods

- Victims may feel grief about lost jewelry, money, or family heirlooms.
- You may lose your home, car, and other items as a result of your incarceration.

Loss of a Job

- Victims may lose their jobs due to crime-related injuries or stress.
- You may grieve the job you lost when you were sent to prison. You may also be unable to return to the same type of work when you are released.

Loss of Physical Self

- Victims who were assaulted may have scars, disabilities, or stress-related health problems.
- You may suffer from stress-related health problems.

Loss of Control

- Victims may lose control in many areas of their lives, especially if they were badly injured.
- You lose control over most parts of your life when you go to prison.

The Face of Grief

People show their grief in many different ways. Grief can make victims feel numb or depressed. Victims may be very angry, lashing out at people for no reason. The amount of time spent grieving will be different from person to person, and it can depend on what was lost.

How Victims Express Grief:

- **Shock:** Being in denial, disbelieving, or feeling numb.

- **Flood of Emotions:** Having emotional reactions like crying or yelling.

- **Anger:** Feeling angry toward people involved in the crime, law enforcement personnel, the legal system, or himself or herself.

- **Depression:** Feeling sad and hopeless; may also include feeling anxious or having panic attacks.

As an offender, you also feel grief. It is important for you to deal with these feelings. Trying to hide your emotions or pretend that your grief does not exist can lead to psychological or physical problems.

Have you ever heard that old saying, "Time heals"? Normal grief does not require any special medical treatment and will pass with time. As you grieve, be sure to take care of yourself, exercise regularly, get enough sleep, and eat a healthy diet. Also, you may want to talk to a good friend or counselor, especially if you feel like you are at a breaking point where you may harm yourself or others.

Understanding Your Own Grief

Directions: Think of the things you have lost as a result of your incarceration. Then, answer the following questions.

1. What is one thing you have lost as a result of your incarceration?

   _____

   _____

   _____

2. In what ways have you felt grief about this loss?

   _____

   _____

   _____

3. What things did you do that helped you deal with your grief? (If you did not use any healthy strategies to deal with your grief, what would you do differently?)

   _____

   _____

   _____

4. Now, imagine you are trying to help a friend deal with grief. What advice would you give him or her, based on what you have learned and your own experiences?

   _____

   _____

   _____

Understanding Others' Grief

We have talked a lot about your grief. Now, let's talk about the grief felt by your family members or friends. Understanding their grief will help you rebuild relationships with them when you return home. Remember that grief can often appear as anger or sudden outbursts of emotion.

You are probably counting the days until you can rejoin your family. Maybe you even imagine the moment when you will go home. In your mind, you see your friends and family smiling, happy to see you. But what happens if things go differently when that big day comes?

Directions: Read the following passage.

> Rachel was happy to be returning home after two years in prison. Rachel knew her time away was hard on her family. Rachel's teenage son had moved in with Rachel's mother, which was hard financially. Because of the money problems, Rachel's mother and son were not able to visit Rachel during her incarceration.
>
> When Rachel arrived at her mother's apartment, she expected a surprise party. There was no party, though. Instead, Rachel's son refused to talk to her, and Rachel's mother cried.

Working with a partner, circle Rachel's best response from the choices below. Then, write your own ideas for how Rachel could respond, based on what you've learned in this class.

1. Rachel's son angrily refused to talk to her. Rachel should:

   A. Take charge by telling him to quit acting like a brat.

   B. Tell her son that she understands how hard her incarceration was on him.

   C. _____

   D. _____

2. Rachel's mother cried and did not seem happy to see Rachel. Rachel should:

   A. Take responsibility and apologize for the pain she caused her mother.

   B. Suggest they go out to dinner, to help her mother forget.

   C. _____

   D. _____

Taking Responsibility

As an adult, you are responsible for your actions and their consequences. Many people try to blame others for things that are not right in their lives. You are lying to yourself and others if you do this. Your actions and decisions help shape your world. If you think about how you got into a bad situation, you can usually name the mistakes you made that got you there. You might say, "If only I hadn't... or "If I would have…"

Once you stop blaming others and accept that you played a part in your situation, you can move forward. Everyone makes mistakes, even very successful people. You can succeed by learning from your mistakes and not giving up.

Always remember: You cannot change your past, but you can take charge of your future.

If you have anger, resentment, or hurt for people or events in the past, it will hold you back. You cannot move forward if you are always looking backward.

It is also important to forgive yourself. Try to understand and forgive others, as well. They probably did the best they could, given their personal circumstances and background.

Directions: Check the actions you have used in the past to avoid responsibility and put blame on others.

- ☐ Pointing out others' weaknesses.
- ☐ Building yourself up by putting others down.
- ☐ Telling others what they want to hear instead of the truth.
- ☐ Lying, either by changing facts or leaving facts out.
- ☐ Diverting attention away from yourself by blaming social issues, like racism or sexism.
- ☐ Confusing others on purpose.
- ☐ Saying "yes" without really meaning it.
- ☐ Not participating; remaining silent.
- ☐ Making a big scene about a minor point.
- ☐ Putting off doing something by saying "I forgot".
- ☐ Arguing with and insulting others so they won't bother you.
- ☐ Accusing others of misunderstanding.

Now that you have identified these bad habits, you can take charge and respond differently in the future.

The Benefits of Taking Responsibility

OFFENDER REALIZATION AND RESTITUTION

When you take responsibility for your actions, you will see improvements in all areas of your life. For example, if you use anger to avoid responsibility, your relationships with your family may suffer. By letting go of that old habit and taking responsibility, you can improve your relationships with family and friends.

Here are some ways you can become more responsible.

- Accept that you are responsible for your choices.

- Don't blame others for your mistakes.

- Ask for help when you need it, and let others help you.

- Examine your fear and irrational thoughts, and don't let them control you.

- Learn how to manage your anger, insecurity, and trust issues.

- Embrace change and take risks that will help you grow.

- Be open to other people—let them earn your trust.

Directions: Read the following passage and answer the questions.

Angie starts a new job as a cashier at a dry-cleaning shop. On Angie's second day at work, she has to work the counter by herself while her supervisor runs an errand. He leaves his phone number in case there's an emergency. When Angie is alone, a customer brings in a large floor rug to be cleaned. Angie does not remember what she is supposed to do when customers bring in large items like rugs.

Angie wants the customer to leave, since she does not know how to help him. She tells the customer that the shop doesn't clean rugs. After he leaves, Angie does not tell anyone about the customer she sent away.

1. Did Angie act responsibly? Why or why not?

   _____

2. What could happen as a result of Angie's actions?

   _____

3. What would be a responsible way to help the customer?

   _____

Responsibility: Test Your Knowledge

Taking responsibility can be hard. Sometimes, it feels easier just to "let it slide" or blame others than to admit your own role in a problem. You may not even realize that you are being irresponsible until later on.

Directions: Read each of the scenarios below. Then, decide if the person is taking responsibility or not. Write "R" by the scenarios that show responsibility. Write "X" by the scenarios that do not show responsibility.

Example	x	Andrew forgot to call his wife to tell her he was running late. When he comes home, she is worried and angry at him. "Quit nagging me!" he yells at her. "I'm not a little kid, you know!"
1.		Sonia is given a new task at her job—to fix a broken window. She is not sure how to do it. Sonia asks her boss for instructions.
2.		Jamal wants to return to community college, but he is afraid he will fail. He waits too long to enroll and blames his friends for not reminding him.
3.		Nikki's church invites her to give a speech to pregnant teens. Nikki was a teenage mom herself, and she knows how hard it can be. Nikki is very nervous about speaking in front of a group, but she decides to do it. She knows she has an important story to share.
4.		A group of Mason's friends is going out dancing and drinking at a club. The group asks him to come, too. Mason knows this will break the terms of his probation. Mason says "no" to his friends and does not go.
5.		Hector is having a hard time dealing with his sadness. He knows he can trust his sister. When she asks him what is wrong, though, he says, "Nothing."

Personal Accountability Guide

Positive affirmations can help you reach any goal, including the goal of being more responsible. When you say a positive affirmation, you are stating your intention. You are focusing on what you want or who you want to be.

The Personal Accountably Guide is made up of 10 simple affirmations that can easily be said every morning when you wake up or every night before you go to sleep.

Directions: Read the 10 affirmations to yourself. Then, read them out loud together as a class.

1. I will take complete responsibility for my actions.

2. I will think before I act and respect the rights of others.

3. I will not blame others for my bad decisions or choices.

4. I will not manipulate, control, or intimidate others.

5. I will be honest with myself.

6. I will make choices for me.

7. I will embrace positive change.

8. I will not purposely do harm to any living thing.

9. I acknowledge that my past choices and actions have caused others pain and suffering.

10. I will seek constructive solutions to my problems and not run from them or turn to drugs and alcohol.

Group Discussion: Talk about how you will put these 10 goals into action once you are released.

Making Amends

Depending on your crime, you may be required to pay restitution or contribute to a victim's assistance fund. Are there other ways you can make amends? In a word, yes.

Restorative Justice

Restorative justice provides additional ways to make amends for your crime. Both the offender and victims must agree to participate. In the process, the offender takes responsibility for his or her actions, apologizing for the harm that has been done. Both sides talk about the impact the crime had on them, their families, and their friends.

Volunteering

Volunteering also provides opportunities for you to make amends, while also helping you reconnect with your community. In fact, you may be able to volunteer with certain organizations while you are incarcerated. Volunteer experience can be included on your resumé and job applications.

Here are some ideas for volunteering and giving back to your community after you are released.

- Working at your local food bank.
- Working with shelter animals that need socialization and training.
- Speaking to at-risk youth about the consequences of criminal activity.
- Repairing donated goods at a local charity thrift shop.
- Planting trees or working in a community garden.

Other Ways to Give Back

You do not have to volunteer to give back. It is important to remember that by simply living a crimefree, productive life and not being a burden on society, you will help the community.

Making Amends

Directions: Imagine that you are taking part in a restorative justice program. The first requirement of the program is that you write a letter to the primary victim. Consider the following questions: What impact do you think the crime had on the primary victim's life? How do you think the crime made that primary victim feel? What might his or her grief look like?

On the lines below, write a letter to the primary victim taking responsibility for your actions and explaining your answers to the previous questions.

_____

_____

_____

_____

_____

_____

_____

_____

_____

_____

_____

_____

_____

_____

_____

_____

_____

_____

_____

_____

_____

_____

_____

Positive Ripple Effects

Do you remember the. story about Mario, who was sent to prison for drug and gun crimes? Let's go back and visit Mario again, now that he has served his time and has been released from prison.

> Mario returned to his old neighborhood. Instead of going back to dealing drugs on the corner, Mario began volunteering at a local youth center. The center had just added a recording studio and needed someone to help the teens produce their own music. Mario was a perfect fit for the volunteer role.

> The youth center staff noticed that Mario was always prepared, on time, and dressed professionally. Mario had a positive attitude and was always willing to help others, too. When the youth center added a new program, they hired Mario to manage it.

> Mario's regular paychecks allowed him to rent an apartment. Mario also began paying child support for his son. Soon, he was able to arrange joint custody, so that his son could visit him during the summer.

As you can see, the ripple effect occurs not just with bad events, like crime. It also happens with good deeds. When you make amends by participating in restorative justice or volunteering, the effects of your actions ripple out.

Let's look at how Mario's decisions created a positive ripple effect in his own life and in his community.

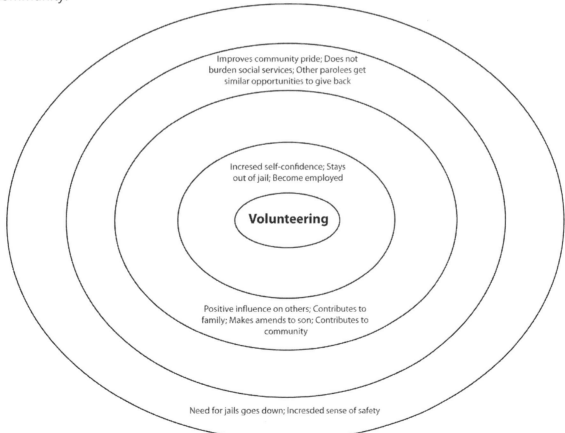

Improves community pride; Does not burden social services; Other parolees get similar opportunities to give back

Incresed self-confidence; Stays out of jail; Become employed

Volunteering

Positive influence on others; Contributes to family; Makes amends to son; Contributes to community

Need for jails goes down; Incresded sense of safety

Now It Is Your Turn

Mario's success after being released from prison was not a miracle. With the right attitude, anyone can do it, including you. Let's look at the choices that Mario made after he was released.

- He found a volunteer job that matched his skills and interests.

- He was responsible, showing up on time.

- He kept a positive attitude.

- He showed empathy, helping others.

- He made amends to his family and community.

Directions: Read the ideas below for how you can give back to your community after you are released. Then, check the types of volunteer activities you would enjoy.

☐ Building or repairing homes for low income families

☐ Repairing donated electronics.

☐ Clearing weeds from parks and trails.

☐ Helping animals.

☐ Speaking to at-risk youth.

☐ Sorting cans at a food bank.

☐ Helping at a recycling center.

☐ Building and maintaining websites.

☐ Other: _____

Making the Most of Volunteering

Your volunteer activities will be more successful and have a greater impact on the community if you match them to your interests, skills, and goals.

Directions: Complete the following items about your goals for volunteering.

1. I have the following skills and experience that I can use when volunteering:

   _____

   _____

   _____

   _____

2. One new skill I would like to learn through volunteering is:

   _____

   _____

3. When I volunteer, I will help the community by:

   _____

   _____

   _____

   _____

4. When I volunteer, I will help myself in these ways:

   _____

   _____

   _____

   _____

Victim Awareness & Restitution Review

Directions: Circle the letter for each correct answer.

1. Drug and prostitution crimes have no victims.
   A. True
   B. False

2. Secondary victims of crime include:
   A. The victim's family.
   B. The offender's family.
   C. Witnesses.
   D. All of the above

3. Tertiary victims of crime include:
   A. The direct victim.
   B. The offender.
   C. Community members.
   D. None of the above

4. What is one ripple effect of crime?
   A. Increased taxes to pay for jails.
   B. Stronger communities.
   C. Happier families.
   D. There is no ripple effect.

5. My crime had a ripple effect on people I do not even know.
   A. True
   B. False

6. "Empathy" is:
   A. Sadness at losing something special.
   B. Selfishness.
   C. The ability to understand others' feelings.
   D. Telling others what to do.

7. Which of these statements show empathy?
   A. "That sounds like it was fun."
   B. "Don't ask me."
   C. "I don't care what you think."
   D. "You need to shut up."

8. Empathy is something that you can learn with practice.
   A. True
   B. False

9. Crime can impact which areas of victims' lives?
   A. Psychological.
   B. Physical.
   C. Financial.
   D. All of the Above

10. Crime can make insurance costs go up.
    A. True
    B. False

11. Telling others what they want to hear is a good way to be responsible.
    A. True
    B. False

12. Which of the following is an example of a positive affirmation?
    A. I will blame others for my mistakes.
    B. I will put others down to make myself look better.
    C. I will not hurt anyone on purpose.
    D. I will lie to avoid trouble with others.

13. You can show responsibility by:
    A. Being open to change.
    B. Dealing with anger without hurting others.
    C. Opening up to others.
    D. All of the Above

14. Both offenders and victims can suffer grief after a crime.
    A. True.
    B. False.

15. The best way to deal with grief is to:
    A. Pretend it doesn't exist.
    B. Deal with your feelings.
    C. Blame others.
    D. Pretend to be happy.

16. Good deeds can have positive ripple effects.
    A. True
    B. False

17. Which of the following are ways to make amends for your crime?
    A. Restorative justice.
    B. Volunteering.
    C. Pretending it didn't happen.
    D. Both A and B

18. Volunteering can:
    A. Help you reconnect with community.
    B. Provide experience for resumés.
    C. Increase self-confidence.
    D. All of the above.

19. It is okay to show up late to volunteer jobs since they are not "real" jobs.
    A. True
    B. False

20. Some people may act angry when they are grieving.
    A. True
    B. False

This page intentionally left blank

CONGRATULATIONS!

Your completion of this material demonstrates an ongoing commitment to personal growth and development.

CERTIFICATE
OF ACHIEVEMENT
THIS CERTIFICATE IS HEREBY AWARDED TO

Your Name Here

FOR SUCCESSFUL COMPLETION OF THE _____ HOUR
EVIDENCE-BASED RECIDIVISM REDUCTION PROGRAM ENTITLED,

Program Title Here

ISSUED AND VARIFIED BY REENTRY ESSENTIALS.
THIS CERTIFICATE ATTESTS TO YOUR KNOWLEDGE AND UNDERSTANDING OF THE CONCEPTS AND
THEORIES EXPLORED DURING THIS COURSE OF STUDY.

AWARDED ON THIS _____ DAY OF _____, 20___.

Certificate verification available online at,
www.reentryessentials.org or via email at
certificate@reentryessentials.org.

Ms. Michaiah
Director of

DEMONSTRATE REHABILITATION

Each of our unique Evidence-Based Recidivism Reduction (EBRR) Programs and Productive Activities (PA) include a transcript and certificate of achievement issued by Reentry Essentials. Ideal for demonstrating rehabilitation to a parole board, case manager, probation officer, judge, potential employer or even your family and friends.

REQUEST YOUR TRANSCRIPT AND CERTIFICATE TODAY!

Simply follow the below instructions based on how your materials were purchased and we will do the rest. We make receiving your certificate and transcript quick and easy!

● **Individual Purchase**
Materials purchased by you directly or on your behalf by family or friends.
Written requests should be submitted to the address below. All requests must include full committed name, inmate number and mailing address. Requests will be verified against our customer purchase history. Please allow 2 - 3 weeks for processing.

● **Organizational Purchase**
Materials purchased by a government agency, nonprofit organization or community service provider. Please contact your program administrator for assistance. Program administrators may forward official requests for certification to, info@reentryessentials.org.

📍 **Reentry Essentials, Inc., 2609 East 14 Street, Suite 1018, Brooklyn, NY 11235-3915**

📞 347.973.0004   ✉ info@reentryessentials.org   🌐 www.reentryessentials.org

CAREER COMPASS
Success in all Directions

Made in the USA
Columbia, SC
15 July 2024